Foreword

By The Secretary of State for the Environment

In the introduction to the Sustainable Development Strategy, which was published in 1994, I said that the United Kingdom was determined to make sustainable development the touchstone of its policies, and that we would need to revise and refine those policies year by year, so that our economy can grow in a way which does not cheat on our children.

If we are to improve our policies, we need to monitor how effective they are. We already collect and publish a mass of environmental information, and a comprehensive range of economic and social statistics. The challenge somehow is to condense this very considerable amount of information into a limited number of key indicators, so that we can see how well we are doing overall, and where we need to make further progress. We hope also to bring home the main messages, not just to government and policy makers but to businesses and individuals. We need to ensure that we all consider how our own actions have an effect on the environment.

That is why I welcome the publication of these indicators. They are a first step, but an important one, in developing measures of our progress. We believe that they will be useful not only in monitoring how we in the United Kingdom are doing, but also in contributing to the international debate on indicators.

Defining what we mean by sustainable development is not easy. Achieving sustainable development presents a considerable challenge. I hope that these indicators will be useful in informing us about our progress, and stimulating us to greater efforts.

Contents

Department of the Environment

Indicators of
Sustainable Development
for the United Kingdom

A set of indicators produced for discussion and consultation by an interdepartmental Working Group, following a commitment in the UK's Sustainable Development Strategy of 1994.

March 1996

The indicators presented in this report are preliminary, intended to stimulate discussion about how we measure whether our development is sustainable.

The Government would welcome views on which indicators are the most useful, and how they might be developed and improved in future.

Comments should be sent to:
Chris Morrey
Indicators Working Group Secretariat
Environmental Protection Statistics and Information Management Division (EPSIM)
Department of the Environment
Room A121, Romney House, 43 Marsham Street, London SW1P 3PY

A publication of the Government Statistical Service

London: HMSO

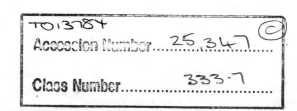

Application for reproduction should be made to HMSO Copyright Unit, Norwich NR3 1PD

Second impression 1996

ISBN 0 11 753174 X

Contents

Chapter 1

Background and introduction

The UK Sustainable Development Strategy

1.1   In 1994 the Government published its Strategy[1] for Sustainable Development, following the commitment made at the Earth Summit of June 1992 in Rio. One of the commitments in that document was the development of a set of indicators to help to inform people, including those in government, industry, non-governmental organisations, and the public, about the issues involved in considering whether our development is becoming more sustainable, and whether the Government is meeting its objectives as set out in the Sustainable Development Strategy. An interdepartmental Working Group was set up to develop a preliminary set of indicators for discussion. This report sets out the conclusions of the Working Group.

What do we mean by sustainable development?

1.2   The principles of sustainable development are now well established. Sustainable development means reconciling two basic aspirations of society:

● to achieve economic development to secure rising standards of living both now and for future generations;

● to protect and enhance the environment now and for the future.

These concepts are embodied in the Brundtland definition of sustainable development:

development that meets the needs of the present without compromising the ability of future generations to meet their own needs.

This was amplified in the UK's 1990 Environment White Paper[2], which said:

Sustainable development means living on the earth's income rather than eroding its capital. It means keeping the consumption of renewable natural resources within the limits of their replenishment. It means handing down to successive generations not only man-made wealth, but also natural wealth, such as clean and adequate water supplies, good arable land, a wealth of wildlife, and ample forests.

What are indicators?

1.3   Indicators are quantified information which help to explain how things are changing over time. For many years, a limited number of key economic measures has been used to judge how the economy is performing - for example, output, the level of employment, the rate of inflation, the balance of payments, public sector borrowing, etc. These are broad brush, aggregated statistics which give an overall picture. They do not explain why particular trends are occurring, and they do not necessarily reflect the

situation in a particular sector of industry or society, or in a geographical area. But, overall they provide to policy-makers and the public reasonable indicators of changes in the economy, assisting economic policy decision-taking and allowing the public to judge for themselves how the economy is performing overall.

1.4   If we are to make good decisions about policy relating to sustainable development, we need reliable information about the state of the environment and the factors which impact on it, including information on relative risks and on costs and benefits of ameliorating any adverse impacts. There is a considerable amount of information available about the environment, much of it already published, and similarly there is a wealth of information about economic and social development. But it is easy to become overloaded with data and to miss the key messages.

1.5   We need a set of summary statistics which highlight the main issues and help both policy-makers and the public better understand them. The objective is to produce a limited number of indicators, so that the main trends are highlighted. The challenge is to strike a balance - the number of indicators should be as small as possible so that the main messages are clear but at the same time the issues must not be over-simplified.

Why do we need indicators?

1.6   There are three basic functions of indicators - simplification, quantification, and communication. Indicators generally simplify in order to make complex phenomena quantifiable so that information can be communicated. More specifically, we need indicators because:

● people are concerned about sustainable development and the environment. They need to be informed about the state of the environment and the economy and how and why they are changing, so that they can understand and monitor government policies, and see how their own personal actions may have an impact. Indicators are therefore needed in a form which is relevant to the general public and can be readily understood;

● they can provide a means of linking environmental impacts to socio-economic activity, and may is some cases provide early warning of potential environmental problems arising from human activity;

● they can help to measure the extent to which policies aimed at sustainable development objectives are being achieved;

● they can help to clarify the confusion caused by the mass of environmental and economic data available.

Uses and limitations of indicators

1.7   The indicators in the preliminary set are based on the objectives set out in the Sustainable Development Strategy. They will be useful in monitoring progress towards the objectives set out in the strategy. They will also help to fulfil the UK's international obligations of reporting to the UN Commission on Sustainable

Development. They should help to focus the public's attention on key issues, and may therefore influence the behaviour of businesses and individuals and encourage them to consider the environmental consequences of their actions.

1.8   However, while indicators certainly help to focus on the key issues and highlight some significant trends, they do not by any means give the whole story. They are by their nature simplifications. They also relate only to areas which can be readily quantified and aggregated in a meaningful way to give national statistics. Some issues are inherently more amenable than others to such quantification - concentrations of pollutants, for example, can be measured with a reasonable degree of precision. Even here, however, there are problems in attempting to summarise a very large amount of information in a few simple series over time. Selection of sites and of parameters to be measured has to be done with care to avoid bias.

1.9   Other areas are inherently more difficult to measure, in particular issues relevant to the quality of land management. There are some environmental qualities which cannot be measured objectively, but which we nonetheless consider to be valuable and wish to preserve - such qualities include factors like natural beauty or tranquillity. Because such qualities are very hard, or even impossible, to quantify, they may be excluded from, or only partially covered in, quantified indicators.

1.10   The concept of sustainable development is inherently about reconciling the benefits of development with the potential environmental costs. While the indicators in the preliminary set measure both environmental and economic change, they do not deal directly with the issue of reconciliation, often because it is difficult or impossible to measure

both on a common basis, such as monetary valuation.

1.11   It is important to recognise these limitations and not to focus solely on quantified indicators as a measure of whether our development is becoming more sustainable. To do so could easily lead to misrepresentation and the distortion of priorities. Qualitative information will also be needed, and judgements will need to be made about the reconciliation between the benefits of development and the potential environmental cost. Nevertheless, quantified indicators are a useful tool, and it is hoped that the set presented in this report will help to inform and stimulate the sustainable development debate, although it is recognised that the process of developing indicators is complex and that this set is very much a preliminary one.

International and other initiatives

1.12   The UK is not alone in developing indicators. Several other countries[3], and international organisations such as the Organisation for Economic Cooperation and Development (OECD)[4] have been working to develop indicators for some time. More recently, the UN Commission on Sustainable Development and the World Bank[5] have produced draft frameworks for indicators for discussion. Work is also going on within Eurostat (the Statistical Office of the European Communities) and the European Environment Agency. In this country the Environment Challenge Group, a group of non-governmental organisations, published in 1994 a set of environmental indicators[6]. Local Authorities, as part of the Local Agenda 21 initiative, are developing a set of indicators for use at local level; the Local Government Management Board published two reports in 1995[7,8]. While much of the earlier work

$\delta\cup\varsigma$

primarily on environmental ... rs, increasingly, countries ... ernational organisations are ... g to develop indicators of ... inable development, although ... e is still no international ... sensus on how such indicators ... ould be constructed and what ... ey should cover.

1.13   The UK has taken into account the ideas of other countries and organisations, but has developed its own framework based on the key issues and objectives set out in the Sustainable Development Strategy. This attempts to go beyond environmental indicators by including indicators which explicitly link environmental impacts with socio-economic activity. However, such linkages are rarely straightforward and great caution needs to be exercised in their interpretation. But the Government hopes that this preliminary set of indicators will prove a useful input to the international debate on the issue. Different indicators will be appropriate for different purposes (for example, issues will vary from country to country and so the selection of indicators can also be expected to vary), but it is useful, where possible, to ensure that the indicators used are consistent with those used elsewhere, so that comparisons can be made and a broader picture presented. A bibliography setting out some of the key publications on indicators which the Working Group considered when developing this preliminary set is included at Annex C.

Environmental accounting

1.14   In the Sustainable Development Strategy, the Government makes a commitment to take forward work on environmental accounts. To this end, a unit has been established in the Central Statistical Office to develop them. It is hoped that pilot

environmental satellite accounts will be published in Summer 1996. These accounts will ultimately adjust measures of income for depletion of natural resources, and report physical quantities of pollutant emissions and expenditure on environmental protection. The accounts aim to comprehensively report pollutant emissions in a manner which is consistent with the conventions and structures of national accounts.

1.15   Environmental accounts present the links between the economic and environmental impacts of different sectors of the economy. They can also be used to model environmental change. Some argue that a modified or, "green GDP" could be used as a comprehensive measure of sustainable development. However, there are significant problems before we can place reliable and robust money values on the cost of environmental pollution. Indicators are able to highlight key environmental issues, such as loss of bioviversity, some of which are difficult to associate with specific sectors of the economy and cannot be easily integrated into the environmental accounts. The Government is therefore taking a joint approach in developing both a set of indicators and a system of accounts which will complement one another. The basic information underlying both measures will, of course, be the same.

Further work

1.16   Some will argue that a set of around 120 indicators included here is too many, and that a much smaller core set is needed if the key messages are to be highlighted. However, the framework within which the indicators have been developed contains 21 "families" of issues. Inclusion of a rounded set of indicators for each of the issues inevitably leads to a relatively larger number of indicators, and it is worth

noting that many of the indicator frameworks proposed by other countries and organisations - particularly those for sustainable development rather than environmental indicators - potentially have a similar number of indicators. The framework proposed by the Commission on Sustainable Development, for example, implies some 140 indicators.

1.17   Nevertheless, with such a large number of indicators, the main trends can still be obscured. During the further work and consultation, the Government will need to consider whether the number of indicators can be cut down, either by selecting a more limited "core" set, or by aggregating the indicators together in some way. However, focusing on a much more limited set of indicators, while it may have more impact presentationally, increases the risk that policy distortions and priorities will result as people may concentrate action on areas which particularly influence the core indicators - a problem which is common to performance measures of any type.

1.18   At this stage, therefore, a relatively large number of indicators has been put up for discussion. This is a preliminary set of indicators, intended to illustrate some of the difficulties and present new ideas and insights. It is not intended to be the final word. The drawing together of the information to evaluate the indicators is in itself useful exercise, and even if some of the indicators are felt in the longer term to be at too detailed a level for a core national set, they may well prove useful to those working in a particular sector or with an interest in a particular area.

Consultation

1.19 The set of indicators presented in this report has been compiled primarily by an interdepartmental Government Working Group. There has also been informal consultation on the indicator framework with groups from outside government, including the UK Government Panel on Sustainable Development and the Sustainable Development Round Table. Individual local authorities and local authority associations have been consulted through the Information Development and Liaison Group (IDLG) and the Scottish Statistical Liaison Committee (SSLC), and academic and research organisations through the DOE's Environmental Statistics Advisory Group (ESAG).

1.20 It is hoped that publication of this report will stimulate wider debate and discussion about how to take the work forward and develop better measures in the future. It will also contribute to the international debate on indicators and the measurement of sustainable development. Further comments and ideas will be welcomed and will be taken into account in developing the indicators.

Comments should be sent to:

Indicators Working Group
Secretariat

Environmental Protection
Statistics and Information
Management Division (EPSIM)

Department of the Environment
Room A121
Romney House
43 Marsham Street
London SW1P 3PY

1.21 The development of indicators is a long and complex process. In some cases, the indicators which should be selected are relatively obvious and easily calculated. In others, either it is not clear which indicators are most appropriate, or the data to evaluate the preferred indicator are not available. Proxy measures have been suggested in such cases, and further work, including further methodological development and data collection, may be needed in the future. The costs of such further work will need to be balanced against the potential value of the indicator, and the views of those using the indicators, both within and outside government, will need to be taken into account in assessing

their usefulness. Also, over time, the issues to be addressed, or scientific knowledge of which issues are particularly significant, is certain to change. The indicators will therefore continue to evolve.

1.22 Unlike the main economic indicators which are tracked on a monthly basis, these indicators are, in most cases, more long-term and short-term fluctuations may not be significant. The majority of these indicators, therefore, are tracked on an annual basis or longer. Some data sets are only collected every five years or longer because of the cost involved. The frequency with which the indicators should most usefully be re-evaluated will be one of the points to be discussed further, but it seems likely that they will be produced at most every two years. As the indicators evolve, we would expect them better to reflect the priorities set out in the Government's annual White Paper, *This Common Inheritance* which began in 1990[2], reporting progress on sustainable development and on further detailed targets or commitments. The Government will also be considering how best the timing of updates of the indicators can be coordinated with the policy development process.

[1] *Sustainable Development: The UK Strategy*. Cm2426, HMSO, 1994. ISBN 0-10-124262-X

[2] *This Common Inheritance, Britain's Environmental Strategy*. Cm1200, HMSO, 1990. ISBN 0-10-112002-8.

[3] See Annex C, Bibliography of related indicator work.

[4] *Environmental Indicators: OECD Core Set*. OECD, 1994. ISBN 92-64-04263-6.

[5] *Monitoring Environmental Progress: A Report on Work in Progress*. The World Bank, 1995. ISBN 0-8213-3365-8.

[6] *Environmental Measures: Indicators for the UK environment*. Environment Challenge Group, 1994. ISBN 0-90-3138-824.

[7] *Sustainability Indicators Research Project - Report of Consultants on the Pilot Phase*. LGMB, 1995. ISBN 0-7488-9702X.

[8] *Sustainable Indicators Research Project: Indicators for Local Agenda 21 - A Summary*. LGMB, 1995. ISBN 0-7488-9744-5.

Chapter 2

Theory underlying development of UK indicators

The indicators framework

2.1 Sustainable development is a very complex concept and there are many interconnections between the environment and socio-economic activity. In some cases environmental improvement and economic development may go hand in hand, for example, where industrial process improvements may make a plant more efficient and reduce pollution. In other cases the benefits to the economy or the environment may be accompanied by costs elsewhere. There may be a range of different impacts on the environment from one particular activity; for example, nitrogen dioxide emissions from transport in urban areas may cause health problems and damage to the built environment, but the gas may disperse and result in acid deposition in far away places, damaging soils, vegetation, and aquatic life. Also, a problem may have several causes; for example, the risk of respiratory disease may increase through exposure to high concentrations of various gases, including nitrogen oxides, ground level ozone, sulphur dioxide, and particles. An indicators framework provides an overview for considering environmental problems and the associated interconnections between them. A framework helps in considering the issues in a systematic way and ensuring that issues have not been overlooked.

2.2 There is no universally accepted definition of what constitutes sustainable development. Nor is there yet a nationally or internationally accepted framework within which to develop measures which will allow us to determine whether our development is becoming more sustainable. As part of the process of drawing up the Sustainable Development Strategy, the Government undertook a very wide consultation exercise which identified the key issues to be addressed in considering sustainable development in the UK. These issues have been taken as the starting point for the development of the indicators, and from this the following framework has been constructed.

Chapter 2

Broad aims		Key objectives and issues	Key indicators
A healthy economy should be maintained to promote quality of life while at the same time protecting human health and the environment, in the UK and overseas, with all participants in all sectors paying the full social and environmental costs of their decisions.	The economy	To promote a healthy economy in order to generate the resources to meet people's needs and improve environmental quality, to further protection of human health and the natural environment. *Current economic growth* *Consumption* *Investment* *Human health*	Gross Domestic Product Structure of the economy Expenditure components of GDP and personal savings Consumer expenditure Inflation Employment Government borrowing and debt Pollution abatement expenditure Infant mortality Life expectancy
	Transport use	To strike the right balance between the ability of transport to serve economic development and the ability to protect the environment and sustain quality of life. *Use of least polluting, practical modes of transport* *Efficient use of transport*	Car use and total passenger travel Short journeys Real changes in the cost of transport Freight traffic
	Leisure and tourism	To maintain the quality of the environment in which leisure takes place, and which is an essential part of the UK's attractiveness to tourists, for future generations to enjoy; thus contributing to the quality of life of those taking part in leisure activities, and maximising the economic contributions of tourism, while protecting natural resources.	Leisure journeys Air travel
	Overseas trade	To ensure that UK activities contribute, to sustainable development in the UK and in other countries as far as possible. *Overseas trade*	UK imports and exports
Non-renewable resources should be used optimally.	Energy	To ensure secure supplies of energy at competitive prices, to reduce adverse impacts of energy use to acceptable levels, and to encourage consumers to meet their needs with less energy input through improved energy efficiency. *Depletion of non-renewable natural resources* *Consumption of fuel to derive economic benefits* *Pollution / impacts caused by energy use* *Energy efficiency*	Depletion of fossil fuels Capacity of nuclear and renewable fuels Primary and final energy consumption Energy consumption and output Industrial and commercial sector consumption Road transport energy use Residential energy use Fuel prices in real terms
	Land Use	To balance competing demands for the finite quantity of land available. *Increasing demand for land for development (especially housing)* *Maintenance of vital and viable town centres*	Land covered by urban development Household numbers Re-use of land in urban uses for development Stock and reclamation of land Road building Out-of-town retail floorspace Regular journeys Regeneration expenditure Green spaces in urban areas

Chapter 2

Broad aims		Key objectives and issues	Key indicators
Renewable resources should be used sustainably.	Water resources	To ensure adequate water resources are available to meet consumers' needs while sustaining the aquatic environment, and to encourage efficient use of water. *Water resources / supply* *Water consumption* *Impacts of water abstraction*	Licensed abstractions and effective rainfall Low flow alleviation Abstractions by use Abstractions for public water supply Demand and supply of public water Abstractions for spray irrigation
	Forestry	To manage forests in a way which sustains their environmental qualities as well as their productive potential. *Preservation of ancient semi-natural forests* *Development of new and environmentally-managed forests* *Tree health*	Forest cover Timber production Ancient semi-natural woodland Tree health Forest management
	Fish resources	To manage the fishing industry to prevent over-exploitation of fish stocks.	Fish stocks Minimum Biological Acceptable Level (MBAL) Fish catches
Damage to the carrying capacity of the environment and the risk to human health and biodiversity from the effects of human activity should be minimised.	Climate change	To limit emissions of greenhouse gases which may contribute to global warming and climate change. *Global emissions* *UK contribution*	Global greenhouse gas radiative forcing rate Global temperature change Emissions of greenhouse gases Power station emissions of carbon dioxide
	Ozone layer depletion	To restrict atmospheric emissions of substances which cause stratospheric ozone depletion. *Global emissions* *UK contribution*	Calculated chlorine loading Measured ozone depletion Emissions of ozone-depleting substances CFCs consumption
	Acid deposition	To limit acid emissions and ensure appropriate land management practices.	Exceedences of provisional critical loads for acidity Power station emissions of sulphur dioxide and nitrogen oxides Road transport emissions of nitrogen oxides
	Air	To control air pollution in order to reduce the risks of adverse effects on natural ecosystems, human health, and quality of life. *Urban air quality* *Photochemical pollution*	Ozone concentrations Nitrogen dioxide concentrations Particulate matter concentrations Volatile organic compound emissions Carbon monoxide emissions Black smoke emissions Lead emissions Expenditure on air pollution abatement
	Freshwater quality	To sustain and improve water quality and the aquatic environment. *Surface water and groundwater quality* *Control of pollution* *Waste water treatment* *Recreational use of water*	River quality - chemical and biological Nitrates in rivers and groundwater Phosphorus in rivers Pesticides in rivers and groundwater Pollution incidents Pollution prevention and control Expenditure on water abstraction, treatment and distribution Expenditure on sewage treatment

Chapter 2

Broad aims		Key objectives and issues	Key indicators
Damage to the carrying capacity of the environment and the risk to human health and biodiversity from the effects of human activity should be minimised.	Marine	To control anthropogenic inputs to the sea. *Marine and estuarial water quality* *Control of pollution*	Estuarial water quality Concentrations of key pollutants Contaminants in fish Bathing water quality Inputs of contaminants Oil spills and operational discharges
	Wildlife and habitats	To conserve as far as reasonably possible the wide variety of wildlife species and habitats in the UK, and to ensure that commercially exploited species are managed in a sustainable way. *Extent and quality of habitats* *Populations and ranges of key species*	Native species at risk Breeding birds Plant diversity in semi-improved grassland Area of chalk grassland Plant diversity in hedgerows Habitat fragmentation Lakes and ponds Plant diversity in streamsides Mammal populations Dragonfly distributions Butterfly distributions
	Land cover and landscape	To protect the countryside for its landscape and habitats of environmental value while maintaining an efficient supply of good quality food and other products. *Rural land cover* *Protection of landscape and habitats of environmental value* *Agricultural productivity* *Nitrogen and pesticide usage.* *Land management.*	Rural land cover Designated and protected areas Damage to designated and protected areas Agricultural productivity Nitrogen usage Pesticide usage Length of landscape linear features Environmentally managed land
	Soil	To protect soil as a limited resource for the production of food and other products and as an ecosystem for vital organisms.	Soil quality Heavy metals in topsoils
	Minerals extraction	To conserve minerals as far as possible while ensuring an adequate supply, to minimise waste production and to encourage efficient use of materials, to minimise environmental damage from minerals extraction, and to protect designated areas from development. *Depletion of resources* *Recycling of waste materials* *Extraction (including fossil fuel minerals)* *Restoration of landscapes after minerals extraction*	Aggregates output Aggregates from wastes Mineral workings on land Land covered by restoration / aftercare conditions Reclamation of mineral workings Aggregates dredged from the sea
	Waste	To minimise the amount of waste produced, to make best use of the waste which is produced, and to minimise pollution from waste. *Waste generation* *Waste recycling* *Energy recovery* *Final disposal of waste*	Household waste Industrial and commercial waste Special waste Household waste recycling and composting Materials recycling Energy from waste Waste going to landfill
	Radioactivity	To ensure radioactive wastes are not unnecessarily created, to ensure radioactive wastes are managed and treated in a manner which does not lead to excessive discharges or radiation doses to members of the UK population, and to ensure that wastes are safely disposed of at appropriate times and in appropriate ways. *Impacts of routine, permitted discharges* *Radioactive waste arisings and disposal*	Radiation exposure Discharges from nuclear installations and nuclear power generation Radioactive waste arisings and disposal

2.3   The framework underlying these indicators is based on the Brundtland definition used in the Sustainable Development Strategy (see para 1.2). This very general definition is then expanded into four broad aims:

● *a healthy economy should be maintained to promote quality of life while at the same time protecting human health and the environment, in the UK and overseas, with all participants in all sectors paying the full social and environmental costs of their decisions;*

● *non-renewable resources should be used optimally;*

● *renewable resources should be used sustainably;*

● *damage to the carrying capacity of the environment and the risk to human health and biodiversity from the effects of economic activity should be minimised.*

2.4   Within each of these broad aims, the key issues identified in the Sustainable Development Strategy have been grouped together. The approach adopted broadly follows the structure in the Strategy and is similar to that used by the OECD. There is no single best way of grouping the issues. Whichever way is chosen there are overlaps between issues and issues which cut across the selected groups; for example, as well as describing the state of wildlife itself in a series of indicators, wildlife is affected by air and water pollution, land use and landscape changes, etc. The indicators are therefore cross-referenced by sector in Annex A to allow the user to identify all indicators relating to, for example, transport, agriculture, or health.

2.5   The order in the framework does not imply any particular hierarchy among the issues or among the indicators themselves. It would be difficult to assign a particular hierarchy since so many of the indicators cut across several

issues. However, the process of consultation and refinement of the indicators may lead to selection of a "core" set of indicators which are widely considered to be the most significant.

The indicator model

2.6   The OECD and several other countries base their work on indicators on the *pressure - state - response concept*. Human activities exert *pressures* on the environment, and change its *state* in terms of its quality and its stocks of natural resources. Society *responds* to these changes through general environmental, economic, and sectoral policies, and through changes in behaviour, thus affecting the *pressures* caused by human activities.

development rather than more limited environmental indicators. The model used is shown in Figure 1. Sectors of the economy generate wealth and welfare for households, enterprises, government and other actors in this country and overseas. Economic activity, and indeed households themselves, can however create pressure on the environment, through consumption of resources and output of pollutants. The quality of the environment in turn can impact on the welfare of households and individuals and other actors. The actors respond to changes in the state of the economy and of the environment, through behavioural and policy changes which either directly affect the environment, or alter the pressures on it from the economic

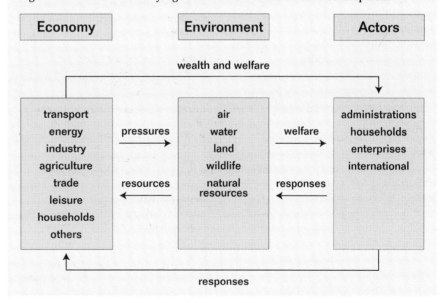

Figure 1: The model underlying the indicators of sustainable development

2.7   In this exercise, although the pressure - state - response concept was found useful in considering the issues in a systematic way, and indeed underpinned the structure of the Sustainable Development Strategy, it was necessary to modify it because of the added dimension involved in considering indicators of sustainable

sectors. Responses which constrain the activity of the economy in order to protect the environment may also be regarded in some senses as pressures, since they may reduce the ability of these sectors to generate wealth and welfare, and this in turn may inhibit the development of solutions to environmental problems.

2.8 "State" indicators have therefore been selected to reflect the state of the economy as well as the state of the environment, since it is reconciling economic development with environmental protection that lies at the heart of the sustainable development debate. State indicators thus attempt to measure the quality of the environment and the stock and quality of natural resources, and also the state of the economy - that is, the wealth and welfare which it generates. Examples of environmental state indicators include concentrations of pollutants in air and in water, stocks of fossil fuels, forests and fish. Economic state indicators include growth in economic output, the rate of inflation and the level of employment.

2.9 "Pressure" and "response" indicators are rather hard to disentangle in the sustainable development model. Both illustrate impacts on the environment and the economy caused by human activities. In the environmental indicator model, pressures are adverse impacts - consumption of resources or output of pollution - while responses are beneficial impacts - actions to reduce pollution or consumption of resources, or investment in environmental protection. Change in the state of the environment cannot be generally linked to a particular factor or pressure, since many factors, including natural factors, will affect it. In developing indicators of sustainable development, where possible, the environmental impact or pressure has been related to a measure of the economic output or benefit of that activity to illustrate the reconciliation that needs to be made between the two objectives of maintaining economic growth and minimising environmental damage. Thus the "pressure" indicators in many cases embody a measure of changes in the "efficiency" with which resources are being used, or

pollution generated in relation to output. To the extent that they show reductions in environmental impacts, or improvements in efficiency of resource use, they also measure the impact of responses. Examples of pressure (or pressure/ response) indicators include emissions from power stations in relation to electricity output, energy consumption by industry in relation to industrial output, household waste arisings.

2.10 Quantified response indicators are particularly hard to develop. There is often a range of policy responses to a particular issue - for example, improvements to urban air quality are being achieved through regulation of pollution from point sources and a range of measures in relation to transport including cleaner fuels, pedestrianisation of town centres, introduction of catalytic converters, etc. Many such responses are not easily quantified directly, but their impact manifests itself as changes in the state or pressure indicators, as discussed above.

2.11 One type of indicator included in this set is expenditure on environmental protection, which may be regarded as both a response to environmental pressure and a pressure on the activity of economic sectors. Total environmental expenditure needs to be interpreted with some caution. Increasing expenditure may imply either that the quality of the environment is improving, because more is being spent on it, or that more needs to be spent on it to maintain quality because the underlying pressures are increasing. Where possible, indicators of this type need to be related to the benefit derived from the expenditure, for example, in terms of amount of pollutant abated. This enables an assessment of cost/ benefit to be made. However, definition of expenditure on environmental protection is very difficult, as is collection of

information. Some of the issues, and the problems over the interpretation of such an indicator, are discussed with the presentation of Indicator a8.

2.12 Another type of indicator which cuts across the pressure/ response boundary is price. In a market economy, changes in price over time can provide very useful indirect indicators of progress towards sustainable development. These may not always be straightforward to interpret in isolation. For example, if the price of a renewable resource rises, it may mean that stocks are becoming depleted, or that demand is increasing for given stocks - that is, resources are not being exploited sustainably. But equally, it may mean that stocks are being exploited more sensibly, perhaps as a result of increased prices driving down demand, or the introduction of a quota which deliberately limits harvesting of the resource. Or a tax may have been imposed to reduce demand and promote sustainability. Similar arguments apply to non-renewable resources and to outputs of goods whose production can involve significant pollution, or are energy intensive. Price indicators should, therefore, often be viewed in tandem with indicators of quantities (for example, demand and supply).

2.13 Examples of response (or response/pressure) indicators include recycling of waste, re-use of previously developed land for new development, expenditure on pollution abatement per unit of pollutant abated, price of fuel.

2.14 Thus, it is particularly through the pressure/response indicators that the link between economic activity and environmental impact has been made explicitly. However, the classification of which of these are "pressure" and which "response" is not straightforward, nor does the nomenclature necessarily matter provided that the issues have been considered in a systematic way. The pressure - state - response concept has therefore been used as a tool in considering how to construct the indicators, but has not been used prescriptively. Annex A illustrates which categories the indicators are considered to represent.

What makes a good indicator?

2.15   Ideally, an indicator should meet the following criteria. It should:

● be representative;

● be scientifically valid;

● be simple and easy to interpret;

● show trends over time;

● give early warning about irreversible trends where possible;

● be sensitive to the changes in the environment or the economy it is meant to indicate;

● be based on readily available data or be available at reasonable cost;

● be based on data adequately documented and of known quality;

● be capable of being updated at regular intervals;

● have a target level or guideline against which to compare it.

2.16   In practice, it is rare for all of the criteria to be met in a single indicator. An indicator which is, for example simple and easy to interpret may be over-simplified and not scientifically valid. Another criterion used in developing the indicators is that overall the package of indicators needs to be as balanced as possible in terms of the coverage and representation of the issues. If we were to choose only indicators which matched all the criteria specified above, then some issues would not be covered at all.

2.17   Among the criteria listed above is that the indicator should be simple and easy to interpret. That is because the indicators ideally, if they are to achieve their objectives of highlighting important issues and possibly influencing behaviour, need to have some resonance, not just with national policy makers and environmental experts, but with businesses, people working in local government, and the general public. In practice, this is hard to achieve, but the Working Group has attempted to tackle the problem by including at least some indicators which will be of interest to certain groups - individuals and householders, businesses, local planners, farmers, etc, so that they can see the impact their own activities have on sustainable development. This has been done by breaking down some of the "pressure" or "impact" indicators by sector, and expressing them where possible in units to which individuals can relate - for example, per capita or per household rather than national aggregates.

Micro or local application of indicators

2.18   These indicators are national ones, and may not adequately reflect, for example, the situation within a particular geographical area, or within an industry sector or individual business. No national figures could ever do this adequately. However, wherever possible, the indicators have been selected with this more local dimension in mind, so that in many cases it should be possible to disaggregate them to a more local level. For example, indicators showing the "state" of the environment nationally in terms of average concentrations of pollutants or proportions of river length of a particular quality standard, could also be calculated for a smaller geographical area, so that locally comparison could be

made with the national "norm". Similarly, many of the "pressure" indicators, for example, relating to emissions of a particular pollutant, or amounts of waste generated, could be calculated for an industry sector or even an individual site or plant level. A manager of an industrial site could, for example, see how his firm's outputs of waste or pollutants compare with the national norm. Similarly, individuals can compare how their own individual behaviour, in terms of energy consumed, waste produced, water used, miles driven, relates to the national figures.

2.19   As mentioned above, local authorities in the UK are developing indicators of sustainability for local use. These are being developed by inviting people who live and work in local communities to say which issues are of most importance to them, and which indicators they would find most useful. This approach is valuable in gaining local acceptance and ownership of the indicators, and may therefore be particularly helpful in influencing people's behaviour. However, if every local area develops indicators in its own way for its own use, all defined and constructed in different ways, no overall national or regional picture can be obtained, nor is it possible for an area to compare its local situation or progress with a national or regional "norm" or with other similar areas.

2.20   It is hoped therefore that over time a consensus will develop, about a core set of indicators which would be useful for all local authorities to monitor, and which will be calculated on a common basis. This will also form part of the national core set. In addition, there will be some indicators which are more relevant at the national level, and which will not be used locally. Locally, however, people will also want to develop indicators which are particularly relevant to their situation, and have particular meaning for the local community.

2.21 Similarly at the international level, there may develop over time a consensus about a set of indicators which it would be sensible for all countries to report on a common basis, while countries will also want to develop indicators for national use which reflect their own particular situation and priorities. The Government hopes through this report to contribute to the development of not only national, but also international and local indicators.

Interpretation of the indicators

2.22 One of the criteria for a good indicator is that it should have a target or guideline level against which to compare it. Ideally, for each indicator one would identify a level or path which can be sustained in the long-term. Although, in some cases, there are already guidelines or targets set - for example, over concentrations of specific pollutants in the air or emissions of particular pollutants to air or water - these are often somewhat arbitrary. Even in cases where an acceptable level of emissions has been estimated with some confidence, our knowledge of the long-term effects is incomplete, and there may be interactions which mean that a level considered acceptable at one point in time may no longer be considered so at a later date. In developing the indicators therefore, the focus is on trends rather than absolute levels.

2.23 Even so, it is not always clear whether or not a particular trend is sustainable in the longer term. There are also judgements to be made about where the optimum balance lies between environmental benefits on the one hand and economic costs on the other. Where possible, however, the trends have been related to any available guideline levels or agreed targets or commitments. The development of indicators will in turn illuminate the possibilities and

problems associated with setting new sustainable development targets and objectives.

2.24 All of the indicators need to be used and interpreted with caution. Their interpretation - what they are telling us about whether our development is becoming more or less sustainable - is not straightforward, and is a matter on which there will be much debate. The Government has not attempted in this exercise to say whether it thinks individual indicators are moving in a more or less sustainable direction. However, some general principles can be stated about the long-term trends we would expect to see in particular types of indicators if development is sustainable:

● levels of pollution would be stable or falling, and at levels below those at which there is an unacceptable impact on the environment or human health;

● the amount of pollution produced, or resource consumed, per unit of output would be stable or falling;

● expenditure on pollution prevention or control in relation to stable environmental quality would be stable or falling (in other words, if it is costing an increasing amount to maintain stable environmental quality, this would not be sustainable in the long-term);

● the relative price of non-renewable resources should be stable or rising, to encourage conservation, and investment in alternative sources;

● stocks of renewable resources should be stable or increasing (that is, we should not be using up resources at a rate faster than they can be replaced).

2.25 While the above principles should apply in the long-term, that does not preclude trends which in the short-term are moving in a less sustainable direction. It may be that

to optimise overall sustainability, it is necessary for some trends to move in a less sustainable direction for a time - for example, in order to boost the economy so that greater environmental protection can be afforded in the longer term. It is also the case, that while such principles may spell out the necessary trends for sustainable development, that does not mean that the achievement of such trends is sufficient for us to achieve sustainable development. As discussed above, the indicators are not fully comprehensive and there are some environmental attributes which are not readily quantifiable, and which cannot be factored into the indicator trends. These also need to be taken into account in assessing whether our development is on a sustainable path.

2.26 In all cases the indicators are simplifications of reality. They cannot describe every local situation, nor should they be taken to imply causation, except where specific factors are linked together. In some cases, ideal indicators are not available, and proxy indicators have been used. In other cases, the data may be less reliable or representative than we would wish. Some indicators, particularly those relating to wildlife, for example, may be subject to significant fluctuations from one year to the next for entirely natural reasons. Along with each indicator there is information which will assist the reader in using and interpreting it.

Chapter 3

Summary of the indicators package

3.1   These indicators are being published as a *preliminary* set, designed to stimulate debate and discussion about which indicators are useful, and how better indicators might be developed in future, rather than as a definitive statement about our progress in achieving more sustainable development. Indeed, although the indicators have been selected because they are informative and help us to better understand some of the underlying issues and driving forces, it is not always readily apparent what the trends are telling us in relation to sustainable development. The indicators will require careful analysis and interpretation. Nevertheless, it is possible to draw some overall messages from those indicators published in this report for which data are currently available.

a   The economy

3.2   Since 1970, output of the economy has grown in real terms by around 60 per cent, an average growth of 2 per cent per year. The structure of the economy has changed significantly; in 1970 the manufacturing sector accounted for one-third of GDP but now accounts for just one-fifth, while there has been a corresponding growth in the service sector which now accounts for two-thirds of GDP. Within the manufacturing sector there have also been changes - a decline in traditional heavy industries and mining and a growth in high

technology industries. This structural change has been accompanied by changes in employment. Over three-quarters of all employees now work in the services sector, while employment in manufacturing industry has fallen by over 40 per cent since 1978. The proportion of the population of working age in work has declined, mirrored by increasing unemployment which currently stands at about 8 per cent of the workforce.

3.3   Investment expenditure adds to the capital stock that will be available to produce goods and services in future years. As a proportion of GDP, investment peaked at over 20 per cent in 1989, but as a result of the recession in the early 1990s has fallen to under 18 per cent of GDP in 1994. The public sector borrowing requirement and total government debt rose sharply as a share of GDP following the recession of the early 1990s, but has started to return towards balance and the long term trend in the ratio of debt to GDP is downwards. Around $2^1/_2$ per cent of GDP is estimated to be spent on environmental protection, although this is difficult to measure and there is an increasing tendency for environmental features to be built into the design of products and processes.

3.4   The rate of inflation fell rapidly from peak levels of over 20 per cent in the 1970s and early 1980s. It has now remained under 4 per cent

since the third quarter of 1992. Consumer expenditure has accounted for a growing share of GDP throughout the 1980s, and reached a peak of 63 per cent in 1993, although there are signs of a decreasing share since then. Consumer expenditure per head has risen in real terms by 73 per cent since 1970. As individuals have become better off their spending patterns have changed. Proportionately less is spent on essentials like food while spending on leisure activities and travel has increased sharply. People are also healthier overall and living longer, as evidenced by the conventional measures of infant mortality (which has declined by almost two-thirds since 1970) and life expectancy (which has increased by over 5 per cent since 1971).

b   Transport use

3.5   Growth in people's income has allowed them to travel more. Since 1970 the amount of car travel has almost doubled to an average of 6,500 miles per person per year, while travel on other road passenger vehicles, mainly buses and coaches, has reduced by a quarter to less than 600 miles per year. Rail travel has remained broadly unchanged at around 400 miles per year. Except for journeys of up to one mile in length, where walking is the most common mode, the car has increasingly dominated, even for short trips. Only 2 per cent of journeys up to five miles long are

Chapter 3

made by bicycle, compared with 4 per cent twenty years ago. Since 1974, the real price of rail and bus fares has increased faster than the 50 per cent growth in real disposable incomes. The real cost of motoring has fallen, and car travel is therefore much more affordable than it was twenty years ago.

3.6 Although amounts of freight transported have not increased greatly over the last twenty years, the kinds of freight carried have changed with the decline of heavy industries, and the distances over which it is carried have increased; 95 per cent of land-based freight is now carried by road.

c Leisure and tourism

3.7 Activities associated with leisure and tourism are among the fastest growing in the economy. The tourism industry in the UK accounts for over 5 per cent of GDP, having doubled in the 1980s. Impacts on the environment of leisure and tourism, being generally concentrated on particular locations at certain times of the year, are not susceptible to measurement at a national level. However, one common impact which can be measured is the growth in travel, particularly by road and air, for leisure activities. Leisure travel has increased by one-third since 1975/76. On average, individuals today make journeys totalling over 2,600 miles per year in pursuit of leisure activities. Half of leisure journeys are social trips involving visiting friends. Overseas air travel has also increased significantly - the number of passengers passing through UK airports has trebled in the last twenty years.

d Overseas trade

3.8 The indicators in this report focus primarily on the UK, but through trade, activities in the UK can impact on the environment in other countries and their economic activities can impact on our

environment. Trade can enable the world to maximise output from a given input of resources, and helps generate wealth needed to invest in environmental protection. But economic activities linked to trade can harm the environment by exacerbating problems of pollution and resource depletion. Indicators in this report are only intended to highlight the issue and act as background indicators which help to explain some of the trends in other indicators. A great deal of further work is required to develop meaningful indicators of the environmental impacts of trade.

3.9 The UK is a net importer of food, wood and wood products, and, since about 1982, of manufactured goods. Imports of food and manufactured goods are increasing. The UK imports around 85 per cent of its timber and wood products. Trends in imports of other basic materials over the last twenty years have been largely dominated by fuels. Exports have increased more than four-fold since 1970, while imports have decreased by a third and the two have been broadly in balance since the early 1980s. Tourism has increased markedly since the early 1970s, and is now a significant component of the UK trade balance. In 1994, UK residents spent £12 billion abroad on holiday, while overseas visitors spent £7 billion in the UK. Other services also contribute to the trade balance, accounting for almost one fifth of total exports and 13 per cent of total imports in 1994. The UK imported around 70 million tonnes of hazardous waste in 1993/94, and amounts imported have been increasing. The UK does not export hazardous waste. Figures are not available to show what proportion of goods and resources imported to the UK are produced sustainably in the country of origin as very few internationally recognised standards exist for classifying goods as sustainably produced.

e Energy

3.10 UK oil and natural gas production has increased over the last two decades, while production of coal has declined. Consumption of the UK's own resources of oil is currently at a rate of 8 per cent of proven and probable reserves per year, while for natural gas the rate is 4 per cent, although additional reserves of oil and gas continue to be identified. In the longer term, as existing energy resources become more scarce, energy prices can be expected to rise, encouraging greater fuel efficiency and boosting incentives to develop alternative sources. Nuclear power stations currently account for 27 per cent, and renewable sources 2 per cent, of the UK's total electricity generation. Over 30 per cent of primary energy is lost in the conversion to electricity and secondary fuels and in the distribution system.

3.11 Primary energy consumption in the UK has remained fairly constant since 1970, despite the 60 per cent increase in GDP, indicating that the economy has become more fuel-efficient overall. This has been attributed in part to the increase in world oil prices in the 1970s and early 1980s. Most of the improvement has been in the manufacturing sector where final energy consumption has fallen by 40 per cent, largely as a result of structural change. Energy consumption in the commercial sector - the fastest growing sector in the economy - has risen by 15 per cent, although some energy efficiency gains have also been made here. Final energy consumption by households has risen by 20 per cent since 1970, mainly because of the increase in the number of households. Fuel consumption is rising fastest in the road transport sector, and there has been no improvement in fuel efficiency over the last twenty years in terms of fuel used for passenger and freight transport, despite increases in the fuel efficiency of individual vehicles. Fuel use for road transport has risen by nearly 90 per cent since 1970, and now accounts for a quarter of total final energy consumption.

3.12   Domestic fuel prices increased by 11 per cent in real terms since 1970, mainly as a result of VAT at 8 per cent in April 1994, while real per capita incomes have increased by 65 per cent. Transport fuel prices have increased by only 2 per cent, although in recent years price rises have been larger as road fuel duties have been increased in real terms by 5 per cent a year. Industrial fuel prices in real terms are 10 per cent lower than they were twenty years ago; price reductions have been particularly marked in recent years as added competition between energy suppliers has exerted downward pressure on prices.

f Land use

3.13   In 1981, land in urban use constituted just over 10 per cent of the area of England, and it is expected that this will have increased to almost 12 per cent by 2016. A key factor behind such growth is a projected increase in the number of households which in turn is caused by a growing population and reducing average household size. The number of households in Great Britain has increased by around 20 per cent over the last twenty years and is expected to continue to increase at a similar rate into the next century. In England, the rate of growth in land in urban use is expected to be about half that of households. This is assuming a continuation of recent trends for around 40 to 50 per cent of new development to take place on previously developed land. Around 800,000 properties in England are vacant, and the Government is encouraging owners to bring these back into residential use. Some reclaimed derelict land is used for new development.

The stock of derelict land declined from 45,700 hectares in 1982 to 39,600 hectares in 1993, despite large scale structural change in industry which produced new dereliction. The growth in transport has led to a greater demand for new roads, and hence land; in the second half of the 1980s an estimated 12,000 hectares of land in England were used for road building, some two-thirds of which was land previously in rural use.

3.14   Patterns of land use have changed over the last twenty years and have contributed to the growth in travel. Increases in income and car ownership have led to people living further away from where they work and shop, and from their children's schools. Average distances travelled to work have increased by 40 per cent to 7.5 miles over the last twenty years. There has been considerable growth of out-of-town shopping centres and business parks which are accessible mainly by car, increasing pressure on roads and distances travelled and contributing to a run-down of many inner city areas. Between 1985 and 1991, the amount of out-of-town retail floor space almost quadrupled.

g Water resources

3.15   Overall the UK has a plentiful natural supply of freshwater, but the distribution of resources does not match that of demand. In Scotland, Northern Ireland, Wales and most of England, there is a substantial margin between the level of effective rainfall (which occurs in drought years) and the total licensed abstractions of water from surface waters and groundwater. The margins are even greater if total actual abstractions are considered. In the NRA Thames and Anglian regions, however, licensed abstractions are more than two-thirds of the effective rainfall, although in both regions there is extensive water re-use. More recently, the hot dry summer of

1995 has highlighted the pressure that peak demands for public water supply has put on the developed resources. In 1993/94, five of the ten NRA regions used 80 per cent of the available resource and one used over 90 per cent of the resource expected to be available under drought conditions once in fifty years. In some areas unacceptably low flows have occurred in some rivers, often as a result of localised over-abstraction under authorisations granted many years ago. In 1990, the NRA identified for remedial action forty reaches of rivers, amounting to 335 km. Subsequent action has reduced the affected length to 207 km. There is a target of further reduction to 79 km by 1996/97.

h Forestry

3.16   Around 10 per cent of the UK is covered by forests, and the Government has announced that it would like to see a doubling of woodland in England over the next half century. Achievement of this will depend on securing changes in the Common Agricultural Policy to allow forestry to compete more effectively with agriculture for land use. Only 1.4 per cent of Great Britain is still covered by ancient, semi-natural woodland. Forest cover has increased in Great Britain by one-third since the early 1970s. Around two-thirds of the forest area is conifer and one-third broadleaved with the former particularly represented in the uplands. In recent years the proportion of broadleaved forest has been increasing. About 15 per cent of the UK consumption of wood products is met from home grown timber.

j Fish resources

3.17   While fishing accounts for only 0.1 per cent of GDP, it is significant in terms of the income of local economies. However, many fish stocks in waters of EC member states are over-exploited and, for nearly 60 per cent of the stocks assessed in 1994, the spawning population was estimated to be at a level where there is a risk of stock collapse.

k Climate change

3.18   Globally, greenhouse gas concentrations have increased over the last 200 years, and the balance of evidence now suggests this has led to discernible global climate change. In the UK, emissions of greenhouse gases declined by around 15 per cent between 1970 and 1993. They are expected to meet and even surpass the internationally agreed target of returning emissions to 1990 levels by the year 2000. Emissions relative to economic output have almost halved since 1970.

l Ozone layer depletion

3.19   Atmospheric chlorine loading from ozone-depleting substances has more than doubled between 1970 and 1994. The ozone layer above the UK has shown a gradual thinning since the early 1980s. International agreements to phase out or limit production of the main ozone- depleters have resulted in substantial reductions in production and consumption of these substances, in the UK and the rest of the EC. Chlorine loading is expected to peak towards the end of the 1990s, although it will be the latter part of the next century before loading returns to pre ozone-hole levels.

m Acid deposition

3.20   The area of the UK where sulphur deposition exceeded the estimated critical load for soil acidity decreased from 38 per cent over the period 1986/88 to 32 per cent in the period 1989/92. In around 17 per cent of freshwater, mainly in sensitive upland areas of north and west Britain, estimated critical loads for acidity are exceeded. Emissions of sulphur dioxide and nitrogen oxides from power stations have fallen by around 30 per cent since 1970. The UK's performance in reducing emissions from large combustion plants is ahead of EC Directive targets. Emissions of nitrogen oxides from road-passenger transport are now more than two and a half times higher than in 1970, although in the last two years emissions have been declining as a result of increased penetration of diesel cars, and because of increases in road fuel duty, and will continue to fall because of the introduction of catalytic converters.

n Air

3.21   Air quality in the UK is generally classified as "good" or "very good" according to environmental quality standards. There have been considerable improvements over the last twenty years as a result of the decline in smoke, sulphur dioxide and nitrogen oxide emissions from large combustion plants. However, episodes of poor air quality continue to occur occasionally, particularly in London and other large urban conurbations, because of the poor dispersion of traffic pollutants under certain meteorological conditions. Ground-level ozone concentrations were particularly high in 1989 and 1990 because of the hot weather in those years, but there is little evidence of changing trends in peak ozone concentrations. Peak nitrogen dioxide levels are highest in major

urban areas and in the last few years have reached highest recorded levels. Particulate matter concentrations from road traffic are likely to be increasing in urban areas because of increased use of diesel vehicles. Emissions of volatile organic compounds from road passenger transport increased by 85 per cent between 1970 and 1990 and emissions of carbon monoxide from road passenger transport more than doubled over this period. Recently, such emissions have been declining as a result of increased penetration of diesel cars and increases in road fuel duty, and they will continue to fall because of the introduction of catalytic converters for new vehicles. The UK is committed to reducing total VOC emissions from all sources by 30 per cent by 1999, compared with 1988. Lead emissions from cars have declined substantially with the reduction in the lead content of petrol and the increasing use of unleaded petrol, which accounted for 65 per cent of petrol consumption by the end of 1995.

p Freshwater quality

3.22   Most UK rivers are classed as good or fair quality (chemically, 91 per cent in England and Wales, 99 per cent in Scotland and Northern Ireland; biologically, 81 per cent in England and Wales, 97 per cent in Scotland, and 89 per cent in Northern Ireland). Quality is generally improving in England and Wales, in large part owing to the level of water industry investment on improved sewerage and sewage treatment and improvements by other industry; 94 per cent of sewage treatment works complied with discharge consents in 1993, compared with 77 per cent in 1986. Compliance rates for private sewage and trade discharges are lower, 51 per cent and 71 per cent respectively. There was a net upgrading in quality of over 26 per cent of total monitored length of rivers and canals in England and Wales between 1990 and 1994. The Government has set a target of upgrading the chemical quality of some 1,000 km of rivers in the UK between 1995 and 2000.

3.23   Sufficient levels of nutrients (nitrates and phosphorus) in water, combined with particular weather conditions, can lead to formation of toxic algal blooms. In the UK, nitrate levels in rivers have generally been fairly constant since 1975, but nitrate levels in some groundwater sites are still rising. Phosphorus levels have in general fallen sharply in lowland rivers in Great Britain since 1989, largely as a result of the increased use of phosphate-free washing powders and liquids, but in Northern Ireland this reduction has been offset by increased phosphorus inputs from agriculture. The Government has a policy to minimise pesticide usage, and most pesticides detected in water are non-agricultural pesticides found in very small quantities, well below any existing or proposed environmental quality standards. The total number of reported water pollution incidents in England and Wales has increased over the last decade, but the number of major and significant incidents fell over the period 1992 to 1994. Expenditure on treatment of drinking water has risen substantially since 1989, primarily because of the need to meet new regulations on drinking water quality which incorporated the requirements of an EC directive. Capital expenditure on sewage treatment works similarly increased from around £5-6 (at 1994-95 prices) per head of the population during the 1980s to nearly £20 per head in the early 1990s in England and Wales. Operational costs of sewage treatment have remained at about £7 per head over the last three years.

q   Marine

3.24   Most estuaries are of good or fair quality (92 per cent in England and Wales, 96 per cent in Scotland, and 88 per cent in Northern Ireland). Concentrations in estuaries of dissolved heavy metals, particularly lead and zinc, have declined over the last three years. Inputs of contaminants to the sea have generally declined substantially over the last decade, although nitrogen inputs increased in the early 1990s, levelling off subsequently in 1993 and 1994. Concentrations of contaminants found in fish in areas considered to be at higher risk have been relatively stable or declining over the last ten years. There were around 680 oil spills from shipping and offshore installations reported in 1993, 99 of which were relatively large incidents with over 100 gallons released. Since 1988, there has been an improvement in the quality of bathing waters, and 89 per cent complied with the EC Directive mandatory coliform standards in 1995, partly reflecting a major programme of investment in sewage treatment plants.

r   Wildlife and habitats

3.25   Many species and habitats in the UK have declined in number or area since 1945. Around a quarter of native species of fish, invertebrates, plants, and mosses are threatened or nationally scarce. However, many species will always be rare simply because the extent of their habitat is naturally very small or because the UK is at the geographical limit of their natural range. Over the last twenty years there have been substantial changes in the population sizes and geographical distributions of many British breeding birds. In woodland, coastal and wetland habitats more species experienced an increase in numbers than a loss. However, this trend was reversed for farmland birds where 22 species experienced

a decline in population size and 10 a decline in geographical distribution. There was a significant loss of plant diversity in hedgerows in lowland pastural landscapes and in semi-natural grasslands in lowland landscapes in Great Britain between 1978 and 1990. The area of chalk grassland has substantially decreased in England over the last thirty years, particularly in Wiltshire. Around 30 per cent of lakes and ponds, which are important havens for some species, have been lost since 1945. The geographical distributions of just over a half of Great Britain species of dragonflies and butterflies have reduced since the 1970s. Over a third of British species of mammals are believed to have declined in population size over the last thirty years (most of these being species of rodents or bats) and about a quarter are believed to have increased (most of these being carnivores or deer, and half being non-native species). The recently published Biodiversity Steering Group report has identified targets and costed action plans for 116 priority species and 14 key habitats of conservation importance. The habitat plans cover about 2 per cent of the UK land area.

s   Land cover and landscape

3.26   Arable land, improved grassland and heath/moorland are the main agricultural land cover types in Great Britain. There were net reductions in these cover types between 1984 and 1990 owing principally to urbanisation and afforestation. In recent years, increasing amounts of rural land have been designated and protected for their natural beauty or their value as wildlife habitats. Damage can still occur within protected sites, but recorded damage represents a tiny proportion of the total area of Sites of Special Scientific Interest and, since 1989, the extent of recorded damage has been decreasing.

Chapter 3

3.27 Agricultural productivity in the UK has almost quadrupled since 1945. Following the post-war drive for increased food production, combined with significant improvements in technology, gross output increased substantially between 1945 and the mid-1980s. Since the mid-1980s, gross output has been more or less stable, with total inputs declining and productivity increasing by about 1 per cent a year. However, output has declined slightly since supply controls were imposed by the 1992 CAP reform. Inputs of nitrogen to agricultural soils increased from 1945 up to the mid-1980s. Over the last ten years, both inputs and outputs of nitrogen and inputs of nitrogen relative to outputs of protein have remained broadly stable. The area of land on which pesticides are applied has also increased since 1945. However, despite an increase in the use of fungicides and growth regulations, the total quantity applied has declined since the mid-1980s. Loss of hedgerows, which are attractive features of the landscape and important havens of biodiversity, is continuing but at a slower rate than before as farmers, in particular, have become more aware of the need to properly maintain hedgerows for wildlife habitats and as barriers against erosion. Most loss of hedgerows arises from lack of management, which causes hedges to be reclassified as lines of bushes or trees. The rate of net loss of hedgerows in England and Wales decreased from 22,000 km per year between 1984 and 1990 to 18,000 km per year between 1990 and 1993. In the latter period, rates of hedgerow planting actually exceeded rates of hedgerow removal which partly compensated for the large losses of hedgerows by management neglect. In Great Britain, the length of walls, which are also important landscape features, decreased from 215,000 km to 195,000 km between 1984 and 1990. Increasing areas of agricultural land are being managed under environmental management schemes, one of whose objectives is to encourage more extensive farming methods. These schemes include the Environmentally Sensitive Areas and Countryside Stewardship schemes, launched in 1987 and 1991 respectively.

t Soils

3.28 Organic matter and nutrients (such as phosphorus and potassium) in soils and optimum pH (acidity) are important for maintaining soil quality and plant growth. Arable farming practices, such as the ploughing up of grasslands, have reduced the organic matter content of some agricultural topsoils in England and Wales. The amount of arable soils with high acidity has declined but there has been some increase in the amount of grassland soils with high acidity, although grassland is less sensitive to acidity than arable land. Phosphorus concentrations below 10 mg/l and potassium concentrations below 60 mg/l in soils can restrict plant growth. Since 1969, there has been a decrease in the proportion of agricultural topsoils in England and Wales with phosphorus concentrations below 10 mg/l, while the proportion of such soils with potassium levels below 60 mg/l has remained broadly stable. Enhanced concentrations of heavy metals in soils are mainly to be found in areas of present or past industrial activity.

u Minerals extraction

3.29 There are extensive geological resources of most minerals worked in the UK, but there is increasing difficulty in finding environmentally acceptable sites for extraction, and a need for sites to be managed and restored to high environmental standards. The annual output of primary aggregates for construction has fluctuated with the economy since the early 1970s, although an increasing demand for aggregates is forecast over the next twenty years. Around 70 million tonnes of demolition and construction waste is generated each year, approximately 4 per cent of which is recycled as high grade aggregates. A further 30 per cent is used in an unprocessed form for construction site engineering and about 30 per cent for landfill site engineering. In 1994, 60,000 hectares of land in England were affected by surface mineral workings or disposal of mineral working deposits, although many sites are now covered by restoration conditions and about 3,400 hectares a year have been restored to beneficial use between 1974 and 1994. Around 1,600 square km of sea-bed around the UK is licensed for the dredging of aggregates.

v Waste

3.30 The UK generates around 400 million tonnes of waste per year. Nearly a quarter of this is mining and quarrying waste, much of which remains on the site at which it was generated. Largely inert construction waste, as discussed above, accounts for a further 70 million tonnes. Around 85 million tonnes are generated annually by the industrial and commercial sectors. Trends are currently uncertain, but the composition of the waste stream is likely to be changing as a result of changes in the structure of the economy. About three-quarters of controlled waste currently produced goes to landfill, but the introduction of the landfill tax will encourage waste producers to use options for their waste which are towards the top of the waste hierarchy, such as minimisation and recycling.

3.31 Waste generated directly by households amounts to around 4 to 5 per cent of the total. While consumer expenditure has increased by 30 per cent over the last ten years, amounts of household waste have increased by only 2 to 3 per cent, probably because of the lightweighting of packaging and substitution of plastics for glass. Only around 5 per cent of household waste is currently recycled, as against a target of recycling 25 per cent of household waste by 2000. Recycling of iron and other metals is well established and rates have changed little over the last ten years. Recycling of glass and of metal cans has been increasing sharply since the second half of the 1980s. Landfill remains the predominant route for waste disposal in the UK, and for some time yet will continue to account for the majority of waste disposal. Around 124 million tonnes of controlled waste, excluding sewage sludge and dredged spoils, goes directly to landfill annually.

w Radioactivity

3.32 The average radiation dose to UK individuals is estimated at 2,600 µSv per year. Around 85 per cent of this dose comes from natural sources, in particular radon, and less than 0.1 per cent comes from radioactive discharges from nuclear installations. Between 1983 and 1993, nuclear power generation increased by 84 per cent. Over the same period, the toxicity of authorised discharges of radioactive waste to air and water fell by 7 per cent and 91 per cent respectively. Arisings of high-level wastes have increased by 38 per cent since 1987, reflecting increased nuclear power generation and fuel reprocessing. Arisings of intermediate-level wastes have increased by 43 per cent since 1987. High-level and intermediate-level waste is not currently disposed of, but is stored, pending development of a new deep disposal site. Arisings and disposal of low-level wastes almost halved between 1986 and 1994.

Chapter 3

chapter 4

The indicators - a preliminary set

4.1 This section of the report presents the indicators themselves. The indicators are presented in the order in which the issues illustrated appear in the framework and, as stated in paragraph 2.5 above, do not reflect any particular hierarchy in terms of the importance related to each issue. Many of the indicators are relevant to more than one issue, but each is shown only once and cross-reference is made to other relevant indicators where appropriate. For those interested in looking at indicators in a different dimension from that shown in the framework (for example, all the indicators relevant to transport) a table showing cross-cutting issues is at Annex A.

4.2 Each indicator "family" is presented along with a brief discussion of the issue, to illustrate why that particular indicator has been selected. Where available, the trend of the indicator going back over time to around 1970 is illustrated in graphical form. For some indicators, a consistent time series over this period is not available, and a shorter series or a point estimate only is shown. Data availability is one of the criteria for selecting an indicator, but in some cases indicators have been proposed for which data are not currently available, but may be collected in the future.

4.3 An interpretation of the trends shown is also given with each indicator. Sources, references and details of measurement of the individual indicators are given in Annex B. A bibliography of related indicator work, in the UK and abroad, is given in Annex C.

a The economy

One of the objectives of sustainable development is to promote a healthy economy in order to generate the resources to meet people's needs and improve environmental quality. This in turn can further the protection of human health and the natural environment.

Promotion of a healthy economy

A wide range of economic indicators is generally available. It is not the purpose of this section to give a fully comprehensive picture of the economy, but macroeconomic data series such as GDP, sectoral employment and output, and indicators of internal balance are included below. They can have direct relevance to sustainable development, some of

them serve as standard comparators for more specific indicators, and they provide the general economic background against which progress towards sustainable development can be assessed. This section also includes estimates of expenditure on pollution control and abatement, which are of direct relevance to sustainable development.

Further economic indicators are included elsewhere in the report. For example, output of the energy sector is included in the *Energy* section, and disaggregated trade series are included in the *Overseas trade* section. Indicators of human health are included in the next subsection.

Indicator a1:
Gross Domestic Product

Since 1970, the output of the economy has grown in real terms by around 60 per cent. Figures for growth in GDP demonstrate the cyclical nature of the economy and its underlying growth. After the recession of the early 1990s, growth accelerated in 1994 but has recently moderated.

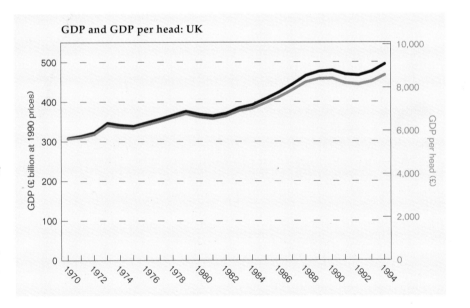

GDP and GDP per head: UK

The rate of growth of GDP is the main indicator of the speed with which the economy is expanding. If sustained over time, growth in GDP per head will lead to general increases in the standard of living. However, the relationship between growth in GDP and sustainable development is not straightforward. Other things being equal, growth is clearly desirable and, indeed, the objective of the Government's economic policy is "to promote

sustained economic growth and rising prosperity". Beyond this, it is hard to generalise. Higher economic activity reflected in higher GDP may increase pollution, or rest upon depletion of scarce natural resources. But, equally growth may raise demands for higher environmental standards and a healthy economy is more able to afford environmental goods, thus improving the future quality of life and promoting sustainability.

Published figures for GDP do not take proper account of factors such as these and in some cases can be positively misleading, eg expenditure on preventing pollution is counted as a positive component of GDP. This has led to calls for the development of environmental or "green" accounts, which make proper allowance for environmental impacts. But the issues involved, such as the valuation of the damage of pollution, are complex and the development of such accounts is still at a very early stage. Even green accounts do not purport to measure overall welfare because they do not take account of other factors relating to quality of life. In any event, both environmental and economic indicators need to be examined in parallel for a proper consideration of sustainable development.

Indicator a1 shows the growth in GDP and in GDP per head of population in the UK since 1970.

Figures for growth in GDP demonstrate the cyclical nature of the economy and its underlying growth. After the recession of the early 1990s, growth accelerated in 1994 but has recently moderated. GDP was 61 per cent higher in real terms in 1994 than it was in 1970. Over the same period, the UK population rose by 5 per cent so that GDP, in 1990 prices, per head of population has risen by 53 per cent from around £5,500 in 1970 to £8,500 in 1994.

Indicator a2: Structure of the economy

Structural changes in the UK economy have resulted in a decline in traditional heavy manufacturing and mining industries and an increased share of GDP from service-based industries.

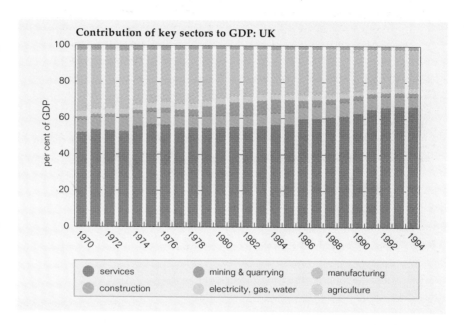

Contribution of key sectors to GDP: UK

Legend: services, construction, mining & quarrying, electricity, gas, water, manufacturing, agriculture

The structure of the economy - that is, the relative size and activity of the various sectors of the economy - has a considerable potential impact on the environment. Consumption of natural resources, use of energy, the types and volumes of pollutants and waste produced are all dependent on the activities of the various sectors. The last 20 years have seen a steady shift in economic activity in the UK in common with other western European countries: a decline in traditional heavy industries in the manufacturing and mining/quarrying sector, and growth in high technology industries. This has been accompanied by a steady growth in the service sector, which now accounts for two thirds of GDP. Innovation and technical advances have given rise to development of more environmentally friendly products -

more energy-efficient appliances and cars, cleaner fuels and processes. There has been stronger growth in the environmental products industries between 1985 and 1992 than in the production industries as a whole.

Indicator a2 shows the contribution of key sectors to UK GDP since 1970.

This indicator has been included to give a background picture of changes in the economy which have an indirect impact on the environment, by influencing the patterns of consumption and generation of pollution and waste in the UK. The share of GDP from manufacturing decreased from 33 per cent in 1970 to 21 per cent in 1994 whereas the share from service-based industries increased

from 52 to 67 per cent over this period. However, interpretation of this indicator is not straightforward. Structural changes may have tended to reduce domestic pollution. But changes in the structure of the UK economy may be compensated by changes in trade - our consumption of our own natural resources may decline but be offset by increased consumption of resources from elsewhere in the world. Similarly, where levels of pollution in this country have changed as a result of changes to the structure of industry, the displacement of UK goods by imports may mean that pollution and consumption of raw materials has been "exported" to the country of manufacture. It would be completely beyond the scope of this report to attempt to quantify such impacts on a global scale but see also Indicator d1 on UK imports and exports in the *Overseas trade* section.

a The economy

a The economy

Indicator a3:
Expenditure components of GDP and personal savings

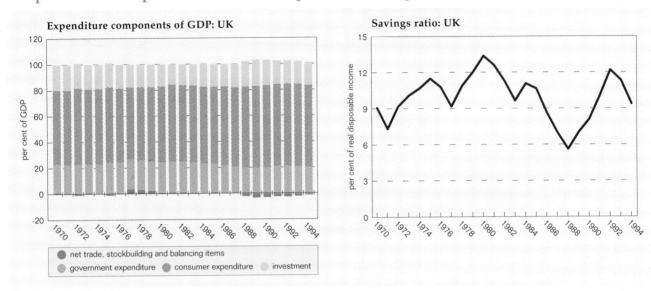

Expenditure components of GDP: UK

Savings ratio: UK

- ● net trade, stockbuilding and balancing items
- ● government expenditure ● consumer expenditure ● investment

Consumers expenditure took a growing share of GDP in the late 1980s but recent growth has been founded more on improvements in the net trade position. The savings ratio fell in the 1980s but is now close to its average level for the past 20 years.

As well as disaggregating GDP by sector, GDP can be broken down by types of spending: investment, consumption, stockbuilding and net trade. Investment expenditure adds to the capital stock that will be available to produce goods and services in future years. Public and private consumption, on the other hand, represent current consumption of resources, although a significant fraction of consumer's expenditure - usually between 5 to 10 per cent - is on durable goods. Investment also uses up resources and ever-higher levels of investment would not be efficient. Stockbuilding can oscillate from year to year and has little implication for sustainable development.

Indicator a3 shows the breakdown since 1970 of GDP by category of expenditure, ie between consumption expenditure by the personal and government sectors, and investment expenditure, and the relationship of saving to personal disposable income.

A rise in the percentage of GDP devoted to consumption reduces the resources available for investment and, other things equal, future levels of consumption. This is not necessarily a bad thing, as current consumption is itself desirable. However, a continually rising share of consumption in GDP would be unsustainable in the long term. Consumer expenditure as a share of GDP increased in the late

1980s reaching 63 per cent in 1993 although there are signs of a decreasing share since then. Government expenditure as a share of GDP decreased from peak levels of nearly 25 per cent in the early 1980s to under 21 per cent in 1994. Investment as a share of GDP peaked at over 20 per cent in 1989 but, as a result of the recession in the early 1990s, has fallen to under 18 per cent in 1994.

It is for people to choose freely how to spend their incomes. To the extent which they choose to save, this may contribute to the amount of finance available to industry. With an aging population, too low a saving rate might jeopardise consumption levels in the future. The savings ratio fell in the 1980s to under 6 per cent of disposable income in 1988 but increased to around 12 per cent in 1993. In 1994, the savings ratio was just over 9 per cent, close to its average level for the past 20 years.

Indicator a4:
Consumer expenditure

Consumer expenditure per head has increased in real terms by 73 per cent between 1970 and 1994 but in some years it has declined reflecting the economic cycle.

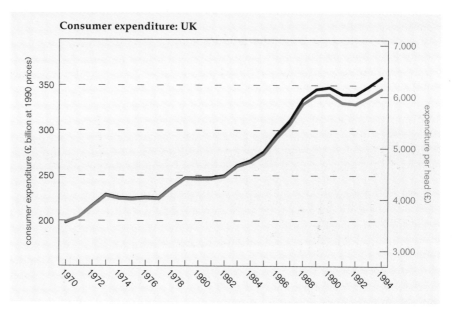

Consumer expenditure: UK

Consumer expenditure is a measure of the economic benefit which people derive from a growing economy in the form of the ability to buy goods and services. It also reflects change in demand, which may impact on the environment directly and indirectly through changing patterns of consumption of raw materials, water and energy, greater production of waste and pollution, greater demand for travel etc.

Indicator a4 shows the trends in consumer expenditure and expenditure per head of population in the UK since 1970.

Consumer expenditure was 81 per cent higher in real terms in 1994 than it was in 1970. Over the same period, the UK population rose by 5 per cent so that, per capita, consumer expenditure has increased by 73 per cent since 1970, around 2.3 per cent per year.

There have also been changes in the pattern of consumption as real incomes have increased. A smaller proportion is spent on food, 11 per cent in 1994 compared with around 20 per cent in 1970. Meanwhile, an increasing proportion is spent on transport and on recreation and leisure activities. In particular, the share of household expenditure spent abroad has more than doubled and expenditure on catering (meals and accommodation) has increased from around 5 per cent to almost 9 per cent of the total over the same period.

Indicator a5:
Inflation

Inflation has now remained below 4 per cent for the longest consecutive period for almost 50 years.

Rate of inflation: UK

Inflation is relevant for economic growth, because economies work most efficiently when inflation is low and stable. If inflation is rising persistently, it may indicate that the economy is overheating and that the rate of growth is therefore not sustainable. Since October 1992 the Government has set an explicit inflation objective of keeping underlying inflation within the range 1-4 per cent, and is now committed to getting inflation below 2.5 per cent by the end of the present parliament.

Indicator a5 shows underlying UK inflation on a quarterly basis since the start of 1976, as measured by the Government's chosen definition - the change in the RPI, excluding mortgage interest payments.

The rate of inflation dropped rapidly from nearly 23 per cent at the start of 1976 to 8 per cent during 1978 but increased to over 20 per cent in 1980. Since then, the rate of inflation has decreased except between 1988 and 1990. Inflation has remained under 4 per cent since the third quarter of 1992, the longest consecutive period for almost 50 years.

Indicator a6:
Employment

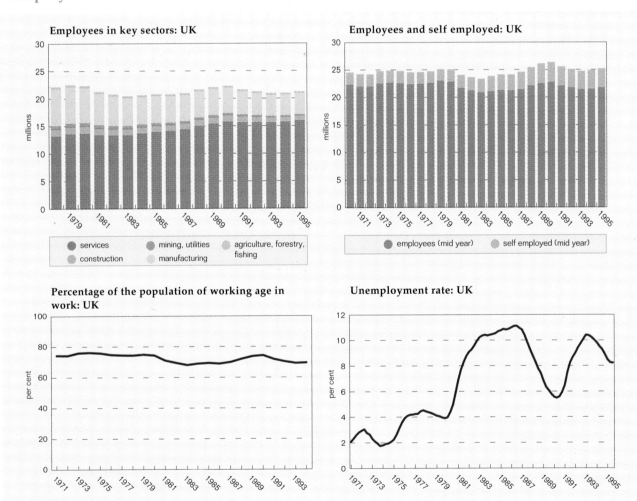

The UK economy has seen a consistent decline in traditional areas of employment, such as manufacturing and mining, and increased employment in the service sector. Self employment has risen by over 50 per cent since 1970. The proportion of the population of working age in work has declined since 1970, mirrored by increasing unemployment which currently stands at about 8 per cent of the workforce.

A healthy economy provides employment (and self employment) which produces income for individuals, businesses and government and enables them to improve living standards. There is no "correct" level of employment, as the size of the workforce depends on the number of people of working age and how many of them are economically active. Some unemployment is also inevitable as members of the workforce move from one job to another. However, ever increasing levels of unemployment, or falling levels of employment, are not sustainable in the long term.

The implications of the split of employment between different sectors for sustainable development are less clear cut, and the considerations discussed under Indicator a2 (the structure of the economy) are also relevant.

Indicator a6 shows trends since the late 1970s of employment in key sectors in the UK and trends since the early 1970s in total employment and the rate of unemployment.

Patterns of employment by sector have changed markedly over the last 18 years (consistent figures are not available prior to 1978 because of a change in the industrial classification). An increasing proportion of people have been employed in the services sector, which accounted for over three quarters of all employees in 1995. Numbers employed in other sectors have generally declined. Employees in manufacturing fell by over 40 per cent between 1978 and 1995. Employees in mining and quarrying fell by two thirds. Employees in the construction industry fell by over 30 per cent, while those working in agriculture, forestry and fishing fell by 26 per cent. These shifts in employment partly reflect changes in the structure of output and production methods (see Indicator a2). Increased contracting out and flexible working will also have resulted in the reclassification of some activities.

Since 1970 the workforce in the UK has fluctuated between 25.1 million and 28.8 million, owing to variation in the number of people of working age and the proportion that is economically active. Of these, around 21.9 million people were employed in the UK in June 1995. The numbers of self employed have increased by over 50 per cent since 1970 to 3.3 million in 1995. As well as sectoral changes, there have been other structural changes in employment. Part-time working has increased, alongside a reduction in male full-time employment and an increase in female full-time employment.

In the 1970s around 75 per cent of the population of working age were in work. By 1994 this had fallen to under 70 per cent. The overall rate of unemployment increased from under 2 per cent of the workforce in 1973 and 1974 to reach a peak of 11.2 per cent during 1986. Thereafter, the rate fell to 5.5 per cent during 1990, before rising sharply during the recession in the early 1990s. In mid-1995, 2.3 million people or 8.3 per cent of the workforce were unemployed.

a The economy

a The economy

Indicator a7: Government borrowing and debt

The PSBR and Government debt rose sharply as a percentage share of GDP following the recession in the early 1990s. But the PSBR has started to return towards balance as the economy recovers and following measures taken in successive Budgets. The long term trend in the ratio of debt to GDP is downwards.

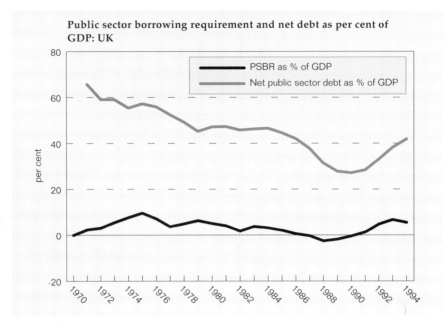

Public sector borrowing requirement and net debt as per cent of GDP: UK

Legend: PSBR as % of GDP / Net public sector debt as % of GDP

The Public Sector Borrowing Requirement (PSBR) is a measure of the Government's annual borrowing. If it is rising persistently, and the ratio of debt to GDP is high and rising, corrective action by the Government would be required, either by raising taxes or cutting expenditure. Servicing high and rising levels of Governments debt could lead to high interest rates for private sector businesses, depressing investment and growth. It is Government policy that the PSBR should be brought back towards balance over the medium term.

Indicator a7 shows the PSBR and the level of net Government debt since the early 1970s as percentages of GDP.

The PSBR fell from a peak level of 7.7 per cent of GDP in 1974, becoming negative in the late 1980s. The PSBR then rose to 6.7 per cent of GDP in 1993, following the recession in the early 1990s, before falling back to 5.6 per cent in 1994. Total Government debt fell from 66 per cent of GDP in 1971 to 27 per cent in 1990, before rising to 42 per cent in 1994.

Other indicators of the public finances, which may have some relevance for sustainable development, are the ratios of public spending and taxes to GDP. High taxation and high Government spending may reduce incentives and so reduce the long run rate of growth of the economy.

Indicator a8: Pollution abatement expenditure

A healthy economy can free up resources, enabling us to spend more on protecting the environment. An indicator of expenditure on environmental protection, viewed alongside indicators of environmental quality, gives an overall measure of the resources expended on dealing with environmental pollution.

Estimates of environmental expenditure in the UK have been made for the period around 1990. It is estimated that around £14 billion (about 2$\frac{1}{2}$ per cent of GDP) was spent each year, covering both capital investment and current spending. Around 60 per cent of the total, some £8.8 billion, was spent on pollution control. It is not at present possible to say whether environmental protection expenditure is increasing or decreasing in the UK. Conventional wisdom suggests that as

economies become wealthier they are able to afford to spend more on protecting the environment. Nevertheless, as scientific knowledge and technology improves, design of goods and manufacturing processes will increasingly reflect higher environmental standards, so that less additional expenditure on protecting the environment is needed. Declining expenditure would not necessarily imply, therefore, that environmental standards are falling; trends in environmental expenditure must be evaluated in relation to environmental quality. In other parts of this report, indicators attempt to explicitly link specific environmental expenditure to the intended effect (see Indicator n8 in the *Air* section showing expenditure on air pollution abatement in 1990, and Indicators p7 and p8 in the *Freshwater quality* section showing expenditure on public water supply and treatment and expenditure on sewage treatment).

Future indicator development:

The Department of the Environment is currently carrying out a pilot survey on environmental expenditure by industry to enable better estimates to be made.

Protection of human health

Much of the policy of environmental protection is intended to protect human health from adverse effects of environmental pollution. However, in most cases it is very difficult to link specific illness with any particular environmental factor. Ill health can be caused or exacerbated by a variety of conditions including lifestyle (eg smoking, lack of exercise, diet), genetic traits, other economic and social factors, as well as by the weather and hazards in the environment. In the UK, incidence of illness which can be directly attributed to specific environmental pollution is, in general, very localised and usually short term. Nevertheless, the health of the population is important to sustainable development, and two widely and internationally accepted measures are rates of infant mortality and average life expectancy.

Indicator a9:
Infant mortality

Advances in health care and medical knowledge and improvements in standards of living have effected steady declines in infant mortality since 1971. Rates of infant mortality have reduced by almost two thirds and are among the lowest in Europe.

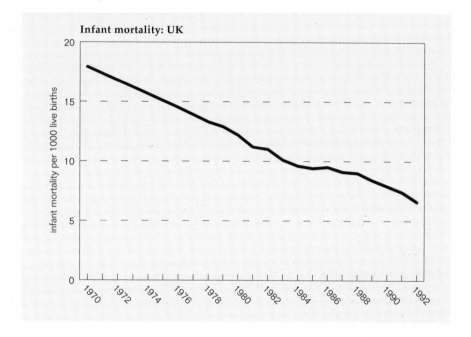

Infant mortality: UK

Indicator a9 shows the infant mortality in the UK since 1970.

The infant mortality rate in 1970 was 17.9. By 1992 this had fallen to 6.6, a drop of 63 per cent. Current levels of infant mortality in the UK are amongst the lowest in Europe, although lower rates in, for example, Sweden (5.2) and Finland (5.2) indicate that there is scope for further improvement.

a The economy

Indicator a10: Life expectancy

Average life expectancy in the UK has increased by over 5 per cent in the last twenty years.

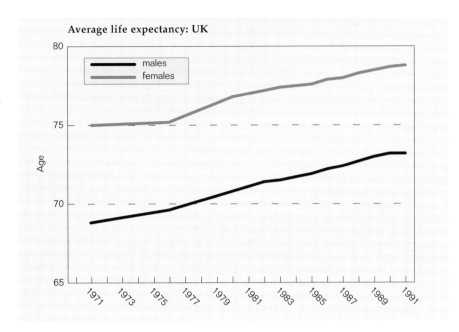

Average life expectancy: UK

Advances in medical treatment and improvements in standards of living have contributed to significant changes in average life expectancy, even over the last 20 years. Not only does this indicate a generally healthier population, but it also has economic and social implications - more people living longer means a larger population of elderly people relative to those of working age. Public provision for pensions, health and community care will need to be financially supported by a relatively smaller population in work.

Indicator a10 shows average life expectancy at birth for males and females in the UK.

Average life expectancy in 1971 was 68.8 years for men and 75 years for women, a difference of 6.2 years. By 1991, average life expectancy was 6 per cent higher for men at 73.2, and 5 per cent higher for women at 78.8 years. Greater longevity still is projected for future years. By 2001, life expectancy is postulated at 75.4 for men and 80.6 for women, and is likely to have increased a further 2 years by 2021.

Future indicator development:

Increasingly, however, attention is focusing not just on total life expectancy, but on the period during which individuals can expect to live a healthy, independent life. Work is going on to define and quantify this in an objective manner, and it may be that for the future this indicator can be supplemented by an indicator of healthy life expectancy.

a The economy

b Transport use

An effective transport system is a necessary part of modern life. Industry and commerce depend on it, and increasing use of the car has shaped today's social and recreational lifestyles. The key sustainable development objective is to strike the right balance between the ability of transport to serve economic development and the ability to protect the environment and sustain quality of life, both now and in the future.

b Transport use

Indicator b1:
Car use and total passenger travel

Since 1970, the amount of car travel per head of population has almost doubled, while travel on other passenger road vehicles, mainly buses and coaches, has dropped by a quarter. Rail travel has remained unchanged.

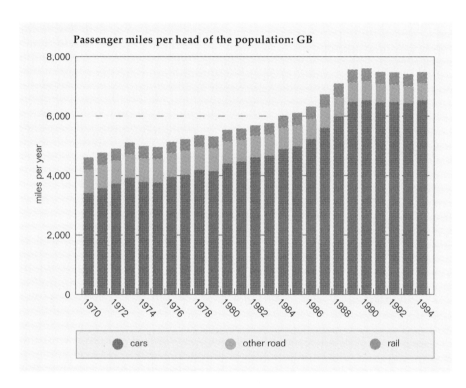

Passenger miles per head of the population: GB

miles per year

● cars   ● other road   ● rail

The Government is taking steps to influence the growth in demand for transport by attempting to ensure that people pay the full social and environmental cost of their transport decisions, so improving the overall efficiency of those decisions for the economy as a whole and bringing environmental benefits. Key indicators included in this section are car use and total passenger travel, mode of travel for short journeys, transport pricing, and the volume of freight transport.

Other transport indicators are included in other chapters of this report. Indicator e6 in the *Energy* section charts the trends in road transport energy use. Indicators m3 in the *Acid deposition* section and n4 to n7 in the *Air* section show trends in emissions of pollutants from road transport. Indicators f5

and f7 in the *Land use* section chart trends in land take for new roads and journey lengths for regular trips. Indicators c1 and c2 in the *Leisure and tourism* section show trends in leisure trips and air traffic.

Much of the growth in passenger transport over the last 20 years has been in car use. Car ownership is now widespread, although the number of cars per household is still less than in many other developed countries; increased incomes has been the main factor driving the growth in car use. The Government's projections show that road traffic is likely to grow between 58 per cent and 92 per cent by 2025 compared to 1994. Traffic congestion is becoming a problem on many parts of the network, particularly in urban areas. This leads to delay and, for

businesses, an increase in costs. The growth in demand for road travel can increase the case for road improvements, which may increase pressures on wildlife and habitats.

Indicator b1 shows the trends since 1970 in passenger miles in GB per year per head of the population.

In this indicator, total miles travelled have been divided by the total population, to give a figure to which individuals can more readily relate their own behaviour. Since 1970, the amount of car travel per head of population has nearly doubled. By 1994, each person in the population was travelling, on average, over 6,500 miles per year by car.

Meanwhile, travel on other passenger road vehicles, mainly buses and coaches, dropped by a quarter, to less than 600 miles per year. Rail travel has remained reasonably constant over the period, at around 400 miles per year. Consequently, the share of car passenger miles to all passenger miles (excluding air travel) has increased steadily from around three quarters of all mileage in 1970

to more than 85 per cent in 1994. The Government has a variety of policies to reduce the impacts of traffic. Through the planning system it attempts to encourage patterns of development in which people live in communities close to where they work and shop (see also Indicator f7 in the *Land use* section). It seeks to encourage people to travel by more environmentally friendly means (see indicator b2 below). The

Government seeks to mitigate the adverse impacts of emissions from transport by setting new vehicle standards and tightening in-service emissions tests, and, for carbon dioxide emissions, by increasing the duty on fuel to encourage greater fuel efficiency (see also indicators m3, n4 to n7 in the *Acid deposition* and *Air* sections, and indicator e6 in the *Energy* section).

Indicator b2:
Short journeys

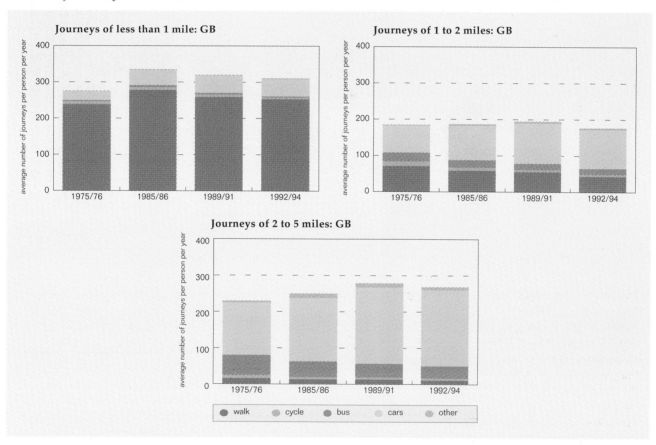

While most journeys of less than a mile are made on foot, the proportion of these being made by car is increasing. Around 60 per cent of journeys of 1 to 2 miles is made by car, and about 75 per cent of journeys of 2 to 5 miles. Only 2 per cent of journeys of up to 5 miles are made by bicycle, compared with 4 per cent 20 years ago.

Government policy is to encourage people to use more environmentally friendly forms of travel. Walking and cycling are the least damaging methods of travel. Research shows that most journeys on foot are less than 1 mile, with some at up to 2

miles. Few people walk further than 2 miles. For cycling, the threshold is around 5 miles. Many people are unable to walk or cycle and for them a bus, where practicable, is often the next best environmental option for short trips.

Indicator b2 shows the number of trips per person per year made by mode of transport for journeys of less than 1, 1 to 2, and 2 to 5 miles.

Not only are most journeys on foot less than a mile, but most journeys of less than a mile are on foot - around 80 per cent between 1992 and 1994. Fewer than 2 per cent are by bicycle or by bus. The majority of the remaining trips are by car. The proportion of these very short trips made by car has increased from 9 per cent in 1975/76 to 15 per cent between 1992 and 1994. For journeys of 1 to 2 miles, about a quarter are made on foot and 3 per cent by bicycle. A larger proportion are made by bus than for very short trips (9 per cent), but for journeys of this length, cars are the most popular. Again, an increasing proportion of these trips is being made by car, rising from around 40 per cent in 1975/76 to around 60 per cent between 1992 and 1994. For journeys of 2 to 5 miles, the car dominates, as it does also for longer trips. The proportion of trips of 2 to 5 miles made by car is around 75 per cent. Again, this proportion has increased significantly over the last 20 years.

Indicator b3:
Real changes in the cost of transport

Since 1974, the real price of rail and bus fares has increased slightly faster than the growth in real incomes. The real cost of motoring has fallen in real terms, and is therefore much more affordable than it was 20 years ago.

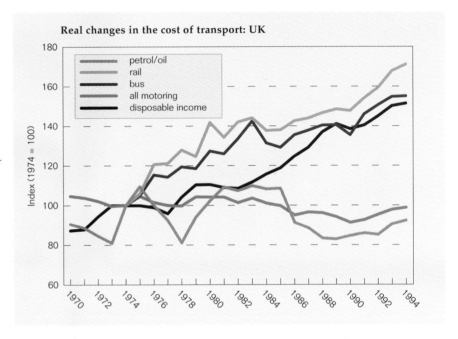

Real changes in the cost of transport: UK

The Government has accepted the need to influence the growth in demand for travel, as part of the wider strategy to stabilise carbon dioxide emissions and to make people pay the full cost of their travel decisions. One of the ways of doing this is through price, and the Government has already announced plans to increase the real price of fuel by increasing fuel duty by an average 5 per cent per year.

Indicator b3 shows the real change in price of passenger fares and motoring, in comparison with the growth in real personal disposable income.

Since 1974, the real increase in bus fares has been 55 per cent and in rail fares, 71 per cent, both higher than the 51 per cent real increase in disposable income. Meanwhile the cost of motoring, which includes all costs like insurance, servicing and repairs, road tax as well as fuel and oil, has fallen by nearly 2 per cent. The real price of fuel and oil only - which is the perceived "marginal" cost for an individual journey once someone owns and runs a car, and is therefore more important to decisions about individual journeys - has fallen by nearly 8 per cent. This demonstrates that the real cost of motoring, particularly the marginal cost of petrol, is very much more affordable, in relation to the real increase in personal disposable income, than it was 20 years ago.

Price change is not the sole factor which has affected the growth in car traffic. Many other factors, including convenience, comfort and security, will influence individual decisions over whether and how to travel. The chart shows that, while public transport fares have increased faster than private motoring costs, they have risen relatively little in relation to personal disposable income. Reducing fares would not necessarily increase the relative use of public transport, but various studies have shown it can have undesirable other effects - eg increasing the attractiveness of living further out of town centres, increasing journeys to work and for shopping, and increasing pressure on demand for housing in out-of-town sites.

Future indicator development:
In planning a more sustainable transport policy, particularly at local level, a wide number of measures have to be considered. These include pedestrianisation of town centres, restrictions on parking

(through cost or availability), accessibility of public transport, and planning decisions about the siting of new facilities. Many of these do not lend themselves to calculation of national scale indicators, though some local authorities are

developing indicators for local use on, for example, parking and accessibility of public transport. In the longer term it might be possible to develop some indicators based on these for use at a national level.

Indicator b4:
Freight traffic

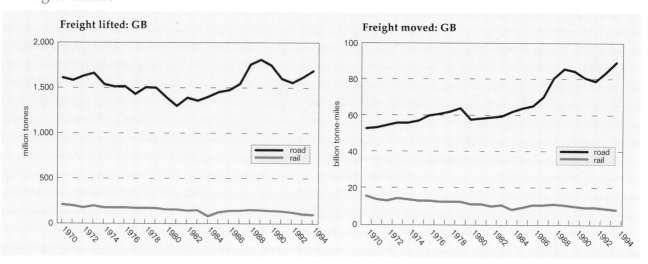

The amount of freight carried has changed relatively little over the last two decades or so, but the distances over which it has been moved have increased by one third. The share of freight carried by road has increased while that carried by rail has declined.

Goods vehicles (over 3.5 tonnes gross weight) account for around 7 per cent of total vehicle traffic. As with passenger transport, the average distance travelled is increasing. There has been strong growth in road haulage, which has been influenced by the removal of quantitative restrictions on road haulage in 1970, larger vehicles and changing distribution methods. In recent years, growth in the number of the heaviest permitted vehicles contributed to an overall reduction in the numbers of goods vehicles. As a result of the diversification of many small, service industries, there has also been considerable increase in the use of light goods vehicles. As a result of the competitiveness and greater flexibility of road haulage and

reductions in traditional staple traffics, particularly coal, the importance of rail freight, in terms of the amounts lifted and moved, has declined. Most long distance traffic goes by road.

Indicator b4 compares the annual trends in road and rail freight lifted and moved since 1970.

The annual tonnages of goods lifted by road and rail together fluctuated between 1.5 and 2 billion tonnes; the amount of freight carried generally declined during the 1970s. During the latter part of the 1980s, freight traffic increased. The sharp decline after 1989 was due to the economic recession and from 1992

amounts carried have increased again. The share of road and rail freight lifted by road vehicles increased from 89 per cent in 1970 to 95 per cent in 1994. The average distance that freight is moved has been increasingly fairly steadily since 1970. Even long distance freight is generally moved by road rather than by rail. Part of the reason for the increase in average distance moved by freight is because retailers, especially food retailers, are moving to central distribution systems.

C Leisure and tourism

The key sustainable development objectives are to maintain the quality of the environment in which leisure takes place, and which is an essential part of the UK's attractiveness to tourists, for future generations to enjoy; thus contributing to the quality of life of those taking part in leisure activities, and maximising the economic contributing of tourism, while protecting natural resources.

Leisure activities are important to people's quality of life, but types of leisure activity are very varied, and their impacts on the environment are similarly diverse. The last 30 years have seen a considerable expansion in leisure activities of all kinds. The tourism industry in the UK currently has a turnover of £36.4 billion, having doubled in the 1980s. It contributes over 5 per cent of GDP and provides work for 1.7 million people. In 1994, earnings from over 21 million overseas visitors on leisure or business travel to the UK contributed £10.1 billion to the UK balance of payments - £7.4 billion on lesiure and £2.7

billion on business; UK residents spent £14.5 billion on business travel and leisure in 1994 in the UK, £9.3 billion of which was soley on leisure activities. In 1991/92, it was estimated that nearly 1 billion day trips with a total of £9 billion were made for leisure purposes. Consumer spending on sports related items amounted to nearly £10 billion in 1992, around 1.6 per cent of GDP, and the sports industry provides employment for nearly 0.5 million people. However, statistics on spending and employment of themselves give little indication of the impacts of leisure and tourism on the

environment. The commonest impacts of leisure have been identified as overcrowding, traffic, wear and tear, disturbance and noise and inappropriate development. Few of these can be quantified meaningfully at the national scale. Most impacts are particular to activities at or nearby specific sites. The most general issue is the amount of leisure travel. Key indicators in this chapter therefore relate to leisure journeys and air travel.

Another related issue is damage to designated and protected areas - see indicator s3 in the *Land cover and landscape* section.

Indicator c1:
Leisure journeys

On average individuals made journeys totalling over 2,600 miles per year between 1992 and 1994 in pursuit of leisure activities. Leisure travel has increased by one third since 1975/76. Half of leisure journeys are social trips, involving visiting friends.

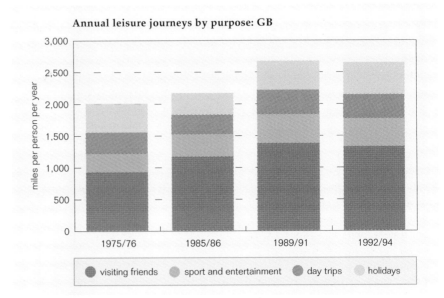

Annual leisure journeys by purpose: GB

y-axis: miles per person per year

x-axis categories: 1975/76, 1985/86, 1989/91, 1992/94

Legend: visiting friends · sport and entertainment · day trips · holidays

Leisure is one of the most significant reasons why people travel, accounting for around 41 per cent of passenger mileage each year. Leisure travel is a fast growing aspect of transport use. As with other passenger travel, most leisure journeys are made by car - 81 per

cent between 1992 and 1994. Leisure includes visiting friends and sporting and entertainment activities which mainly take place locally, day trips to the countryside or the coast, and longer trips, including trips abroad, on holiday.

Indicator c1 shows the average miles travelled per person per year for each of the main leisure purposes.

On average, individuals made journeys totalling over 2,600 miles per year between 1992 and 1994 for leisure purposes. Half of all journeys - around 1,300 miles - had a primarily social purpose: visiting friends either in their home or elsewhere. Over 500 miles per year were for domestic holidays and almost 450 miles per year for sport and entertainment. Since 1975/76, the annual distance travelled per person for leisure has increased by around one third. The growth in leisure travel reflects both greater distancing apart of where people live in relation to their friends and places they frequent for entertainment, and an increase in the number of trips made. The number of leisure trips per person per year has risen from around 250 in 1975/76 to around 280 per year between 1992 and 1994, an increase of about 12 per cent. Over half the number of trips made are to visit friends.

Indicator c2:
Air travel

The number of air passengers passing through UK airports on overseas leisure trips has trebled since 1975.

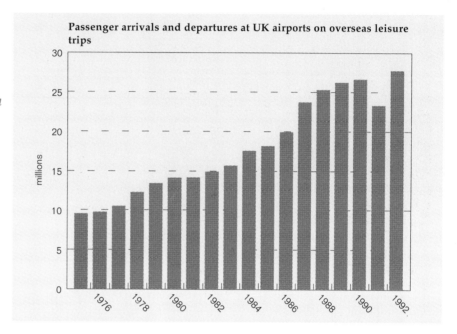

Passenger arrivals and departures at UK airports on overseas leisure trips

millions

Trends in leisure travel can be useful indicators not simply of the direct impacts of transport, but also of the wider impacts of tourism and leisure destinations (eg economic impacts, changes in land use and overcrowding). Looking at air travel can give some idea of the trends in international tourism as well as domestic. Air travel itself has direct impacts on sustainable development. Carbon dioxide emissions per passenger-mile and per freight tonne-mile are generally higher for air transport than for most other modes. Other types of emissions from aircraft, especially nitrogen oxides, can contribute to atmospheric and local air quality problems (although emissions per passenger-mile are expected to fall as a result of technological developments, fuel efficiency improvements and internationally-agreed regulations). The most significant local environmental impact of aviation is noise. Unlike some other impacts noise has only a transistory effect. But the development of transport infrastructure can have long-term implications for noise.

Indicator c2 shows numbers of passengers per year arriving at and departing from UK airports on overseas leisure trips since 1975.

One useful indicator of wider impacts of travel on sustainable development, including the impacts on holiday destinations of growing international tourism, is the number of people travelling to and from the UK by air. The number of passengers arriving and departing from UK airports on overseas leisure trips increased between 1975 and 1992. Numbers of aircraft movements over the same period increased rather less because of the increasing capacity of aircraft.

c Leisure and tourism

d Overseas trade

The key sustainable development objective is to ensure that UK activities contribute to sustainable development in the UK and in other countries as far as possible.

An open, fair and stable world trading system makes possible a more efficient use of natural resources in both economic and environmental terms. It enables us to maximise output from any given input of resources, thus diminishing demands on the environment. By increasing efficiency, and improving living standards from higher incomes, trade can help both to generate the wealth and resources needed to invest in environmental protection, and to foster awareness of, and appreciation for, environmental values. Increased trade liberalisation can mean the maintenance of higher environmental standards, removal of market-distorting subsidies and pricing policies, thus improving further the efficiency of resource allocation, and encouraging the spread of environment-friendly technology.

There is no reason why trade liberalisation and sustainable development policies should be in conflict. International trade in general is not the root cause of environmental problems, but may act as a magnifier of environmental policy failures, particularly in the transport sector. It is in the absence of effective domestic policies that economic activity linked to trade can in practice sometimes harm the environment by exacerbating problems of pollution and resource depletion. What is important is that policies necessary to promote sustainable development are in place at the national level, including where possible the reflection of environmental impacts in economic decision-making, and the establishment and enforcement of effective environmental regulations.

We are not in a position at present to assess the full impact that trade might, indirectly or directly, have on sustainable development. Furthermore, trade in itself is not a root cause of unsustainable management, but rather production and consumption patterns in the UK and its trading partners. It would therefore be premature, in the absence of indicators for other countries' sustainable development, to attempt to assess the relationship between trade and sustainable development. To set the issues in context however, imports and exports for key sectors of the UK economy have been presented below. Trade flows and balances provide background information, but do not in themselves enable one to draw conclusions about whether development is sustainable.

Indicator d1:
UK imports and exports

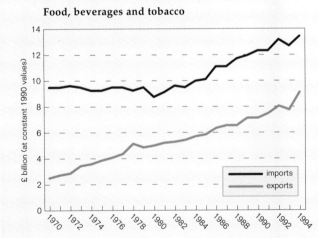

Food, beverages and tobacco

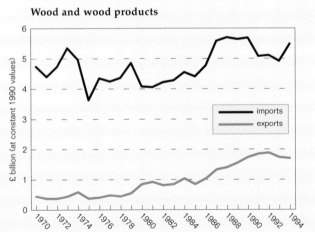

Wood and wood products

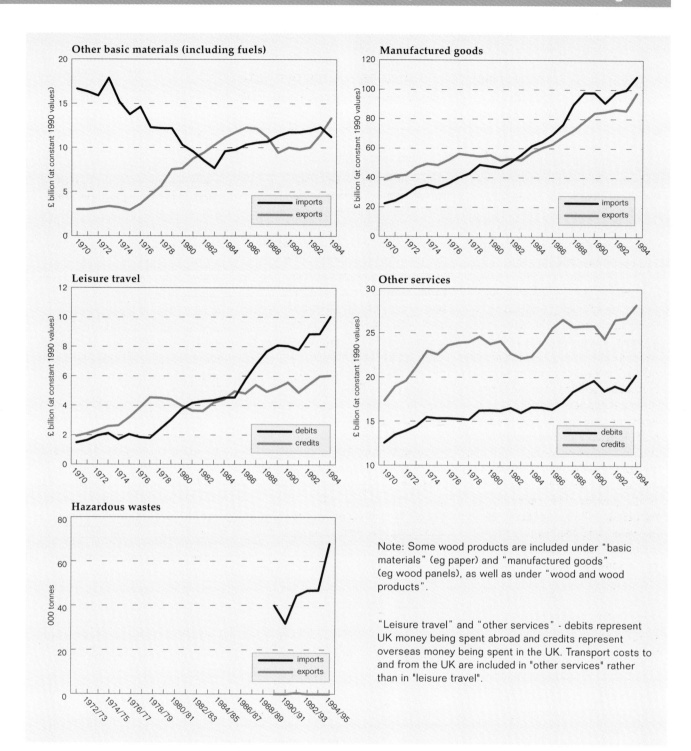

Other basic materials (including fuels)
£ billion (at constant 1990 values)

imports
exports

Manufactured goods
£ billion (at constant 1990 values)

imports
exports

Leisure travel
£ billion (at constant 1990 values)

debits
credits

Other services
£ billion (at constant 1990 values)

debits
credits

Hazardous wastes
000 tonnes

imports
exports

Note: Some wood products are included under "basic materials" (eg paper) and "manufactured goods" (eg wood panels), as well as under "wood and wood products".

"Leisure travel" and "other services" - debits represent UK money being spent abroad and credits represent overseas money being spent in the UK. Transport costs to and from the UK are included in "other services" rather than in "leisure travel".

d Overseas trade

The UK is a net importer of food, wood and wood products and, since 1982, manufactured goods. In volume terms, trade in each of these elements is increasing. Trends in imports and exports of other raw materials are largely dominated by fuels; imports have decreased and exports increased since 1970 and the two are now broadly in balance. Tourism is increasing, particularly travel abroad by UK residents; their expenditure overseas in 1994 was £12 billion, nearly 70 per cent higher than income from foreign visitors to the UK. Other services (which have a relatively lower environmental impact than other sectors of the economy) contribute increasingly to the UK's trade balance with the rest of the world. Hazardous waste imports have increased since the late 1980s, while the UK does not export hazardous waste.

It is not possible to encapsulate the issues discussed above in simple quantified indicators. However, in conjunction with the indicators on consumption of UK resources, it is relevant to consider what proportion of the UK's consumption is met by imports and how this is changing, and also how exports contribute to the UK economy.

Indicator d1 shows UK imports and exports of food, wood, basic materials, manufactured goods, leisure travel and other services, and hazardous wastes.

Food, beverages, and tobacco

Around 8 per cent of UK imports (some £14.6 billion in 1994) consist of food, beverages, and tobacco, an increase in volume terms of about 40 per cent since 1970. Around 60 per cent comes from the EC and 40 per cent from non-EC countries. Imports account for about 60 per cent of all food and feed consumed in the UK. The UK exported around £10.1 billion of food, beverages, and tobacco in 1994, some £4.6 billion less than we imported. Exports have increased in volume by three and a half times since 1970, and so have grown at a much faster rate than imports. Principal items exported are beverages (29 per cent), cereals (15 per cent), meat (12 per cent), and tobacco (9 per cent). As with imports, about 60 per cent of export trade is with the EC and 40 per cent with the rest of the world.

Wood and wood products

The UK imports around 85 per cent of its wood and wood products in volume terms, more than 80 per cent of which is softwood. Wood and wood pulp make up more than half the imports by volume, but only around one-third by value; the rest are paper, panels, and other wood

products. Imports of paper increased between 1970 and 1994, while wood imports have fluctuated with construction industry activity, peaking in the late 1980s. Around 14 per cent of imports comes from tropical hardwood forests, with the remainder, both hardwood and softwood, from temperate and boreal forests. Domestic timber production, which has met an increasing proportion of UK consumption is covered by Indicator h2 in the *Forestry* section. The UK exports some paper, but very little wood or other products. These amounts have been steadily increasing since the early 1980s.

Other basic materials (including fuels)

Imports of raw materials (mainly non-fuel minerals) amounted to around £4 billion in 1994 (2 per cent of total imports), while some 38 per cent of UK consumption of fuels is met through imports (accounting for £6.2 billion in 1994, around 3 per cent of all imports). Raw material imports, mainly metal ores (28 per cent) and animal and vegetable materials (16 per cent), have generally been increasing in volume since the early 1980s, although the recession caused a dip in the early 1990s. Around 40 per cent comes from the EC. Exports, mainly metal ores (27 per cent), textile fibres (23 per cent), and fertilisers (17 per cent), are at a lower level, some £2.6 billion in 1994, but have been fairly steadily increasing since 1970. Fuel import volumes fell by about 60 per cent between 1970 and 1983 following the discovery of North Sea oil and gas, but have since increased slowly. Despite these recent increases, the UK is a net exporter of fuels; exports have increased 5-fold since 1970 and exceeded imports by £2.8 billion in 1994. Fuels account for over 5 per cent of total exports. Most fuel imported and exported is petroleum, although a small amount of coal, gas, and electricity is also traded.

Manufactured goods

Manufactured goods account for around 66 per cent of total imports and 64 per cent of exports. Until 1982, the UK was a net exporter of manufactured goods, after which the pattern reversed, although there is little difference overall between import and export levels. Significant components of import and export trade are road vehicles (16 per cent of imports, 10 per cent of exports), office machinery and computers (11 and 10 per cent), and electrical machinery excluding domestic appliances (10 and 10 per cent). The proportion of imports coming from non-OECD countries has remained around 15 per cent over the last 15 years, while most exports go to developed countries (around 40 per cent in total go to Germany, the USA, and France).

Leisure travel

Expenditure by UK residents on holiday abroad counts as a trade debit (the equivalent of imports), while expenditure by overseas visitors on holiday in the UK counts as a trade credit (the equivalent of exports). The increase in people's real incomes has enabled them to spend more on leisure activities generally, including overseas travel (see also Indicator c2 in the *Leisure and tourism* section). Leisure travel contributes to people's quality of life, but has diverse environmental impacts - beneficial as well as adverse. Tourism is often an important source of income for the countries to which UK residents travel and can encourage them to protect their environment in order to continue to attract visitors. Expenditure on leisure abroad by UK residents has increased more than 5-fold in real terms since 1970. In 1994, UK residents spent £12 billion on leisure travel abroad. Expenditure by overseas visitors in the UK has increased at a slower rate and amounted to £7 billion in 1994.

Other services

This represents UK residents buying services from abroad (debits, the equivalent of imports) and other countries buying UK services (credits, the equivalent of exports). As discussed under indicators a2 and a6 in *The economy* section, the service sector has grown in recent years. As services increase and other more polluting, resource-intensive sectors of the economy diminish (such as manufacturing and mining/quarrying), environmental benefits can result. The growth in services is reflected by the increases in trade between 1970 and 1994. Credits have been at a higher level throughout the period, and in 1994 represented over £33 billion while debits were £24 billion.

Hazardous wastes

Imports of hazardous wastes have been steadily increasing during the early 1990s. Between 1990/91 and 1991/92 approximately 500 tonnes of hazardous wastes were exported from Northern Ireland to the Irish Republic. Exports then ceased and there are now no exports from the UK under the Transfrontier Shipment of Hazardous Wastes Regulation 1988. Around 90 per cent of imports came from Germany, Ireland, the Netherlands, Luxembourg, and Italy in 1993/94, with Greater London, Greater Manchester and Hampshire accepting almost two-thirds of the total imports. Nearly 60 per cent of the wastes imported were destined for incineration in 1993/94, with most of the rest being physically or chemically treated at specialist facilities before going for final disposal.

Future indicator development:

This area requires much future work, including internationally, as the issues involved are very complex. In the longer term, we will need to consider, in conjunction with other countries and international organisations, whether more appropriate indicators might be developed to illustrate the role of trade in global patterns of consumption and production.

Regarding wood and wood products, the "Statement of Forest Principles" adopted at Rio in 1992 by developed and developing countries has been refined further by the development of "Criteria and Indicators" for sustainable forest management by groups of countries in a number of regional initiatives. Reports on the progress on these indicators should be available by 1997. In a number of countries, including the UK, there has been some market-led development of mechanisms to provide information about timber sources and evidence of sustainable management, but as yet these have not had a major impact on international trade.

d Overseas trade

e Energy

The key sustainable development objectives are to ensure supplies of energy at competitive prices, to reduce adverse impacts of energy use to acceptable levels, and to encourage consumers to meet their needs with less energy input through improved energy efficiency. Indicators relevant to these objectives concern the depletion of fossil fuel reserves, the capacity of nuclear and renewable energy sources, energy usage by sector, and fuel prices.

Depletion of non-renewable resources

Indicator e1:
Depletion of fossil fuels

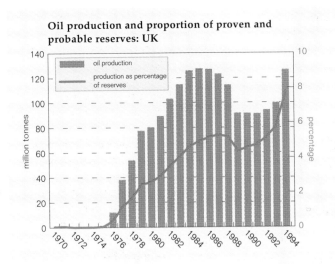

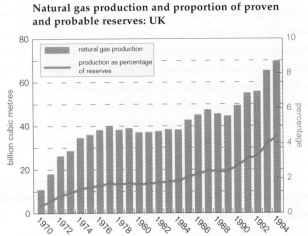

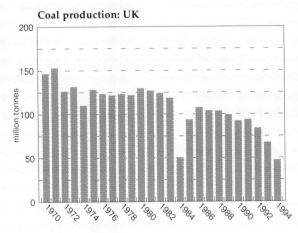

UK oil and natural gas production has increased over the last 2 decades whereas there has been a marked switch away from coal as an energy source. Depletion rates of oil and gas reserves have increased in recent years, although additional reserves of both fuels continue to be identified each year. The prospects for future coal production are limited not by the resource base but by the economics of opening new mines.

Developed economies such as the UK are critically dependent on the supply of energy and a prime sustainable development aim is to ensure that future generations can enjoy a quality of energy services comparable to that enjoyed today. The way in which energy is produced, supplied and consumed is one of the major ways in which human activity affects the environment. The UK has 4 main sources of primary energy: coal, oil, natural gas and nuclear, of which the first 3 are based on finite fossil fuel reserves. However, additional reserves of oil and gas continue to be identified or confirmed in the UK continental shelf.

The UK has abundant supplies of fossil fuels and the potential to extend use of nuclear and renewable sources of energy. UK production of fuels has increased and considerably diversified over the past 30 years and is currently just over 230 million tonnes of oil equivalent (MTOE) per annum. More than half the total is oil, more than a quarter natural gas and an eighth coal. As existing energy sources become more scarce, energy prices can be expected to rise, encouraging greater fuel efficiency and boosting incentives to develop alternative sources.

Indicator e1 gives the total indigenous production of oil, natural gas and coal together with resource depletion rates since 1970.

Oil

Following the discovery and extraction of North Sea oil in the early 1970s, annual oil production rose steadily to nearly 130 million tonnes in the mid-1980s. In the late 1980s, production declined, following the Piper Alpha accident, but has recently returned to the mid-1980s levels. Although 8 per cent of the UK's proven and probable reserves were consumed in 1994, the ratio of production to reserves should not be taken as a measure of the future life of reserves. It is likely that the reserves still to be discovered or confirmed will enable the UK to sustain its current levels of production for much longer than a decade.

Natural gas

Annual natural gas production has risen steadily since 1970 to 70 billion cubic metres in 1994. Outside the transport sector, natural gas - a relatively cheap and clean fuel - has become the dominant fuel, accounting for 65 per cent of domestic fuel use, 42 per cent in the commercial and public sector, and 33 per cent in industry. Recently, its use for electricity generation has grown sharply; by the end of 1995 it accounted for more than 15 per cent of the fuel used. The depletion rate, at 4 per cent in 1994, is about half that for oil although, as with oil, this depletion rate should not be taken as an indication of how long the reserves will last. Additional gas reserves continue to be discovered and it will be possible for production to continue at current levels for longer than suggested by the current depletion rates.

Coal

The relative benefits of greater convenience and competitive pricing offered by other cleaner fuels, plus the pressures of Clean Air legislation, have effected a severe squeeze on the use of coal. The proportion of total fuel demand satisfied by coal has shrunk from over 40 per cent in the early 1970s to about 25 per cent in 1994. The depletion rate of economic coal reserves, at about 5 per cent in 1994, was similar to the rates for oil and gas. Data on this basis for earlier years are not available. Unlike oil and gas, the future prospects for coal do not depend on new discoveries, because substantial additional coal reserves are already known. However, the greater part of these resources are not considered economic at current energy prices. Any development of these resources will depend on future energy prices, and perhaps on the development of cheaper exploitation technologies.

e Energy

Nuclear and renewable resources

Indicator e2:
Capacity of nuclear and renewable fuels

The total capacity of nuclear power stations is currently about 12,000 megawatts or 17 per cent of the UK's total generating capacity. The capacity from renewable sources is a little under 2,000 megawatts or 3 per cent of the UK total.

Target:
to work towards 1,500 megawatts of new generating capacity from renewable resources by the year 2000.

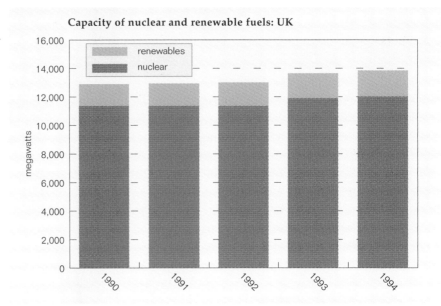

Capacity of nuclear and renewable fuels: UK

e Energy

Use of nuclear and renewable sources of energy has considerable benefits, not only in reducing demand for non-renewable fossil fuels, but also in producing lower environmental impacts in terms of carbon dioxide emissions and air pollution. However, possible environmental disadvantages of particular schemes in terms of the effect on landscape or noise, for example, also have to be considered through the planning system. Nuclear power generation also generates radioactive waste which needs to be disposed of safely (see Indicator w3 in the *Radioactivity* chapter).

Indicator e2 shows the net capacity of nuclear and renewable resources for electricity generation from 1990 to 1994.

In total, nuclear and renewable energy resources contribute around 10 per cent of total energy consumption in the UK; however, the technology for the use of many renewable energy sources is in the relatively early days of development. The main impact is in the area of electricity generation where the proportion of UK electricity provided by nuclear and renewable sources has been slowly increasing. In 1994, nuclear and renewable resources amounted to nearly 13,900 megawatts of Declared Net Capacity. The proportion of electricity generated by these resources has reached 29 per cent, of which nuclear represents 27 per cent and renewables 2 per cent. The Government is working towards 1,500 megawatts of new generating capacity from renewable sources by the year 2000. The proportion of electricity produced by nuclear generation is expected to increase up to the year 2000, but thereafter may decline as the old magnox reactors come to the end of their operational life.

Fuel consumption

Indicator e3:
Primary and final energy consumption

Primary energy consumption in the UK has remained fairly constant at around 200 to 220 million tonnes of oil equivalent (MTOE) per year since 1970. Over 30 per cent of primary energy is lost - largely in the conversion of fossil fuels to electricity and secondary fuels and also in the distribution network.

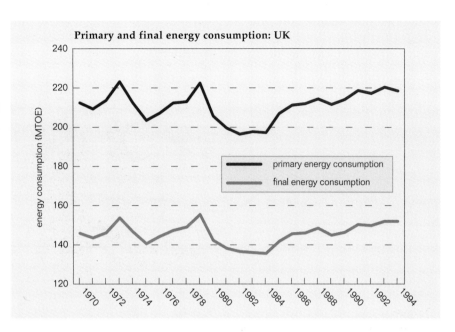

Primary and final energy consumption: UK

e Energy

An examination of the trends in primary and final energy consumption, in total and by sector, can illuminate the way in which energy is used to derive economic benefits for the community. The major user categories which are examined are industry, services, transport and households. While trends in the amounts of fuel consumed are relevant, it is also important to monitor their relationships with other indicators to determine their effectiveness of use. Comparisons are therefore made with GDP and value added, traffic growth and, for domestic consumption, with the number of households.

Indicator e3 shows the trends in primary and final energy consumption since 1970.

Primary energy consumption has remained relatively static over the last 25 years though it has been influenced by sudden changes in external factors affecting price levels, such as wars in the Middle East, the OPEC oil crisis as well as the economic cycle in general. Following peaks of around 220 million tonnes in 1973 and 1979, primary energy fell below 200 million tonnes in the early 1980s but has since climbed back to around 220 million tonnes. Over 30 per cent of primary energy is lost in the conversion to electricity, to other secondary fuels and in the distribution network. The ratio of primary to final consumption has hardly changed over the period. Use of waste heat from power generation can increase the efficiency of fuel use up to 80 to 90 per cent and the Government has a target of installed capacity of Combined Heat and Power (CHP) of 5,000 megawatts by the year 2000.

Indicator e4:
Energy consumption and output

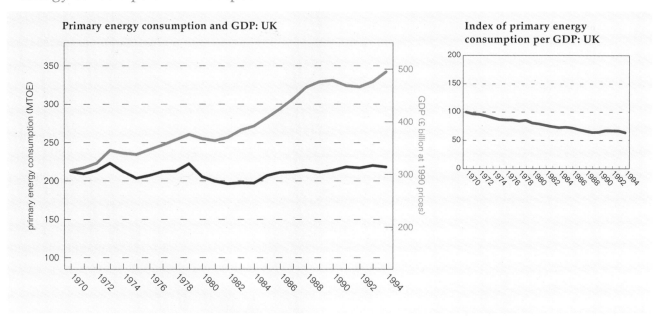

Primary energy consumption and GDP: UK

Index of primary energy consumption per GDP: UK

Primary energy consumption has remained broadly stable while the economy has grown by 60 per cent. As a result the energy ratio has followed a generally downward trend since 1970.

Indicator e4 shows the relationship of primary energy consumption to GDP since 1970.

Despite real growth in the economy of over 60 per cent since 1970, the consumption of energy has hardly changed, showing that it is possible to uncouple energy growth from economic growth. A variety of factors, for example, have contributed to this - the increase in world oil prices in the 1970s and early 1980s, improvements in energy efficiency; saturation in the ownership levels of the main domestic appliances; the unresponsiveness of certain industrial uses, like space heating, to long run output growth; and a structural shift away from energy intensive industries, such as steel production, towards lower energy users, such as the service sector.

Indicator e5 shows industrial, commercial and public sector energy consumption since 1970 compared with the value added by the two sectors.

Industrial sector

Despite the relative shrinking in the size of the industrial sector within the economy, particularly in manufacturing and mining industries, output has increased in real terms by around 40 per cent since 1970. At the same time, however, there has been a 40 per cent fall in the consumption of energy. Cuts have been made in operating costs, and more capital-intensive methods of production, higher levels of mechanisation and energy-saving technologies have been adopted. The switch away

from heavy industry and energy efficiency measures were the main reasons for the improvement in the energy ratio.

Services sector

In contrast to the industrial sector, the commercial sector has been growing in terms of its size and contribution to the economy overall, and its energy consumption has increased by 15 per cent between 1970 and 1994. Although overall, the energy ratio has declined for the commercial sector, the decline is less marked than for the industrial sector.

Indicator e5:
Industrial and commercial sector consumption

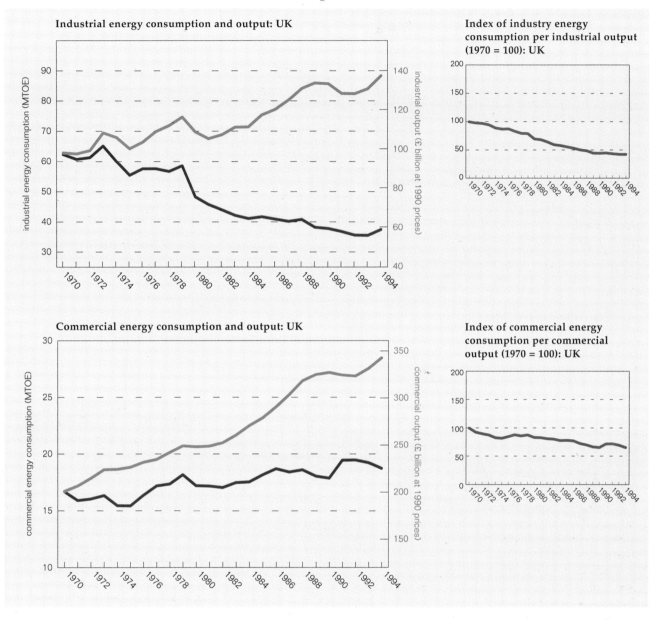

Industrial energy consumption and output: UK

Index of industry energy consumption per industrial output (1970 = 100): UK

Commercial energy consumption and output: UK

Index of commercial energy consumption per commercial output (1970 = 100): UK

e Energy

The amount of energy used by the industrial sector has decreased by 40 per cent since 1970 despite a 40 per cent growth in output. At the same time energy used by the commercial sector has increased by 15 per cent compared with a 70 per cent growth in output. In both sectors, the energy ratio has improved considerably since 1970.

Indicator e6:
Road transport energy use

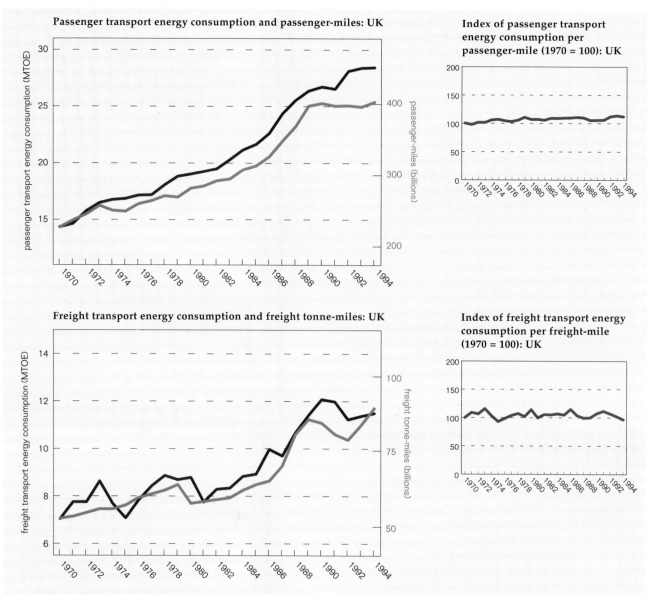

Road passenger energy consumption has nearly doubled since 1970 and road freight transport energy consumption has increased by over 60 per cent. The growth in energy consumption to a large extent has been mirrored by the growth in traffic with the result that there has been little, if any, improvement in energy efficiency over the period.

Indicator e6 compares road passenger vehicle fuel consumption with the number of passenger-miles travelled, and road freight vehicle fuel consumption with the number of tonne-miles moved since 1970.

Fuel use for road passenger transport has nearly doubled since 1970 and has increased by over 60 per cent for freight. The volume of traffic, measured in terms of passenger-miles and freight tonne-miles has increased by about the same amount, showing that there is little change in efficiency of fuel use, in marked contrast to the industrial and commercial sectors. For passenger traffic, vehicle engines are more fuel efficient than they used to be, but the advent of unleaded petrol, catalytic converters, higher safety standards, higher specifications and performance have all tended to counter the fuel efficiency gains from improved engine design. These factors, together with a fall in the average numbers of passengers per car and a fall in bus use, have decreased the overall fuel efficiency of road passenger transport. Similar factors have affected freight transport. Vehicles have become more fuel efficient but average loading for most freight vehicle types has fallen. Larger, more fuel efficient vehicles are now available and are being used for some types of operation, but economic conditions have led to an overall increase in the age of the fleet and consequently to lower overall efficiency.

e Energy

Indicator e7:
Residential energy use

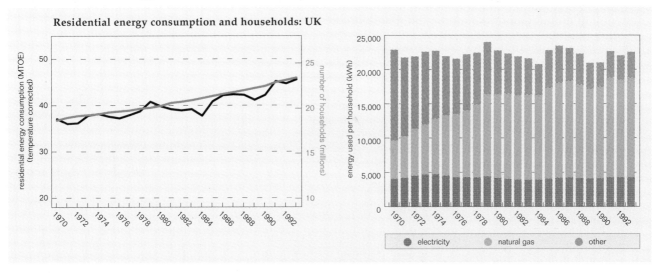

Residential energy consumption and households: UK

Residential energy consumption has increased by over 20 per cent from 1970 to 1993. However, the amount used per household has remained relatively stable and the overall growth is driven more by the increase in number of households.

Indicator e7 contrasts the trends in domestic energy consumption with the number of households.

Annual energy consumption for domestic use, adjusted for yearly temperature fluctuations, has increased from 37 million tonnes of oil equivalent in the 1970s to nearly 46 million tonnes in 1993, a growth of over 20 per cent. However, per household energy consumption has changed little although there have been year to year fluctuations. Trends in domestic energy consumption also reflect other changes, such as the increasing use of natural gas for central heating and improvements in the energy efficiency of dwellings.

Fuel prices

Indicator e8:
Fuel prices in real terms

The real price of fuel in the UK has been largely influenced by trends in world oil prices. UK fuel prices peaked in the early 1980s but have subsequently fallen. More recently, Government policy has been to increase the level of road fuel duties in real terms to encourage greater efficiency of use.

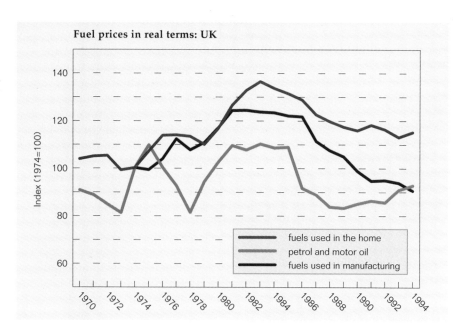

Fuel prices in real terms: UK

Index (1974=100)

fuels used in the home
petrol and motor oil
fuels used in manufacturing

Although the proportion of UK fuel consumption supplied from UK resources has increased during the last 25 years, the prices of fuel have largely been influenced by trends in world oil prices and, in particular, the sharp rises in 1974 and 1979.

Indicator e8 shows the trends in fuel prices since the early 1970s.

In real terms, the prices of fuels used in the home during the early 1980s were 30 per cent higher than in 1970. Following a series of world oil price shocks they have generally fallen since then, but remained 11 per cent higher in 1994 than in 1970. VAT at 8 per cent was imposed on domestic fuel and power in 1994. The price of fuels used in manufacturing has followed a similar pattern but the price falls over the last decade have been somewhat stronger, as added competition between energy suppliers has exerted downward pressure on prices. Petrol and motor oil prices in real terms in 1994 were similar to those in 1970. As part of the UK Climate Change Programme, road fuel duties are being increased by 5 per cent on average in real terms each year to encourage reduced consumption and improved fuel efficiency.

e Energy

f Land use

The key sustainable development objective is to balance the competing demands for the finite quantity of land available. The main issues are to minimise the loss of rural land to development and to maintain the vitality and viability of town centres with people living close to where they work. The indicators relevant to these issues are the area of land covered by urban development, household numbers, re-use of urban land for development, reclamation of derelict land, the amount of land used to build new roads, the growth in out of town shopping centres and vacant retail space in town centres, regular journeys by car and other modes for shopping and commuting and for taking children to and from school, money spent on urban regeneration, and green spaces in urban areas for recreation.

Loss of land in rural uses to development

Indicator f1:
Land covered by urban development

Land in urban uses in 1981 constituted just over 10 per cent of England's land area and is projected to account for just under 12 per cent of the country by 2016.

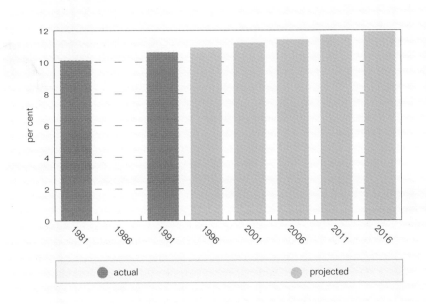

actual   projected

The spread of urban development, the consequent loss of rural land and the associated impacts on the environment are important areas of concern. There is a continuing need to reconcile the requirements for additional land for important uses such as housing, industry, commerce and retailing with a desire to protect the countryside and agriculture. More recently, concern about sustainable development, and in particular about the need to reduce travel demand through land use planning controls, has added to interest in the extent and location of urbanization.

Indicator f1 shows the proportion of land in England which was in urban use in 1981 and 1991 and projections up to 2016.

The area of England in urban uses in 1991 is estimated to have been around 10¹/₂ per cent compared with just over 10 per cent in 1981. This equates to a change from land in rural uses to land in urban uses of around 6,800 hectares per year on average since 1981. In the mid-1980s, around 48 per cent of all urban development took place on

land in rural uses, increasing to around 50 per cent in 1987 and 1988. This proportion fell to only 44 per cent in 1989 with 34 per cent of development occurring on agricultural land, and 10 per cent on land in other rural uses. These proportions were maintained in 1990.

Recent projections suggest a further 169,000 hectares (1.3 per cent of the land area) of England will change from rural to urban uses between 1991 and 2016, equivalent to around 6,800 hectares per year. This represents an increase of around 12 per cent or a growth rate of less than ¹/₂ per cent per year.

Most of the development on land in rural uses can be linked directly to the increasing demands for housing (see Indicator f2). Government policy in recent years has focused on minimising residential development on land in rural uses through recycling land already in urban use (see Indicator f3). A target has been set by the Government of building half of all new homes in England on re-used sites by 2005.

Indicator f2: Household numbers

The number of households in Great Britain has increased by around 20 per cent over the last 20 years and is expected to continue rising at a similar rate into the next century.

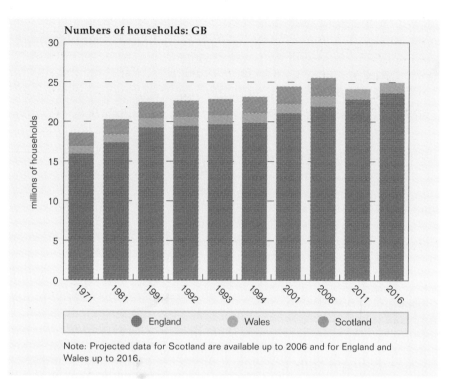

Numbers of households: GB

Legend: ● England ● Wales ● Scotland

Note: Projected data for Scotland are available up to 2006 and for England and Wales up to 2016.

Demand for housing constitutes the main pressure for increased use of rural land for development. This demand is being driven more by changes in lifestyle than by an increasing population. Over the last century the population has doubled but the number of houses has quadrupled, reflecting a large decline in household size. People are living longer and increasingly on their own, through choice, or through death of a partner, or as a result of marriage break-ups. The pressure for new housing is expected to continue in the first part of the next century, as overall population increases and current trends in the age structure and marital status of the population are maintained.

Indicator f2 shows past trends and projections in household formation for England, Wales and Scotland.

Over the 20 years to 1994, the number of households in GB is estimated to have increased by around 4 million to just over 23 million. Between 1994 and 2006, the number of GB households is projected to grow by nearly 2.5 million (11 per cent) to around 25.5 million. Further increases in household formation are expected in England and Wales up to 2016. The pressure for new household formation is expected to be greatest in the south of England.

f Land use

**Indicator f3:
Re-use of land in urban uses for development**

On average, some 7,000 hectares of land in urban uses in England were re-used for new development each year between 1985 and 1990. Re-use of land in urban uses accounted for an estimated 40 to 50 per cent of all changes in land to urban uses over this period.

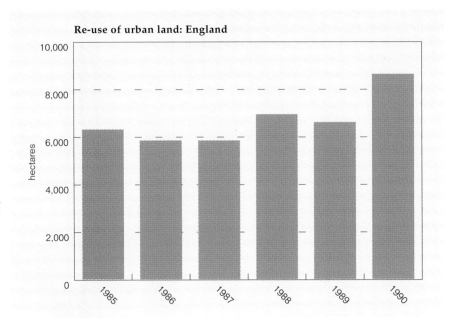

Re-use of urban land: England

f. Land use

The re-use of land in urban uses, particularly for housing and commercial development, contributes to reducing the pressures on the countryside to accommodate new development. Commercial and residential redevelopment within existing urban areas helps to maintain their vitality and viability. It can also improve the general quality of life and also accessibility for those people without a car by increasing and widening the range of services and facilities available and thereby reducing the need for people to travel to other towns for work, shopping and leisure.

Indicator f3 shows how much previously developed land in England was re-used for development in the second half of the 1980s.

Data on the amounts of land in urban uses recycled for new development are subject to uncertainty owing to time lags in recording change and the resultant difficulties in assigning change to the year in which it occurred. Data for 1990 are considerably higher than in any previous year partly because some of the change recorded as taking place in 1990 is thought to have occurred in the years around 1990. The recycling of previously developed land in urban uses in England for new development averaged around 7,000 hectares per year between 1985 and 1990. Recycling of land in urban uses accounted for between 40 to 50 per cent of all land changing to urban use over this period. Data for the early 1990s are not yet available owing to the inevitable time lags in recording urban change.

Indicator f4:
Stock and reclamation of derelict land

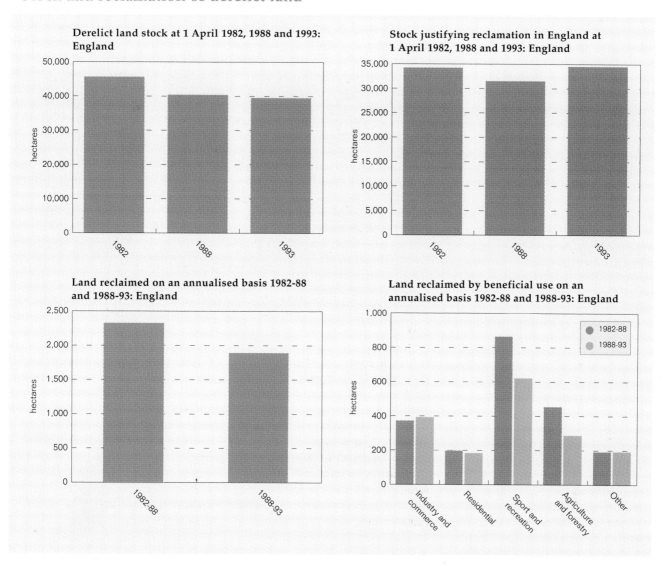

Derelict land stock at 1 April 1982, 1988 and 1993: England

Stock justifying reclamation in England at 1 April 1982, 1988 and 1993: England

Land reclaimed on an annualised basis 1982-88 and 1988-93: England

Land reclaimed by beneficial use on an annualised basis 1982-88 and 1988-93: England

f Land use

The stock of derelict land in England declined steadily between 1982 and 1993. This reduction was achieved against a background of large-scale structural change in industry, which produced new dereliction. The area justifying reclamation remained broadly constant over the same timescale. The area of derelict land reclaimed on an annualised basis decreased by almost a quarter between 1982-88 and 1988-93. Some 9,500 hectares of derelict land were reclaimed between 1988 and 1993.

Reclamation and regeneration of derelict land in both urban and rural areas minimises the pressure to develop greenfield sites. It can also help to revitalise local environments, particularly urban areas, by removing unsightly developments and providing land suitable for housing, employment and leisure uses.

Indicator f4 shows the stock of derelict land in England and the area justifying reclamation from surveys undertaken in 1982, 1988 and 1993. It also shows the area of derelict land reclaimed on an annualised basis and the area of derelict land which has been brought into beneficial use on an annualised basis during 1982-88 and 1988-93.

The amount of derelict land in England decreased steadily from 45,700 hectares in 1982 to 39,600 hectares in 1993. At the same time, there was an estimated 34,600 hectares of derelict land in England justifying reclamation in 1993, slightly more than in 1982. An

estimated 9,500 hectares of land was reclaimed between 1988 and 1993, equivalent to 1,900 hectares per year on average, compared with 14,000 hectares (2,300 hectares per year on average) reclaimed between 1982 and 1988. Local authorities reclaimed 55 per cent of the 9,500 hectares of derelict land between 1988 and 1993. Over 90 per cent of this reclamation was aided by Government grants.

Expenditure on the Derelict Land Grant (DLG) rose from £67.9 million in 1988/89 to £103.9 million in 1993/94. The amount of land reclaimed, with DLG funding, rose from 1,187 hectares in 1989/90 to 1,540 hectares in 1993/94. The DLG was subsumed within English Partnerships unified Investment Fund in 1994/95. English Partnerships reclaimed some 1,700 hectares of derelict land in 1994/95.

Between 1988 and 1993, an average of almost 1,700 hectares per year (8,400 hectares in total) was brought back into beneficial use, compared with an average of just over 2,000 hectares per year (12,570 hectares in total) between 1982 and 1988. The most common use to which reclaimed land was put was sport and recreation (41 per cent of all land reclaimed between 1982 and 1988 and 37 per cent between 1988 and 1993). Other uses include industry and commerce

and agriculture and forestry. Hard end uses, eg commercial development, predominated in urban areas while soft end uses, eg recreation, were more prevalent in rural areas.

The Scottish Vacant and Derelict Land Survey showed that in 1994 there were just over 9,000 hectares of derelict land, and that during the previous year almost 500 hectares were reclaimed. The main uses of reclaimed land were agriculture (137 hectares), residential (61 hectares), mineral activity (60 hectares), recreational and leisure (61 hectares) and nature conservation (37 hectares).

Future indicator development:

The data on amounts of derelict land reclaimed only give a rough indication of reclamation performance. Higher standards in recent years in terms of the removal of contamination, together with inflation, has meant that less land has been reclaimed on an annualised basis even though the money spent through reclamation grants, etc has increased over the years. A better indicator of reclamation performance would be one which takes full account of costs and the quality of derelict land reclamation undertaken.

Indicator f5: Road building

In the second half of the 1980s, an estimated 12,000 hectares of land in England (0.1 per cent of the total land area) were used for road building, some two thirds of which was land previously in rural use.

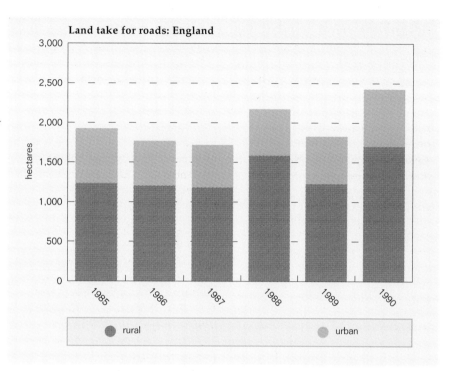

Land take for roads: England

Businesses and communities need to have reasonable access to goods, services and other people, and an adequate road network is part of the solution. The pressure to build roads has increased in recent years with the growth in car ownership. Economic growth has allowed people to make more use of their cars and has also resulted in rapid increases in the amount of freight transported by road. These factors have increased the pressure for using rural and previously urban land for building new roads in GB.

Indicator f5 shows the area of urban and rural land in England used to build new roads during the second half of the 1980s.

Data on road lengths and the area of urban and rural land changing to roads are subject to uncertainty owing to measurement difficulties and problems of classification. An estimated 12,000 hectares of land was used for road building between 1985 and 1990. Over 8,000 hectares of these new roads were built on land previously in rural use and nearly 4,000 hectares on land which was either previously developed for urban purposes or vacant urban land. Road building is estimated to have accounted for 13 per cent of all changes in land use in England between 1985 and 1990. The majority of new roads are unclassified roads providing access to new development, rather than trunk roads.

f Land use

Vitality and viability of town centres

Indicator f6:
Out-of-town retail floorspace

Between 1986 and 1990, the amount of out-of town retail floorspace almost tripled, but reduced economic activity resulted in a slower rate of increase thereafter.

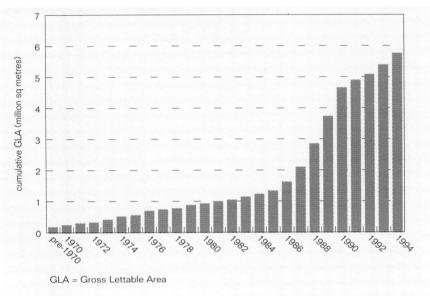

GLA = Gross Lettable Area

f Land use

The development of out-of-town shopping centres and retail parks has contributed to the rundown of town and city centres. Reduced retail activity in urban areas can have a knock-on effect on other services, such as entertainment, leisure, banking, etc. Out-of-town retail developments also encourage people to travel longer distances for shopping, mainly in cars, which causes increased congestion, pollution and noise.

Indicator f6 shows the growth in the gross lettable area (GLA) of out-of-town shopping centres between 1970 and 1993.

Out-of-town retail centres in the UK, larger than 5,000 sq metres, covered an estimated 200,000 sq metres of floorspace by the end of the 1960s, rising to an estimated 900,000 sq metres by the end of

the 1970s and a total of nearly 1.4 million sq metres by 1985. Total out-of-town floorspace almost tripled in the following 5 years to nearly 4.7 million sq metres by the end of 1990. Since 1990, reduced economic activity has caused a slowdown in out of town development with only an additional 850,000 sq metres of floorspace opened between 1991 and 1994.

Under "Planning Policy Guidance Note 6: Town Centres and Retail Developments", issued in 1993, the Government asks that local authorities take account of the possible impact on village and town centre shops of proposed new out-of-town retail developments. This has already resulted in a slowdown in the number of planning applications granted for new developments. The impact of this policy is not reflected in the data shown in Indicator f6 because of the time required in dealing with planning applications.

Future indicator development:

Vitality and viability of town centres is a difficult area to measure and the indicator presented is very partial. It is difficult to analyse, with limited data, the complex pattern of changing lifestyles. A more rounded picture of the effect of out-of-town developments on the vitality of city and town centres could be provided by having trends on the development of leisure and entertainment facilities, eg cinema multiplexes, skating rinks and bowling allies outside urban areas.

There are around 800,000 empty houses in England, with over 700,000 of them in private ownership. Similar information, including trends, is not available on the amount of vacant retail/office/other business floorspace in town and city centres. Such information would provide a useful indication of the effect out-of-town development is having on urban centres.

Indicator f7:
Regular journeys

Over the last 20 years the average journey length for commuting has increased by around 40 per cent. The average journey lengths for shopping and for taking children to and from school are much less than for commuting. Nevertheless, average journey lengths for these purposes increased by 35 per cent and 40 per cent respectively over the same period.

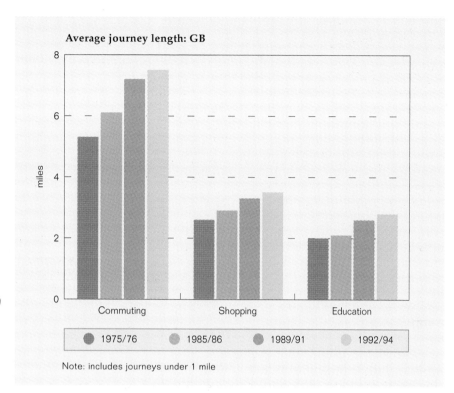

Average journey length: GB

Note: includes journeys under 1 mile

Cars account for around 59 per cent of all journeys. More people are able to afford cars and are using them for commuting and travelling greater distances, as a result of changes in the location of residential and retail development, and employment patterns. People are also using their cars more for leisure purposes (see Indicator c1 in the *Leisure and tourism* section). In addition, more parents are driving their children to schools, many of which are further from home.

Indicator f7 shows trends in the average lengths for commuting, shopping and taking children to and from school.

The length of the average journey for commuting was $7^1/_2$ miles in the period 1992 to 1994 compared with 5.3 miles in 1975/6, an increase of some 40 per cent. More and more commuting journeys are now made by private car and less and less by public transport. The length of the average shopping trip was 3.5 miles between 1992 and 1994 compared with 2.6 miles in 1975/76, an increase of 35 per cent. This increase has been mainly resulted from the growth in out-of-town shopping centres and retail parks which are easier to access and therefore more convenient (see Indicator f6). The average journey for taking children to and from school increased by 40 per cent to 2.8 miles between 1992 and 1994 compared with 2 miles in 1975/76.

f Land use

Indicator f8:
Regeneration Expenditure

Expenditure on regeneration programmes in England more than doubled from £0.77 billion in 1989/90 to a peak of £1.56 billion in 1993/94, then fell slightly in 1994/95. Planned expenditure of £1.32 billion in 1997/8 will be some 17 per cent below the 1993/4 peak, as time-limited agencies such as the Urban Development Corporations complete their work and are wound up.

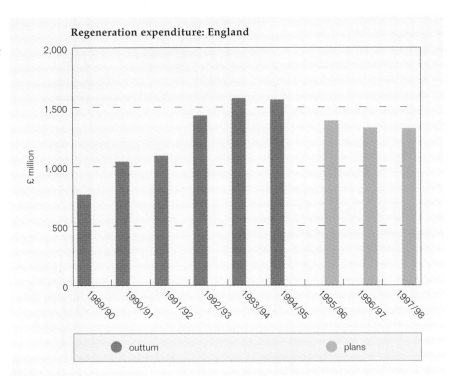

The Government promotes sustainable regeneration, economic development and competitiveness in England through the targeted Single Regeneration Budget (SRB). The SRB Challenge Fund supports comprehensive regeneration strategies developed by local partnerships between the public, private and voluntary sectors to help improve the quality of life of local people. In deprived rural areas, support is mainly channelled through the Rural Development Programme and Rural Challenge. The amount spent by Government on such regeneration programmes gives an indication of the rate at which urban and rural land is being regenerated and put to beneficial use.

Indicator f8 shows the amount of actual and planned Government funding for regeneration in England between 1989/90 and 1997/98.

Following the creation of the SRB in April 1994, programme expenditure is being re-focused on the broader objectives and priorities of regeneration. As inherited commitments are fulfilled and programmes come to an end, an increasing proportion of the overall budget will fund new partnership schemes directed at comprehensive strategies.

Indicator f9:
Green spaces in urban areas

Future indicator development:

Green spaces in urban areas are important for recreational purposes and for generally enhancing the quality of life of people who live in urban areas. It is therefore important that they are maintained and developed both in terms of area and environmental quality, and not lost to development or allowed to fall into disrepair.

No comprehensive and validated data exist on the extent of urban green spaces. New initiatives such as the proposed Land Use Stock System for England may provide suitable data for this important area. Developing indicators on the quality of urban green spaces will prove a much more difficult task.

f Land use

g Water resources

The key issues for sustainable development are to ensure that adequate water resources are available to meet consumers' needs, to meet the demand for water from households, agriculture and industry whilst sustaining the aquatic environment, and to improve the efficiency of water use. Key indicators include comparisons between overall demand and the available resource, rates of use for particular purposes and the efficiency of remedial measures.

Freshwater is a renewable natural resource comprising rivers, lakes and groundwater. The inland freshwaters of the UK are put to many and varied uses. They are the source of water put into the public water supply system to meet basic daily requirements for drinking and washing and are also a vital resource for use in agriculture and industrial processes. Large quantities of water are used in the transport of human wastes to treatment plants and freshwaters are also a recipient of waste from industry and agriculture after appropriate treatment. Many rivers and lakes are also valued for their recreational and amenity value. The availability and quality of freshwater is important in shaping the ecology and the environment of the UK.

There are important potential conflicts between these uses of the freshwater resource and protection of the aquatic environment.

Indicator g1:
Licensed abstractions and effective rainfall

There is a high utilisation of resources in the Anglian and Thames regions where the total annual licensed abstraction is similar to or even exceeds the effective rainfall in severe droughts. The balance is taken from reservoir and groundwater storage.

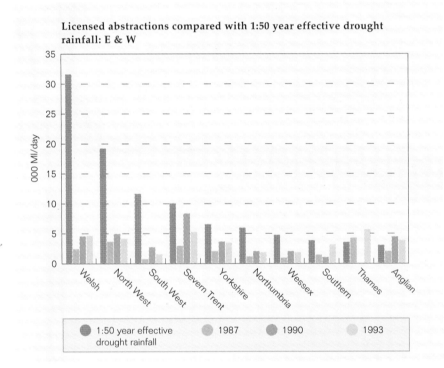

Licensed abstractions compared with 1:50 year effective drought rainfall: E & W

000 Ml/day

Legend:
- 1:50 year effective drought rainfall
- 1987
- 1990
- 1993

Regions: Welsh, North West, South West, Severn Trent, Yorkshire, Northumbria, Wessex, Southern, Thames, Anglian

Although in total the available water resources in the UK well exceed demand, the balance between these varies widely from region to region. Many parts of the UK have had to develop river basin management systems to ensure that water can be reused between its falling as rain and its eventual return to the sea. This occurs particularly in the Thames basin where recycling of abstracted water takes place along the whole length of the Thames.

Indicator g1 compares licensed abstractions and effective drought rainfall

Indicator g1 illustrates the much higher resource potential of the wetter north west and west of England and Wales compared with the south east and east of England, by showing the effective rainfall in a drought of a severity which can be expected to occur once in every 50 years compared with licensed abstractions in 1987, 1990 and 1993 in each of the National Rivers Authority (NRA) regions. In 8 of the 10 regions the ratio of abstractions to effective rainfall is less than one-third. In the Thames region, licensed abstractions can appear to exceed the 1:50 year effective rainfall because of re-use and storage in reservoirs and groundwater.

Indicator g2:
Low flow alleviation

Between 1990/91 and 1994/95 128 km of river affected by low flows have been restored. Expenditure since 1993/94 is some £6 million.

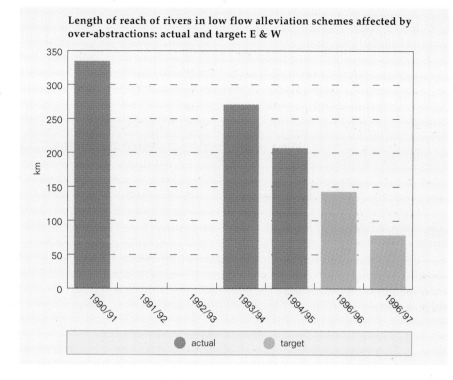

Length of reach of rivers in low flow alleviation schemes affected by over-abstractions: actual and target: E & W

River flows in Britain reflect, not just the balance between rainfall and evaporation, but also the effects of abstractions to meet demand from the domestic, industrial, and agricultural sectors. The effects of increasing demand can give rise to unacceptably low flows in rivers, thereby damaging wildlife habitats and having adverse effects on water quality, and recreational and amenity value.

Indicator g2 shows the length of rivers in low flow alleviation schemes in England and Wales affected by over-abstractions since 1990/91.

The NRA plays a significant role in augmenting river flows to support abstractions and to protect the environment through its water transfer and river regulation schemes. In 1990/91 the NRA identified 335 km of affected reach in 40 rivers in England and Wales. Subsequent action to alleviate low flows at a cost of £6 million has reduced the affected reaches to a total of 207 km. There is a target to further reduce the affected reaches to 79 km by 1996/97.

8 Water resources

Indicator g3:
Abstraction by use

Total abstractions have remained steady over the past 10 years. OFWAT predict that demand for water from the Public Water Supply will remain unchanged until 2014-15, but that there will be further falls in industrial demand.

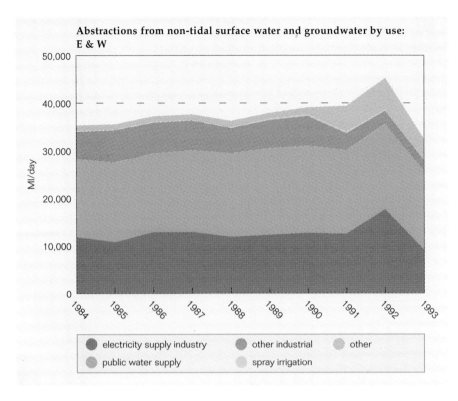

Abstractions from non-tidal surface water and groundwater by use: E & W

g Water resources

Water is drawn from both surface freshwater resources, such as rivers and lakes, and from groundwater resources held in water-bearing rocks known as aquifers. Substantial amounts of water are also drawn from estuarial waters, although these are excluded from the discussions here. Many industrial abstractions, such as those for hydro-electric power by electricity companies and for cooling , agricultural abstractions and for fish farming do not consume water resources. Virtually all of the water abstracted is later discharged back to surface water and the total volume abstracted is therefore of less importance environmentally. However, the quality of the water discharged is not necessarily of the same quality when it is discharged as it was when abstracted. In contrast, uses such as spray irrigation and abstractions for evaporative cooling represent a loss to the water resource.

Indicator g3 shows abstraction by use in England and Wales since 1984.

In 1993, just over half of the water abstracted from surface and underground sources in England and Wales was taken and distributed by the water companies. Approximately half of the remainder was abstracted by the electricity supply industry, mainly for hydropower: other industry accounted for a further 12 per cent of abstractions. Only a small proportion of national abstractions (less than 1 per cent) was used for spray irrigation in agriculture. A general decline in the amount of water abstracted for industry and general agricultural purposes over the last 10 years has been accompanied by an increase in demand for abstractions for spray irrigation of crops, fish farming and hydropower. The declines are

attributed partly to the introduction of more efficient processes and partly to the shift in the national economy away from production towards service industries. A study by OFWAT in November 1994, predicted virtually no growth in overall demand for water from the Public Water Supply to the year 2014-15 in England and Wales. It also predicted further falls in industrial demand and an increase in domestic demand. The Government is however doing further work with the NRA, OFWAT and the water industry to test these assumptions in the light of recent experience of demand.

Indicator g4:
Abstractions for public water supply

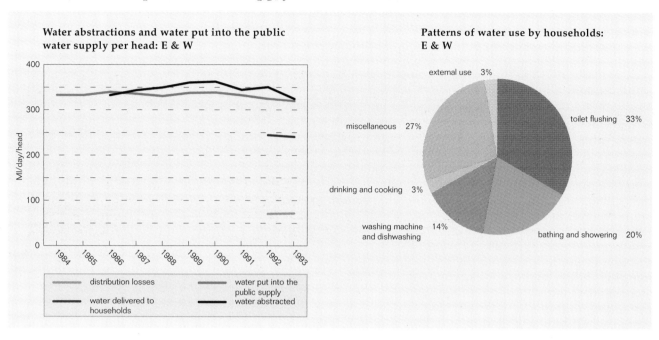

Water abstractions and water put into the public water supply per head: E & W

Patterns of water use by households: E & W

Changes in water demand patterns may be placing greater stress on supplies at times when they are already under pressure from abnormal weather patterns.

Much of the population is concentrated in the drier parts of south and east of England where river flows and water resources are particularly vulnerable to variations in climate. Increasing affluence and higher standards of living are changing water demand patterns. The main increases in domestic water use are for personal hygiene and for watering of gardens in summer, when supplies are under most stress.

Indicator g4 shows abstractions for public water supply per head in England and Wales since 1984 together with present patterns of water use by households.

Household use accounts for half the water used from public supplies, equivalent to about 40 per cent of all the water abstracted. The average household uses about 380 litres a day or 160 litres for every man, women and child. Toilet flushing and miscellaneous uses each account for approximately one-

third of water used (around 50 litres each day). Only around 5 litres is used each day for drinking and cooking: Almost a quarter of the water put into supply by the water companies (70 ml /person/day) never reaches the customer. Losses for individual companies vary from 15 per cent to 38 per cent of the total water put into the supply. These figures represent treated water losses due to leakage from company supply pipes. Major reductions in that proportion, if they could be achieved at economic cost, would considerably reduce the amount of water companies need to abstract and enable the development of new resources to at least be deferred.

Indicator g5:
Demand and supply of public water

The margin between average demand for public water supply and the resource available in dry years is reasonable in most areas.

g Water resources

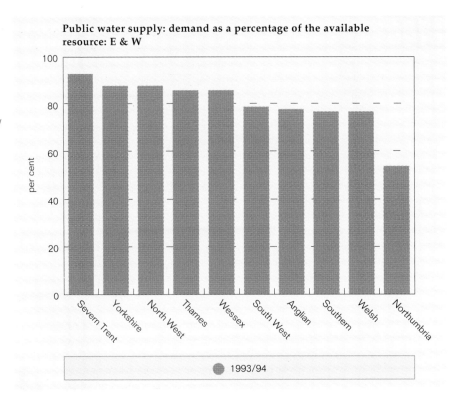

Public water supply: demand as a percentage of the available resource: E & W

● 1993/94

The exceptionally low winter rainfall in parts of south and east England between 1988 and 1992 and hot, dry summers of recent years have shown that the margin between the available resource during a severe drought and the demand for public water supply during a drought may become sufficiently narrow in some areas to require restrictions on water use during periods of exceptional weather. This picture is however clouded by factors such as standards of service and customer behaviour. There remains some uncertainty over the possible effects of climate change on water resources over the next few decades, although recent research suggests that climate change could result in an increase of up to 4 per cent in the demand for water in the south and east of the country up to 2021.

Indicator g5 shows the demand for public supply water in England and Wales in 1993/94 as a percentage of the available resource.

Indicator g5 shows that in 1993/94 5 of the 10 NRA regions used over 80 per cent of the available resource and 1 used over 90 per cent of the resource expected to be available under drought conditions expected to occur once in 50 years. In 1993, rainfall was higher than the 1961-90 average in all except the North West region.

Indicator g6:
Abstractions for spray irrigation

Irrigation rates have doubled between 1982 and 1992, largely in response to demands for higher quality agricultural produce.

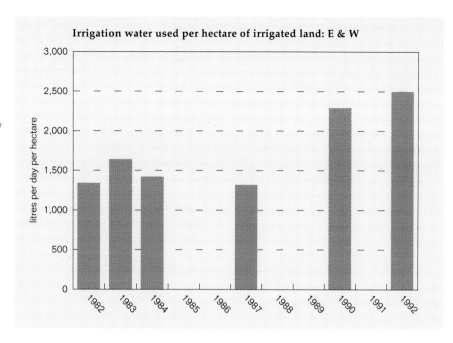

Irrigation water used per hectare of irrigated land: E & W

Although abstractions for spray irrigation represent only a small proportion (less than 1 per cent) of annual abstractions they can be significant because they are immediately consumptive (ie little water is returned to the system due to retention in the crop and/or evapotranspiration), they occur in a concentrated period usually in the drier parts of the country and can vary greatly from year to year, peaking in dry years when surface water is scarcest. Agricultural irrigation in England and Wales has increased and changed considerably over the last 40 years. The original emphasis on yield increase has been superseded by a need to secure better quality produce and reliable product supply.

Indicator g6 shows abstractions for spray irrigation in England and Wales since 1982.

Potatoes account for most of the water used for irrigation (59 per cent in 1992) closely followed by vegetables. Irrigation rates have doubled from approximately 1,300 litres per day per hectare in 1982 to 2,500 litres per day per hectare in 1992, although the level of abstraction for spray irrigation varies markedly from year to year and is dependent on the prevailing weather conditions in the growing season. There is an underlying trend towards irrigation of a larger area of agricultural land in dry years.

8 Water resources

h Forestry

The key sustainable development issue for forestry is to manage forests in a way that sustains their environmental qualities as well as their productive potential.

This means that UK forests should be valued not only for their commercial potential, which currently produce some 7 million cubic metres of wood each year - about 15 per cent of our total consumption, but also for recreation, nature conservation and landscape enhancement. Indicators relevant to this objective are therefore the extent of forest cover and timber production in the UK, the areas of ancient semi-natural woodland remaining, the health of trees, and indicators of whether forests are being managed in an environmentally beneficial way.

Forest cover and timber production

Indicator h1:
Forest cover

The area of forest and woodland cover in GB has increased by one third since the early 1970s. Coniferous species have been favoured in increasing forest cover particularly in the uplands although now there is greater emphasis on broadleaved species and planting on better quality land.

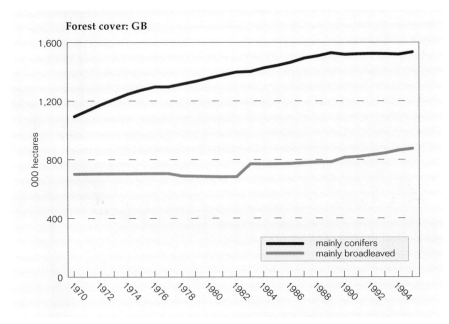

Forest cover: GB

Indicator h2:
Timber production

Post war forestry expansion in the UK has created conifer forests which are now of an age to contribute a rapidly increasing component of home grown timber to the British market. The thinning and felling of conifers in GB has increased by 72 per cent since 1984.

Thinning and felling of conifers: GB

Forestry makes a small (almost 0.2 per cent) but growing contribution to GDP and around 35,000 people are employed in the forestry sectors. However, only around 15 per cent of UK consumption of timber is met from our own resources (see also Indicator d1 in the *Overseas trade* section). Growing trees also remove carbon dioxide from the air and store the carbon in wood.

Over many centuries there has been a gradual loss of forest cover in the UK, which fell to its lowest level of 5 per cent of the UK's area at the start of this century. These losses led to an overdependence on imported timber which was the catalyst after the first world war for the initiation of a UK forest expansion programme. Today, 10 per cent of the UK land area is covered by forests but this is significantly less than the 25 per cent average for the EC. Most of these new forests have been established on land of low agricultural quality in the remoter upland areas of the UK, and non-native coniferous species have generally been favoured because of their high productivity.

Concerns about the impact on the landscape and on the ecology of semi-natural habitats have led to greater emphasis on securing multiple benefits by planting "down the hill" on better quality land and increasing the amount of broadleaved planting and new native woodlands. Felling is regulated through licences which require that felled areas be replanted, implementing the principle that woodland that is currently broadleaved is expected to remain so.

Indicator h1 shows trends since 1970 in the area of GB covered by coniferous and broadleaved species.

Forest cover in GB has increased from 1.8 million hectares in 1970 to 2.4 million hectares in 1995, 64 per cent of which is mainly conifer. Broadleaved cover remained stable at about 0.7 million hectares up to the early 1980s but has risen gradually since then to a level of 0.87 million hectares in 1995, reflecting an increase in new planting each year of broadleaved species from a few hundred hectares to nearly 11,000 hectares over the same period. The marked increase in new broadleaved plantings since 1985 follows introduction of the Broadleaved Woodland Grant Scheme to provide incentives for private forestry and its successor the Woodland Grant Scheme (WGS) in 1988. The Farm Woodland Scheme and its successor the Farm Woodland Premium Scheme (FWPS) have also contributed to encourage a productive alternative use of farmland and to the increase in the new planting of broadleaved woodland.

In the Rural White Paper launched in October 1995, the Government has indicated that it would like to see a doubling of woodland in England over the next half century, and that achieving this will depend on securing changes in the Common Agricultural Policy (CAP) to allow forestry to compete more effectively with agriculture for land use.

Future indicator development:

A key aim of woodland policy is to encourage the regeneration and extension of native woodland. While most of the UK's native tree species are broadleaved, native Scots Pine forest is a particularly important habitat in the Scottish Highlands. The Forestry Commission has introduced a new system for an inventory of all types of woodland which, together with the Countryside Surveys carried out by the Department of the Environment (CS1990), will provide detailed information about woodlands and their management. Woodland plant species richness could be monitored in future using sample plots comparable to those in CS1990, taking particular account of species characteristic of different woodland types or conditions.

Indicator h2 shows trends since 1984 in the volume of conifers thinned and felled in GB.

The post war expansion of forest area has created conifer forests which are now of an age to contribute a rapidly increasing component of home grown timber to the British market. This has allowed a rapid expansion and modernisation of the wood processing industry with major investment in sawmills, pulp, paper and panel board mills in the UK. Thinning and felling of conifers in GB has increased by 72 per cent since 1984 and softwood production from these forests is expected to double over the next 20 to 25 years. The rate of production of hardwood timber from broadleaved forests has been steady but may increase if more profitable markets can be found for the timber much of which it is in stands of high environmental value but low quality for timber production.

h Forestry

Ancient semi-natural woodland

Indicator h3:
Ancient semi-natural woodland

Ancient semi-natural woodland by size: GB

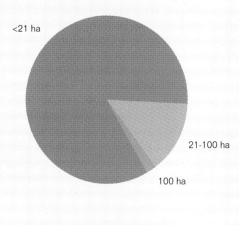

Area of ancient semi-natural woodland: GB

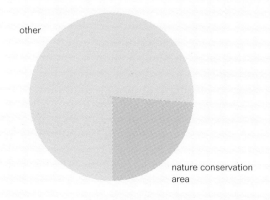

35,000 ancient woodlands in GB
containing semi-natural stands

316,000 hectares of ancient semi-natural
woodland in GB of which 75,000 hectares
are within nature conservation areas

Ancient semi-natural woodlands, the majority of which are smaller than 21 hectares, cover less than 1.4 per cent of the area of GB, a fraction of the original natural woodland which once covered the country. The depletion of such woodlands has now largely ended. Around one quarter of such woodlands today are within nature conservation areas.

Ancient semi-natural woodlands are areas which have been continuously wooded since 1600 and contain tree and shrubs composed of native species including oak, ash, hazel, birch and Scots pine which have regenerated naturally from seed. These woodlands tend to be richer in plants and animals than other woodland areas and contain many rare and vulnerable species. It is therefore important to preserve what remains of these forests which are often important for cultural as well as ecological reasons.

Indicator h3 shows the number and area of ancient semi-natural woodlands in GB in 1992.

There are many remaining pockets of ancient semi-natural woodlands throughout the UK, but they occupy today only 1.4 per cent of the area of GB. About one quarter of such woodlands are contained in nature conservation areas - Sites of Special Scientific Interest, National Nature Reserves, Local Nature Reserves and reserves owned or managed by voluntary nature conservation organisations. Ancient semi-natural woodlands are highly fragmented with 84 per cent of the 35,000 sites less than 21 hectares and under 2 per cent of sites being larger than 100 hectares. The greatest concentrations of such woodlands now are in south east England, the southern Welsh borders and the central Scottish Highlands. Some 7 per cent of the area of ancient semi-natural woodland present in around 1930 have been cleared for other land

uses, mainly for agriculture, while 38 per cent by area has been replaced with plantations, usually of non-native species. Over the last decade, both clearance and unsympathetic forestry practices in such woodlands have declined and depletion has now largely ended.

Future indicator development:

Further work to track more accurately changes over time in the area of ancient semi-natural woodland might involve use of up-to-date aerial photography coupled with field analysis of a structured sample of sites, together with linkages to other surveys, eg the Forestry Commission's National Inventory of Woodlands and Trees and the DoE Countryside Surveys. It will be important to incorporate some assessment of management status of ancient semi-natural woodlands.

Tree health

Indicator h4:
Tree health

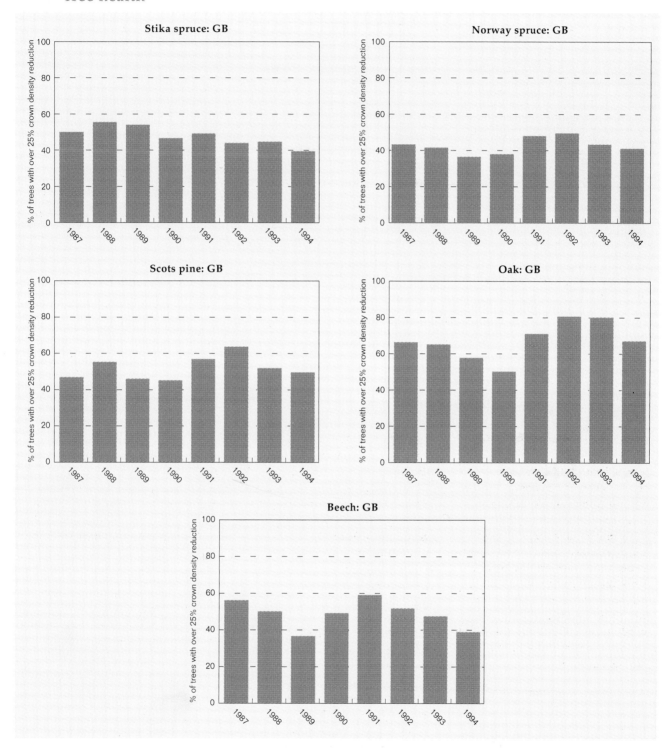

In general, tree health in GB declined in the late 1980s but since 1992 there has been an improvement. Drought, insect defoliation and storm damage are thought to be the principal influences on crown density.

Tree health is characterised by *crown density* - the amount of light passing through the crown - and needle or leaf discolouration. The health of the tree is assessed by comparing its crown density with that of a "perfect" tree. Besides air pollution, other factors such as frost, drought, wind and nutrient deficiencies can cause discolouration and reductions in crown density, as can fungi and insects.

Indicator h4 shows the trends in crown density reductions for selected tree species in GB since 1987.

This indicator shows the proportion of trees whose crown density is 25 per cent or more below what would be expected if the tree were "perfect". Thus, a decline in the proportion illustrated by the bar on the chart implies an improvement in tree health. The condition of 4 of the 5 species surveyed - Norway spruce, Scots pine, oak and beech declined between 1989 and 1992, but since 1992 there has been an improvement for all species. Sitka spruce has been the exception showing a gradual increase in crown density since 1987. In beech, the improvement began a year earlier than in the other three declining species. In oak, foliage loss has

been particularly severe with around 80 per cent of trees surveyed showing crown density reductions of over 25 per cent in both 1992 and 1993. Since 1987, crown density has fluctuated either annually or on a slightly longer cycle, revealing little evidence so far of a long term trend. The results are consistent with variations caused by a number of well-known biotic or climatic factors. Drought, insect defoliation and storm damage are thought to have been the principal influences on crown density.

Forest management

Indicator h5:
Forest management

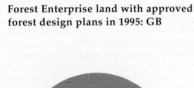

Forest Enterprise land with approved forest design plans in 1995: GB

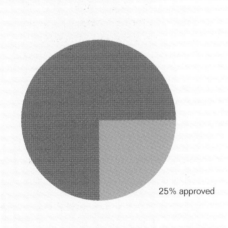

25% approved

Area of private woodland covered by the Woodland Grant Scheme: GB

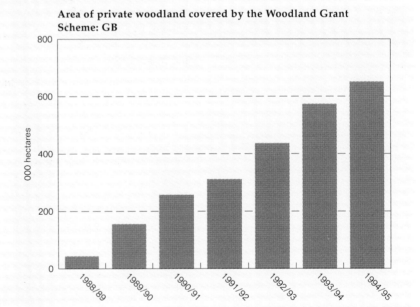

25 per cent of Forest Enterprise land in GB had approved design plans in 1995 and will continue to expand until all the estate is covered. The area of private woodland with plans approved under the Woodland Grant Scheme has increased rapidly since 1988.

h Forestry

It is important to measure not only the extent of forest cover but also its quality. Current techniques and data do not allow this to be measured on a comprehensive basis but, as a proxy, we can measure the amount of forestry in approved grant schemes and design plans for Forestry Enterprise woodland, since such schemes ensure forests are managed in an appropriate way.

The concept of multipurpose forestry is central to Government forestry policy objectives. Government grants for forestry are aimed at increasing the recreation, nature conservation and landscape benefits of forests as well as timber production. The Government is supporting a number of community-based multipurpose forestry initiatives including the National Forest in the Midlands, the 12 Community Forests throughout England, the Central Scotland Woodlands and the Welsh Valleys Initiative. These initiatives also have specific targets for afforestation of the areas they cover.

Indicator h5 shows the percentage of Forest Enterprise woodland in GB with design plans approved by the Forestry Authority and the area of private woodland with plans approved under the Woodland Grant Scheme.

All new forestry proposals must be accompanied by a comprehensive plan to identify special status and other sensitive areas to be protected or specially managed. These plans must show that management and environmental guidelines covering landscape design, nature conservation, archaeological sites, effects on water supply and catchment, and recreation are being followed.

The Forest Enterprise estate is regulated by the Forestry Authority through approval and monitoring of Forest Design Plans. These plans set out integrated proposals for multi-objective forestry over design units which can be very extensive and take a long term view. The approval system was introduced during 1993 and by April 1995, 25 per cent of Forest Enterprise land in GB had approved Forest Design Plans. Forest Enterprise forest design planning will continue to expand until all the estate is covered. The Forest Service in Northern Ireland produces Landscape Plans for forests on sensitive sites and to date these plans cover about 25 per cent of the forest area.

The main vehicle for grant aid to the private sector is the Woodland Grant Scheme. This scheme is structured according to the nature of the planting proposed and the environmental benefits that will be achieved. For example, broadleaf planting benefits from a higher rate of grant to reflect higher establishment costs but planting which provides particular opportunities for nature conservation and recreation may attract supplementary payments.

In addition, the Farm Woodland Premium Scheme offers annual payments to farmers to abate the loss of farming income consequent upon converting agricultural land to woodlands. The rates of annual payment vary according to the quality of agricultural land involved. Unimproved land, the type most likely to be valuable for nature conservation, attracts the lowest rates. The number of annual payments depends on the tree species planted - predominantly broadleaved woodland attracts payments for a longer period.

The area of private woodland covered by grants under the Woodland Grant Scheme has increased rapidly from 45,000 hectares in 1988/89 to over 640,000 hectares in 1994/95. The area in this scheme includes existing woodland including that transferred from earlier grant schemes. The Forestry Authority considers proposals under the Woodland Grant Scheme and former grant schemes against the same environmental guidelines. However, the Woodland Grant Scheme provides a wider range of incentives for multipurpose forestry than former schemes, stimulating nature conservation and recreation, as well as more planting on better land and on land surplus to agricultural requirements.

Future indicator development:

Periodic sample checks of Design Plans and Grant Schemes will be developed to ensure that what takes place on the ground does meet multipurpose forestry and will permit refinement of existing guidelines. Trial work in this area is being undertaken by the Forestry Authority.

h Forestry

j Fish resources

Fishing has a major impact on the living resources of the sea and most of the fish stocks in the waters of EC member states are currently over-exploited. The key issue for sustainability is therefore to prevent over-exploitation of fish stocks and to balance fishing effort against the natural ability of fish stocks to regenerate. Indicators relevant to this issue are fish stocks and catches in UK waters.

Indicator j1: Fish stocks

Some stocks in the waters of EC member states are at historically low levels and most are over-exploited.

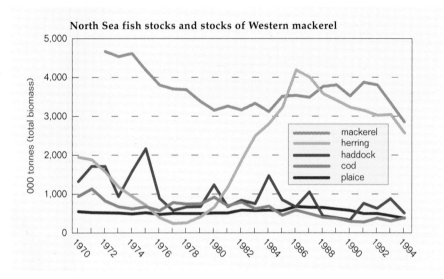

North Sea fish stocks and stocks of Western mackerel

As well as fishing activity, fish stocks are also affected by natural factors, but are largely unaffected by anthropogenic inputs to the sea because concentrations of contaminants in the sea are generally low.

Indicator j1 shows trends since 1990 in total biomass stocks of fish in the North Sea and in Western mackerel

Most stocks in the waters of EC member states are over-exploited and some stocks are at historically low levels. Recent trends vary from species to species. North Sea

herring stocks have been in decline since the peak in the mid 1980s. North Sea cod stocks have been in general decline over the last 25 years and are currently a third of the peak level in 1971. Stocks of North Sea haddock have fluctuated considerably. Western mackerel stocks have been increasing since the early 1980s but have declined since 1991.

Indicator j2: Minimum Biological Acceptable Level (MBAL)

42 per cent of stocks fished by the UK fishing fleet and other international fleets in the waters of EC member states, in 1994, were above MBAL

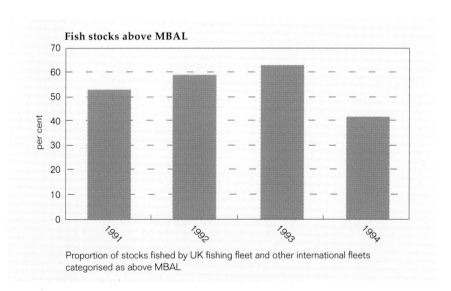

Fish stocks above MBAL

Proportion of stocks fished by UK fishing fleet and other international fleets categorised as above MBAL

j Fish resources

Biomass estimates of major, internationally assessed, fish stocks are produced by the International Council for the Exploration of the Sea (ICES) based on data on international catches and fishing effort and estimates of abundance from research vessel surveys. These estimates are used to evaluate whether the spawning biomass of each stock is above its Minimum Biological Acceptable Level (MBAL). This is the level of the mature stock size below which there is an increasing risk that the reproductive potential of the stock will collapse. For some stocks, for which information is more limited,

estimated spawning stock is compared with previous years' estimates and categorised as above MBAL only if the estimated spawning stock is above the lowest level so far recorded. The percentages for each year are not directly comparable because the stocks for which ICES has made these estimates have varied from year to year.

Indicator j2 shows the proportions of stocks fished by the UK fishing fleet and other international fleets above MBAL

The low level of MBAL indicates the over-exploitation of fish stocks of interest to UK fishermen. The percentage of stocks fished by the UK fishing fleet and other international fleets which ICES has categorised as being above MBAL (in either of the ways discussed above) was 53 per cent in 1991, 59 per cent in 1992, 63 per cent in 1993 and 42 per cent in 1994. The variations from year to year reflect, to some extent, changes in the make-up of the indicator.

j Fish resources

Indicator j3: Fish catches

Balancing fishing effort against the natural ability of fish stocks to regenerate is one of the main objectives of the EC Common Fisheries Policy and a range of measures have been adopted aimed at conserving fish stocks including a system of setting Total Allowable Catches.

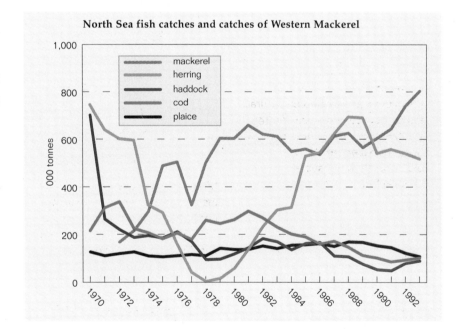

North Sea fish catches and catches of Western Mackerel

Legend: mackerel, herring, haddock, cod, plaice

000 tonnes — 1,000 / 800 / 600 / 400 / 200 / 0
Years: 1970, 1972, 1974, 1976, 1978, 1980, 1982, 1984, 1986, 1988, 1990, 1992

Fishing is important to the local economy in certain coastal areas both directly and through the industries dependent on them, including food processing. There are some 20,750 fishermen engaged in the UK sea fishing industry whilst another 19,400 people are employed in fish processing. Industry estimates suggest that there are in total, about 3 jobs in ancillary and supporting industries for every

fisherman. Most of the fish stocks in the waters of EC member states are over-exploited. The size of the mature stock (its spawning biomass) which represents the stock's reproductive potential is particularly important.

Indicator j3 shows trends in international catches of fish in the North Sea and Western mackerel

International catches of cod and haddock have declined substantially since peak levels in the early 1970s. Mackerel catches have increased fourfold over the same period.

k Climate change

The key sustainable development objective is to limit emissions of greenhouse gases which may contribute to global warming and climate change. Indicators of relevance are greenhouse gas radiative forcing rates, global temperature change, and UK emissions of greenhouse gases.

Global greenhouse gas radiative forcing rates and global temperatures

Indicator k1:
Global greenhouse gas radiative forcing rate

Total average greenhouse gas radiative forcing has increased steadily over the last 200 years, largely because of increases in atmospheric carbon dioxide concentrations and, to a lesser extent, methane and nitrous oxide. Since 1960, atmospheric concentrations of chlorofluorocarbons (CFCs) have contributed to the overall warming rate.

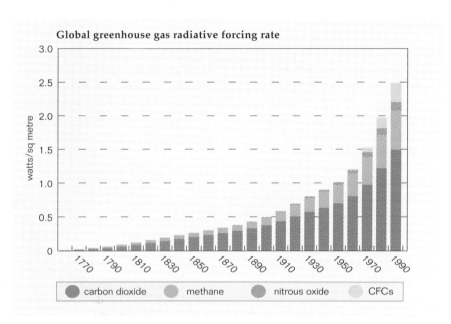

Indicator k2:
Global temperature change

Observed global temperature increases are consistent with the expected increase estimated from enhanced levels of greenhouse gases.

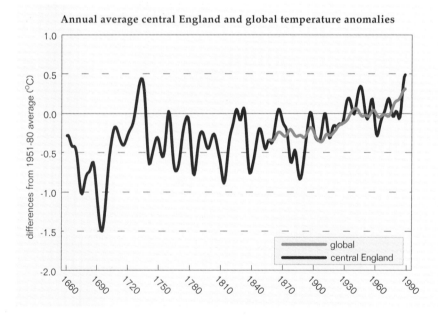

k Climate Change

The earth absorbs solar radiation mainly at its surface and this energy is then redistributed by the atmosphere and the oceans and re-radiated to space. Some outgoing infrared radiation is absorbed by naturally occurring greenhouse gases and by clouds, and some of this is re-radiated to the earth's surface. The result of this, the *natural greenhouse effect*, is that the surface of the earth is some 33°C warmer than it would be without greenhouse gases in the atmosphere. Increases in the atmospheric concentrations of greenhouse gases, because of human activity, contribute to an *enhanced greenhouse effect*. *Radiative forcing* is the term given to the effect which greenhouse gases have in altering the energy balance of the Earth-atmosphere system - a positive radiative forcing caused by increased concentrations of greenhouse gases tends to warm the earth's surface and the lower atmosphere.

Indicator k1 shows the average greenhouse gas radiative forcing since 1760.

The main greenhouse gases emitted because of human activity are carbon dioxide, methane, nitrous oxide, and, since the 1960s, the halocarbons of which chlorofluorocarbons (CFCs) are the most significant. The human-induced greenhouse gas radiative forcing has increased from virtually zero in the pre-industrial era to around 2.5 watts per square metre today. Carbon dioxide contributes most to the overall warming rate at approximately 1.5 watts per square metre at present. Contributions from methane, nitrous oxide and CFCs are about 0.6, 0.1 and 0.3 watts per square metre respectively.

Ozone is also an effective greenhouse gas whose concentration is altered by human activity. Ozone in the lower atmosphere is probably increasing because it is generated by chemical reactions involving nitrogen oxide and hydrocarbons and emissions of these compounds are increasing. By contrast, ozone in the upper atmosphere is being destroyed as a result of emissions of CFCs and other halocarbons. Therefore, the net contribution of CFCs to greenhouse radiative forcing could be substantially reduced if the indirect effect of destroying ozone in the upper atmosphere is taken into account.

Indicator k2 shows global annual temperature variations since 1858 and annual temperature variations over central England since 1660.

Global temperatures have been increasing over the last 130 years and this change is consistent with the expected increase in temperature estimated to result from increasing greenhouse gases. The Intergovernmental Panel on Climate Change (IPCC) estimates that if nothing is done to limit greenhouse gases, the global average temperature could increase by between 0.2°C and 0.5°C each decade over the next 100 years. The central England temperatures over the last three centuries show greater fluctuations, as would be expected for a small area. It is too soon to tell whether the recent warming over England is a reflection of global changes. Other temperature fluctuations are known, in part, to be due to changes in atmospheric circulation.

k Climate Change

UK greenhouse gas emissions

Indicator k3:
Emissions of greenhouse gases

Target:
To return UK emissions of carbon dioxide and other greenhouse gases to 1990 levels by the year 2000.

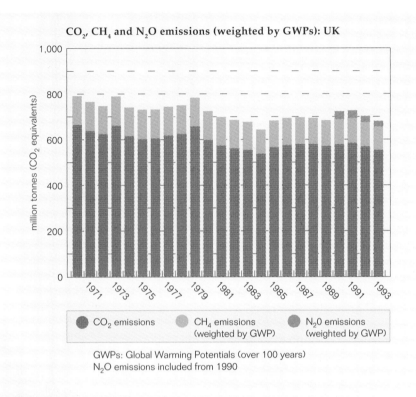

CO_2, CH_4 and N_2O emissions (weighted by GWPs): UK

- CO_2 emissions
- CH_4 emissions (weighted by GWP)
- N_2O emissions (weighted by GWP)

GWPs: Global Warming Potentials (over 100 years)
N_2O emissions included from 1990

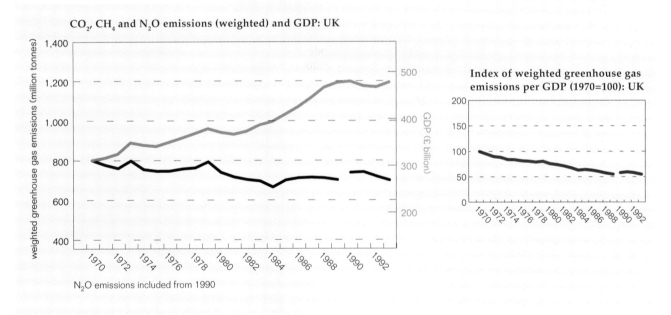

CO_2, CH_4 and N_2O emissions (weighted) and GDP: UK

N_2O emissions included from 1990

Index of weighted greenhouse gas emissions per GDP (1970=100): UK

UK emissions of greenhouse gases have gradually decreased over the last two decades and are on course to meet the internationally agreed target to return emissions to 1990 levels by the year 2000 for each greenhouse gas. Carbon dioxide is by far the most significant greenhouse gas for the UK. Emissions relative to economic output have almost halved since 1970.

k Climate Change

The major greenhouse gas is carbon dioxide and the UK contributes, largely through burning of fossil fuels, about 2 per cent to global man-made emissions. UK methane emissions arising mainly from landfilled waste, animals, coal mining, gas pipe leakage, and offshore oil and gas operations contribute about 1 per cent of global man-made emissions. UK nitrous oxide emissions, mainly from industry and agriculture, also contribute about 1 per cent of man-made emissions. CFCs, which are also powerful greenhouse gases with generally long atmospheric lifetimes, are being phased out under the Montreal Protocol because of their important role in the depletion of the ozone layer.

Indicator k3 shows the trends since 1970 in UK estimated emissions of greenhouse gases and total emissions in relation to the change in GDP.

Global Warming Potentials (GWPs) provide a relative index which allows the radiative effects of emissions of each greenhouse gas to be compared. Relative to carbon dioxide (GWP = 1.0), the latest GWP estimate for methane is 24.5 and for nitrous oxide 320 over a 100-year time horizon, although considerable uncertainty surrounds these figures. These weights have been applied to annual estimates of UK emissions of carbon dioxide and methane since 1970 and to nitrous oxide since 1990, the earliest year for which UK estimates are available, to give an overall UK global warming index. Although the GWP for carbon dioxide is lower than for other greenhouse gases, emissions of carbon dioxide are much larger so carbon dioxide has the greatest impact on global warming.

UK emissions of carbon dioxide have decreased from 664 million tonnes in 1970 to 554 million tonnes in 1993, a drop of 17 per cent. The UK's target is to return carbon dioxide emissions to 1990 levels by the year 2000; in 1993, emissions were already nearly 25 million tonnes below this target.

UK methane emissions have fallen from 126 million tonnes (CO_2 equivalent) to 102 million tonnes in 1993, a decrease of 19 per cent since 1970. The relative importance of UK nitrous oxide emissions is small at between 25 and 35 million tonnes (CO_2 equivalent) per annum.

Whereas emissions of greenhouse gases have decreased since 1970, economic output as measured by GDP has increased by around 57 per cent in real terms over this period. The UK economy has become substantially more carbon efficient over the period, in terms of producing greater output without increasing carbon dioxide emissions. This is in part due to the use of less carbon intensive fuels, to changes in the structure of the economy (see Indicator a2 in *The economy* section) and in part because of other trends and measures affecting energy efficiency (see Indicators e4, etc in the *Energy* section).

k Climate Change

Indicator k4:
Power station emissions of carbon dioxide

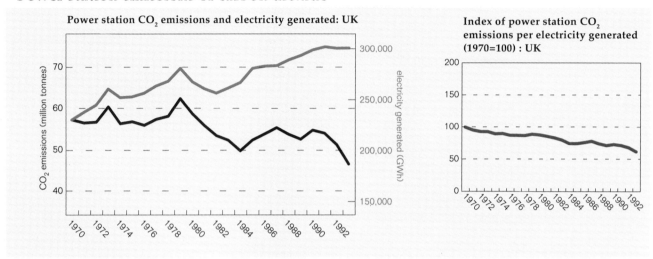

Power station CO$_2$ emissions and electricity generated: UK

Index of power station CO$_2$ emissions per electricity generated (1970=100) : UK

Carbon dioxide emissions from power stations have declined by around 20 per cent between 1970 and 1993 whereas electricity generated from all major power producers has increased by around 30 per cent over the period. The ratio of emissions to electricity output has fallen by almost 40 per cent since 1970.

In the UK, electricity generation from fossil-fuelled power stations, other industry and road transport are the major sources of carbon dioxide accounting for 31 per cent, 24 per cent and 20 per cent respectively of total emissions. Domestic emissions account for a further 16 per cent of total emissions.

Indicator k4 shows emissions of carbon dioxide from power stations between 1970 and 1993 in relation to the amount of electricity generated from UK sources.

Carbon dioxide emissions from power stations and the amounts of electricity generated have fluctuated since 1970, reflecting demand for energy that can alter according to weather conditions but which has been partially offset by supply fuel switching, mainly from coal to gas. Overall, carbon dioxide emissions have declined to about 80 per cent of the 1970 level in 1993, whilst electricity generation has risen to about 130 per cent of

the 1970 level. The ratio of emissions to the number of units of electricity generated has declined steadily to about 62 per cent of the 1970 level, as a result of switching from coal to other energy sources which produce less carbon dioxide.

Energy trends for other industry, commercial, transport, domestic sectors and energy efficiency measures are given in the section on *Energy* (see Indicators e5, e6 and e7).

k Climate Change

1 Ozone layer depletion

The key sustainable development objective is to restrict atmospheric emissions of substances which cause stratospheric ozone depletion. Indicators of relevance are chlorine loading in the atmosphere, ozone depletion over the UK and consumption and emissions of ozone-depleters in Europe.

Calculated chlorine loading in the atmosphere and extent of ozone depletion over the UK

Indicator I1:
Calculated chlorine loading

The atmospheric chlorine loading from ozone-depleting substances has more than doubled since 1970.

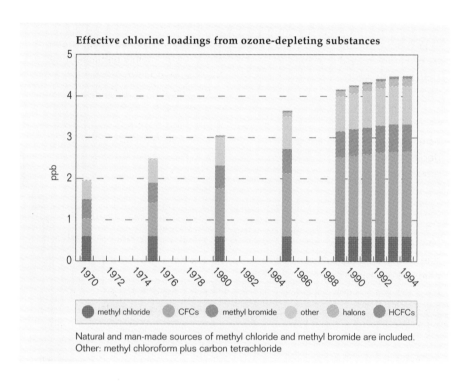

Effective chlorine loadings from ozone-depleting substances

legend: methyl chloride, CFCs, methyl bromide, other, halons, HCFCs

Natural and man-made sources of methyl chloride and methyl bromide are included. Other: methyl chloroform plus carbon tetrachloride

Indicator I2:
Measured ozone depletion

Column ozone measurements at Lerwick and Camborne in the UK have shown some fluctuations but there has been a general trend of decreasing ozone levels since the early 1980s.

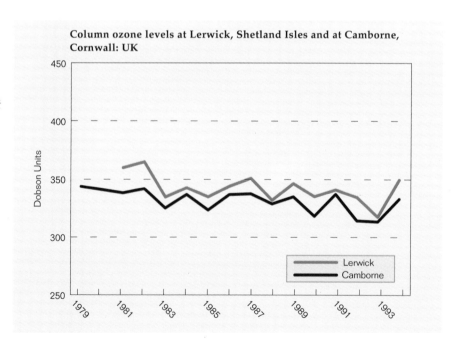

Column ozone levels at Lerwick, Shetland Isles and at Camborne, Cornwall: UK

legend: Lerwick, Camborne

1 Ozone Layer Depletion

The ozone layer is found approximately 15 to 50 km above the earth's surface and protects the earth from harmful ultraviolet radiation from the sun. Depletion of the ozone layer may allow more of this radiation, which can increase the risk of skin cancer and reduce crop yields, to penetrate to the earth's surface. Most of the depletion currently occurs over the polar regions. Although the depletion of ozone recorded so far over the UK is unlikely to have any significant effect on human health or on crop yields, action is needed to restrict emissions of ozone-depleting substances to respond to the global threat of ozone depletion. Ozone in the stratosphere also acts as a greenhouse gas and its depletion can partly offset any global warming caused by the accumulation of man-made greenhouse gases.

Some man-made halocarbons, chemicals that contain carbon and one or more halogen (fluorine, chlorine or bromine) atoms are ozone depleting substances (ODS). Their photochemical breakdown in the upper atmosphere releases chlorine and/or bromine which catalyse in the destruction of ozone. The most well known ODS are chlorofluorocarbons (CFCs) and halons, emitted as a result of their use as spray-can propellants, refrigerants, foam blowing agents and fire extinguishers. Other ODS are carbon tetrachloride, methyl chloroform (a solvent) and methyl bromide (an agricultural fumigant). More recently, other less-damaging halocarbons have been developed as replacements for CFCs. These are hydrochlorofluorocarbons (HCFCs) and hydrofluorocarbons (HFCs). HCFCs have similar properties to CFCs but are significantly less damaging to the ozone layer, mainly because they are destroyed in the lower atmosphere, thus reducing the amount reaching the stratosphere. HFCs are similar to HCFCs but do not contain chlorine or bromine and therefore do not deplete the ozone layer, although they are greenhouse gases.

Indicator 11 shows the trend in effective chlorine loading in the atmosphere since 1970.

One measure of the potential damage to the ozone layer is given by the effective chlorine loading in the atmosphere. This indicator is a global one and shows total chlorine loading in the atmosphere from all sources. Some chlorine and bromine-containing species occur naturally but, owing to human activity, the overall chlorine loading has more than doubled from just under 2ppb in 1970 to 4.5ppb in 1994. Well over half of this increase arises from CFCs. Natural emissions of methyl chloride and methyl bromide account for around 30 per cent of the total loading. Assuming global compliance with the current provisions of the Montreal Protocol to phase out the production and consumption of ODS, the chlorine loading is expected to peak towards the end of the decade and decline thereafter to pre-ozone hole levels in the second half of the next century.

Indicator 12 gives annual column ozone levels above Camborne, Cornwall since 1979 and above Lerwick, Shetland Isles since 1981.

Column ozone levels are measured at 2 sites in the UK, Camborne in Cornwall and Lerwick in the Shetland Isles. Although the annual average levels fluctuate from year to year, the overall trend shows a reduction of ozone above both UK sites.

1 Ozone Layer Depletion

European emissions and EC consumption of ozone depleting substances

1 Ozone Layer Depletion

Indicator 13:
Emissions of ozone depleting substances

European emissions of all major ozone-depleting substances have decreased since 1987.

EC Targets:
Phase out of production of halons by 1994, CFCs and carbon tetrachloride by 1995, methyl chloroform by 1996; 25 per cent cut in methyl bromide by 1998; and cap on HCFC consumption in 1995 and phase out in 2015.

Indicator 14:
CFCs consumption

EC consumption of CFCs has fallen dramatically within the last decade, particularly their use as spray-can propellants. Emissions and consumption will continue to fall to very low levels, allowing for only limited essential uses of ozone-depleting substances.

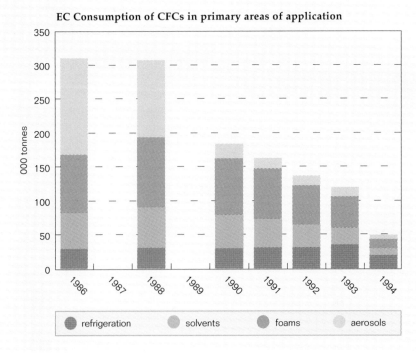

Estimated European emissions of ozone-depleting substances (weighted by ODPs)

CFC - 11
CFC - 12
Methyl chloroform
Carbon tetrachloride
CFC - 113

ODPs: Ozone Depleting Potentials

EC Consumption of CFCs in primary areas of application

refrigeration · solvents · foams · aerosols

International agreements, ie the Montreal Protocol and EC regulations are cast in terms of limiting the *production and supply to the market* of ozone-depleting substances. There will of course be time-lags between *production* and *consumption*, and between *consumption* and *emission* particularly for longer-lived goods such as refrigerators (if the CFCs are not recovered at the end of the refrigerators' lifetime). Except for limited essential uses, production of CFCs, halons and carbon tetrachloride in the EC has now ceased and production of methyl chloroform will cease by 1996. EC regulations for phasing out HCFCs and reducing methyl bromide have been agreed which are tighter than the terms of the Montreal Protocol.

Indicator 13 shows the trends in European emissions of ozone-depleting substances since 1987.

Ozone Depleting Potentials (ODPs) have been developed to compare the relative potential of CFCs and other halocarbons to damage the ozone layer. Estimated European emissions of ODS have fallen sharply since 1987 as a consequence of agreements to phase out their use. The fall of around 120,000 tonnes of CFC-11 and over 70,000 tonnes of ODP-weighted CFC-12, between 1987 and 1994, have been particularly noteworthy. ODP-weighted emissions of CFC-113 and carbon tetrachloride have also fallen by nearly 50,000 tonnes and over 30,000 tonnes respectively over this period. The decrease of 6,000 tonnes of methyl chloroform since 1987 has, however, been more modest.

Indicator 14 shows EC consumption of CFCs in primary areas of application since 1986.

CFCs consumption for aerosol use has fallen dramatically from 142,000 tonnes in 1986 to around 6,000 tonnes in 1994. Consumption for foam blowing and solvents has decreased by over 80 per cent over this period, while for refrigeration the decrease has been somewhat less. It is expected that future consumption will fall to very low levels, allowing only for limited production to meet essential uses.

1 Ozone Layer Depletion

m Acid deposition

The key sustainable development issues are to limit acid emissions and ensure appropriate land management practices. Indicators of relevance are exceedences of provisional critical loads for acidity, UK emissions of acidifying pollutants from major sources, and expenditure on pollution abatement.

Critical load exceedences

Indicator m1:
Exceedences of provisional critical loads for acidity

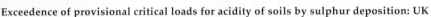

Exceedence of provisional critical loads for acidity of soils by sulphur deposition: UK

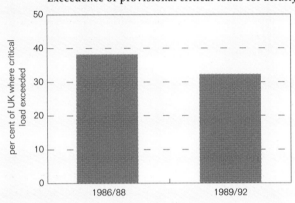

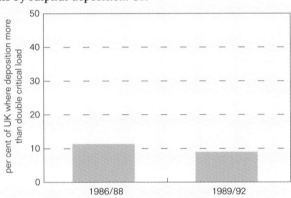

Exceedence of provisional critical loads for acidity of freshwaters by sulphur and nitrogen deposition: UK

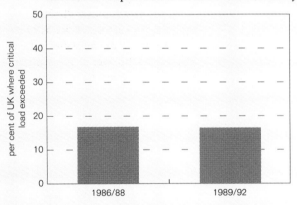

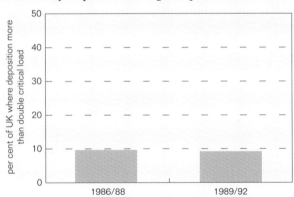

The area of the UK where sulphur deposition exceeded the critical load of acidity for soils decreased from 38 per cent over the period 1986/88 to 32 per cent in 1989/92. The intensity of this deposition likewise decreased. The area of the UK where deposition exceeded the critical load for freshwaters, although lower than for soils, has remained at around 17 per cent since the mid 1980s.

"Acid rain" is the term used to refer to the various processes by which man-made emissions of sulphur dioxide, nitrogen oxides and ammonia, are deposited on land and water, often at long distances from the sources of pollution. Through acidification of soils in geologically sensitive areas, acid rain can inhibit plant nutrition and restrict the range of flora and fauna. Freshwaters in such areas can be made toxic to aquatic plants, invertebrates and fish. Acid rain also damages building materials such as stone, concrete and metal. Acid deposition occurs through both wet processes (polluted rainfall) and dry processes (interception of gases and particles at the surface).

Indicator m1 shows exceedences of provisional critical loads for total acidity of soils by sulphur deposition and of freshwaters by sulphur and nitrogen deposition.

The concept of critical loads is used to make a scientific assessment of the risk of harmful effects of acid deposition. A critical load is the estimated level of deposition below which present knowledge indicates that there are no significant harmful effects on a specified, sensitive element of the environment. Critical loads for total acidity have been provisionally estimated for soils and freshwaters in the UK, maps of which can be compared with those of annual deposition, averaged over a number of years to remove short term weather fluctuations, to assess where environmental damage may occur. The mapped data of critical load exceedences on a grid square basis have been aggregated to the UK level to form the basis of this indicator.

The top two charts show the percentage area of the UK where critical loads for total acidity of soils are exceeded by average annual sulphur deposition over the periods 1986 to 1988 and 1989 to 1992, and the degree of exceedence in terms of deposition being at least

double critical loads. The bottom two charts relate to critical load exceedences of sulphur and nitrogen deposition for freshwaters.

For soils, 38 per cent of the area of the UK exceeded these critical loads over the 1986-88 period but this has reduced to 32 per cent over the 1989-92 period. The area for which deposition was over twice critical loads decreased from over 11 per cent to under 9 per cent between these two periods. For freshwaters, around 17 per cent of the area of the UK exceed critical loads with little apparent improvement since the mid 1980s either in overall exceedences or in the degree of exceedence. The most vulnerable soils and freshwaters are to be found in upland areas of north and west Britain.

Future indicator development:

In future, it should also be possible to produce indicators for soils on critical load exceedences by nitrogen deposition once methodologies have received international approval. It also remains to establish links between exceedences of calculated critical loads and the nature, timescale and extent of any resulting ecological changes.

m Acid deposition

UK emissions of acidifying pollutants

Indicator m2:
Power station emissions of sulphur dioxide and nitrogen oxides

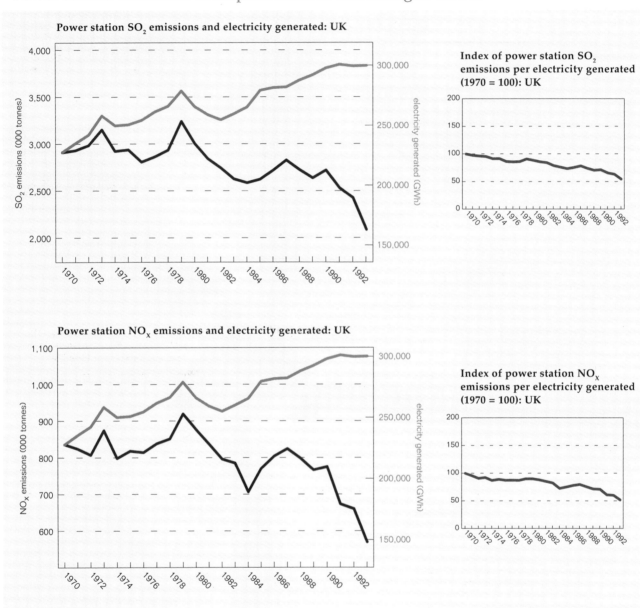

m Acid deposition

Whilst electricity generation has increased between 1970 and 1993, sulphur dioxide and nitrogen oxide emissions have decreased and hence the amount of sulphur and nitrogen released per unit of electricity generated has declined substantially over this period.

Indicator m3:
Road transport emissions of nitrogen oxides

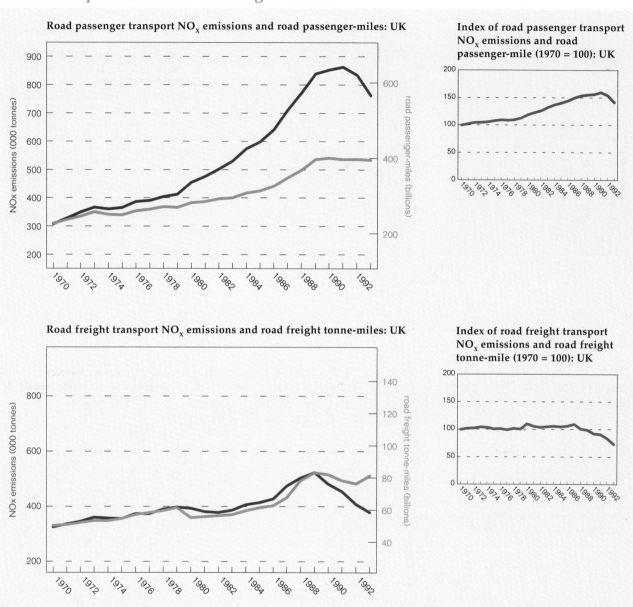

Road passenger transport NO$_x$ emissions and road passenger-miles: UK

Index of road passenger transport NO$_x$ emissions and road passenger-mile (1970 = 100): UK

Road freight transport NO$_x$ emissions and road freight tonne-miles: UK

Index of road freight transport NO$_x$ emissions and road freight tonne-mile (1970 = 100): UK

The growth in nitrogen oxide emissions from road passenger transport has outstripped the growth in road passenger traffic. Recently emissions have declined as a result of increased penetration of diesel cars and increased road fuel duty and will continue to fall because of the introduction of catalytic converters for new petrol cars. Emissions from freight transport have grown steadily but have fallen sharply since 1989.

m Acid deposition

The main human activities which result in the emission of acidifying pollutants and hence may enhance acid deposition are electricity generation, road transport, and agriculture. Electricity generation from fossil-fuelled power stations is the major source of sulphur dioxide accounting for 66 per cent of all emissions. It also accounts for 24 per cent of nitrogen oxide emissions, although road transport is the main source of these at 49 per cent of emissions. Other activities, such as industrial processes, also result in such emissions, but these are not as significant. Agriculture is the principal source of ammonia, accounting for 70 to 90 per cent of all UK emissions.

Indicator m2 shows the trends since 1970 in emissions of sulphur dioxide and nitrogen oxides from power stations in relation to the amounts of electricity generated.

Both sulphur dioxide and nitrogen oxide emissions from power stations have declined to around 70 per cent of the 1970 level in 1993, whilst electricity generation has risen to about 130 per cent of the 1970 level. The ratio of sulphur dioxide and nitrogen oxide emissions to unit of electricity generated has declined to about 55 per cent and 50 per cent, respectively, of the 1970 level. The principal reason for the reduction in emissions has been due to the switch towards the use of gas in electricity generation.

The EC Large Combustion Plants (LCP) Directive requires a reduction in sulphur dioxide emissions from existing combustion installations with an annual capacity greater than 50 megawatts thermal of 20 per cent by the end of 1993, 40 per cent by 1998 and 60 per cent by the year 2003, taking 1980 emissions as the baseline. Target

reductions for nitrogen dioxides are 15 per cent by the end of 1993 and 30 per cent by 1998. These targets are currently in the process of revision. Emissions from power stations in 1993 accounted for around 90 per cent of LCP emissions, for both sulphur dioxide and nitrogen oxides. From 1991 onwards, actual emissions from individual LCPs are available; prior to 1991, such emissions were estimated and may have been overestimated. UK emissions suggest that the 1998 EC targets for both sulphur dioxide and nitrogen oxides were met five years ahead of schedule.

The UNECE Second Sulphur Protocol sets reduction targets for total sulphur dioxide emissions of 50 per cent by the year 2000, 70 per cent by 2005 and 80 per cent by 2010 from a 1980 baseline. By the end of 1993, the UK had achieved a 35 per cent reduction of total sulphur emissions from 1980 baseline levels.

Indicator m3 shows the trends since 1970 in emissions of nitrogen oxides from road passenger and road freight transport in relation to the growth in traffic.

Nitrogen oxide emissions from road passenger transport have nearly trebled since 1970 reaching a peak in 1991 but have since declined as a result of increasing numbers of diesel cars which emit less nitrogen oxide than non-catalyst equipped petrol-fuelled cars and because of increases in road fuel duty. Emissions will continue to fall following, in 1993, the fitting of catalytic converters to all new petrol cars. However, since diesel vehicles emit more nitrogen oxides than cars with catalytic converters, the magnitude of the improvement will depend on the amount of future diesel penetration into the fleet. Road passenger traffic has grown less steeply, by around 75 per cent since 1970, with the result that

emissions per unit of passenger transport rose by 60 per cent between 1970 and 1991, but are now starting to decrease. Nitrogen oxide emissions from freight transport up to 1989 have tended to grow in line with the growth in the amounts of goods moved, but since then emissions have decreased sharply, as a result of tighter emissions standards for heavy goods vehicles. The ratio of emissions from road freight transport per goods moved in 1993 was over a quarter less than the rate in 1970.

Future indicator development:

UK emissions

Because of scientific uncertainty surrounding their measurement, it is not possible at present to produce a similar indicator for ammonia emissions.

Expenditure on sulphur dioxide and nitrogen dioxide abatement at power stations per unit abated

Important response indicators are expenditures on abating air pollution. Some overall estimates are given in the *Air* section but comprehensive information on expenditure to abate sulphur dioxide and nitrogen dioxide emissions from power stations linked to the amounts of the pollutants abated is not readily available at present.

National Power initiated its environmental investment programme five years ago and cumulative expenditure on projects to improve environmental performance to date amounts to around £1.5 billion. Retrofitting of flue gas desulphurisation (FGD) equipment and its combined cycle gas turbine (CCGT) programme accounted for a substantial part of this investment. FGD adds around 25 per cent to the production cost of each unit of electricity sold. Powergen has also initiated FGD and CCGT programmes. With over £1 billion investment in FGD at Drax and Ratcliffe power stations, this should reduce their combined sulphur dioxide emissions by over 90 per cent.

n Air

The key sustainable development objective is to control air pollution in order to reduce the risks of adverse effects on natural ecosystems, human health and quality of life. Key issues are to reduce pollutant emissions to improve local air quality, especially in urban areas, and to control photochemical pollution. Indicators to illustrate these issues are concentrations of pollutants at selected sites, UK emissions of pollutants, and expenditure on pollution abatement.

Air quality in the UK

Indicator n1:
Ozone concentrations

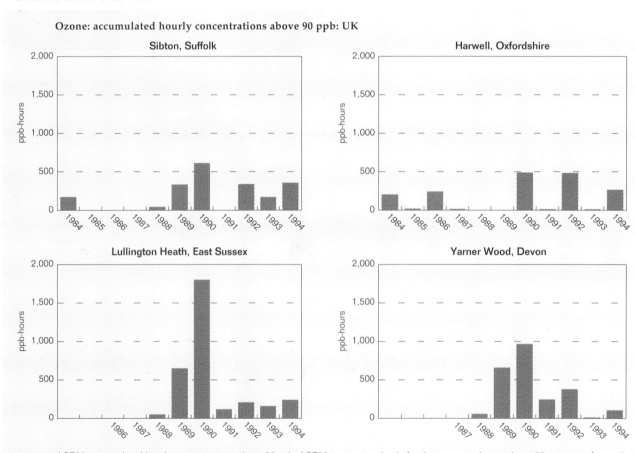

AOT90: accumulated hourly concentrations above 90 ppb. AOT90 is presented only for those years where at least 75 per cent of annual hourly recordings were ratified. Monitoring of ozone concentrations at Lullington Heath and Yarner Wood started in 1986 and 1987 respectively. No ratified recordings were made at the Sibton site in 1986 and 1987.

Peak ozone concentrations are determined by meteorological conditions acting on man-made emissions and can vary significantly from year to year. These peaks are added to a baseline (of about 35 ppb in the UK) which has roughly doubled in the Northern Hemisphere since the turn of the century. Average ozone concentrations in the areas of the UK remote from nitrogen oxide emissions appear to be increasing in recent years. Elevated concentrations of ozone occurred in 1989 and 1990 and reflect the hot summer temperatures recorded in those years. There is as yet little evidence on changing trends in peak ozone concentrations.

Indicator n2:
Nitrogen dioxide concentrations

Peak nitrogen dioxide levels are highest in major urban areas because of high road traffic levels, and have been highest in the last few years. However concentrations are expected to fall in future as the proportion of catalyst-equipped cars increases.

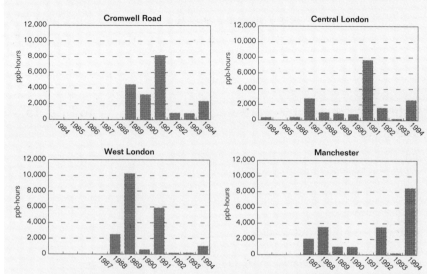

Nitrogen dioxide: accumulated hourly concentrations above 100 ppb: UK

AOT100: accumulated hourly concentrations above 100 ppb. AOT100 is presented only for those years where at least 75 per cent of annual hourly recordings were ratified. Monitoring of nitrogen dioxide concentrations at the Earl's Court site in west London and Manchester sites started in 1987. No ratified recordings were made at the Cromwell Road site in 1987 and 1988.

Indicator n3:
Particulate matter concentrations

Particulate matter (PM_{10}) concentrations from road traffic are likely to have been increasing in the 1980s but levels are expected to fall in future as a result of measures already in place. Concentrations in Belfast, where solid fuel is still commonly used for domestic heating, are higher than in many other UK cities.

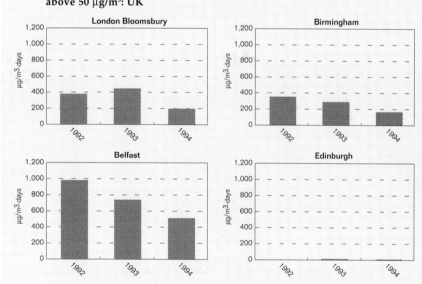

Particulate matter (PM_{10}): accumulated daily concentrations above 50 $\mu g/m^3$: UK

AOT50: accumulated daily concentrations above 50 $\mu g/m^3$. AOT50 is presented only for those years where at least 75 per cent of annual daily recordings were ratified.

Good air quality is essential for human health and the well-being of the environment as a whole. There have been major changes in UK air quality since the 1950s and 1960s. Widespread coal burning in the home has declined substantially with the move to cleaner fuels such as gas and electricity. Cleaner fuels, less polluting processes and pollution abatement equipment have

all contributed to lower emissions from industry. However, motor traffic has increased substantially to the extent that vehicles are now major sources of nitrogen dioxide and particulate matter in urban areas. Peak ozone levels tend to be highest in rural areas, although health-related guidelines are also exceeded in urban areas. A useful aggregate statistic for measuring air

quality at a given site is Accumulated exposure Over a Threshold x (AOTx). Such a statistic combines both the magnitude and length of time that concentrations are above any given threshold. The thresholds chosen are the DOE "poor" air quality thresholds for ozone and nitrogen dioxide. These may change in future if the bandings change.

n Air

Indicator n1 shows trends in ozone concentrations at selected sites in the UK since 1984.

Ground level ozone can be increased through chemical reactions involving nitrogen oxides and volatile organic compounds driven by sunlight, and may be carried for considerable distances and persist for several days. In the UK, the highest concentrations occur in southern rural areas on hot, sunny and relatively windless days in summer. Medical evidence indicates that ozone has irritant effects on the lungs, resulting in certain circumstances in cough or discomfort in breathing, which may be promoted by physical exercise, though such effects are not expected to be severe at UK levels. It may exacerbate symptoms in some asthma sufferers, though there is no clear evidence that anyone, including children or people with asthma, suffer long term damage from exposure to the levels of ozone that are encountered in the UK. For ozone, AOTs have been calculated against the hourly UK criterion for "poor" air quality of 90 ppb, set at the EC level for informing the public. Trends in AOT90 for ozone are given for 4 monitoring stations in southern England, Sibton near the Suffolk coast, Harwell in Oxfordshire, Lullington Heath near the Sussex coast, and Yarner Wood in Devon which are susceptible to summer ozone pollution episodes. Concentrations were particularly high in 1989 and 1990 and largely reflect the hot summers in those years. The number of days on which at least one hourly ozone concentration of "poor" air quality have been recorded since 1984 are relatively few, eg a maximum of 15 days at Lullington Heath in 1989. Underlying trends in ozone concentrations increased during the 1980s but the widespread introduction of catalytic converters and of exhaust emission controls to

reduce emissions of the precursor gases should bring about improvements.

Indicator n2 shows trends in nitrogen dioxide concentrations at selected sites in the UK since 1984.

Nitrogen dioxide has been shown to have adverse effects on the respiratory system. People with pre-existing chronic respiratory disease are most at risk and long-term exposure has been linked with an increased risk of respiratory infections in children. At current UK levels, none of these effects is expected to be severe, nor is there any evidence that they are indicative of a serious or lasting effect upon health. For nitrogen dioxide, AOTs have been calculated against the hourly UK criteria for "poor" air quality of 100 ppb. Trends in AOT100 for nitrogen dioxide are given for a kerbside monitoring site in Cromwell Road in London, urban background sites at Bridge Place near Victoria Station and near Earls Court in London and at a central Manchester site. The Earls Court and central Manchester sites were established in January 1987. Monitoring at the Cromwell Road site was suspended during 1987/88 because of refurbishment to the building where the monitor is located and, prior to this, recordings did not meet the 75 per cent data capture criteria. Recorded concentrations are typically higher in London than elsewhere in the UK as a consequence of the very high levels of road traffic in London. As with ozone, meteorological conditions can occasionally mean that traffic pollutants are poorly dispersed, leading to episodes of poor air quality. The number of days on which at least one hourly nitrogen dioxide concentration of "poor" or "very poor" air quality have been recorded since 1984 are usually few, eg a maximum of 61 days at the Earls Court site in 1989. However, underlying concentrations

of nitrogen dioxide were rising throughout the 1980s and, despite the introduction of catalytic converters and stricter exhaust emission controls, episodes of poor air quality continue to occur.

Indicator n3 shows trends in concentrations of particulate matter at selected monitoring sites in the UK since 1992.

Airborne particulate matter is the primary cause of visibility loss on hazy days and on the soiling of buildings. High particulate matter concentrations are now being linked with premature mortality from respiratory conditions. For particulate matter, AOTs have been calculated against a baseline daily concentration of 50 µg/m^3, an indicative threshold for assessing trends in elevated concentrations. Monitoring of fine particles, PM_{10} (particles less than 10 µm in diameter) was added to the UK's Automated Urban Network in 1992. Trends in AOT50 are given for 4 city centre sites - Bloomsbury in London, Birmingham, Edinburgh and Belfast. In general, concentrations in Belfast are higher than for other sites because of the continuing reliance there to use solid fuel for domestic heating. AOT50 in Edinburgh is very small. Monitoring has not been carried out for long enough to give trends, but estimates of emissions suggest that throughout the 1980s, urban PM_{10} concentrations from road traffic have been increasing in the 1980s. Measures already in place are expected to lead to decreases in PM_{10} in future.

Future indicator development:

Presenting site-specific information on pollutants is not ideal and should be seen as short-term proxy indicators. Work in future will concentrate on developing aggregate UK indicators of the population at risk from exposure to pollution concentrations.

n Air

UK air emissions

Indicator n4:
Volatile organic compound emissions

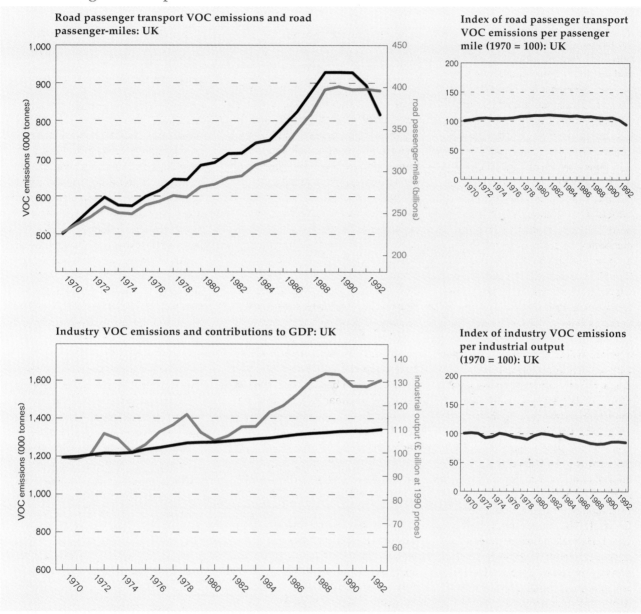

Road passenger transport VOC emissions and road passenger-miles: UK

Index of road passenger transport VOC emissions per passenger mile (1970 = 100): UK

Industry VOC emissions and contributions to GDP: UK

Index of industry VOC emissions per industrial output (1970 = 100): UK

n Air

VOC emissions from road passenger traffic have increased steadily over the 1970s and 1980s matching largely the growth in the volume of traffic. Recently, emissions have declined as a result of increased use of diesel cars and increased road fuel duty and will continue to fall because of the introduction of catalytic converters for new petrol cars. There has been a modest increase in industrial VOC emissions since 1970.

Indicator n5:
Carbon monoxide emissions

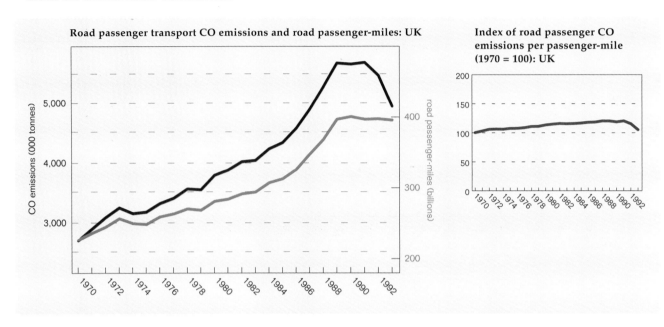

The growth in carbon monoxide emissions from road passenger transport has outstripped the growth in road passenger traffic. Recently emissions have declined as a result of increased penetration of diesel cars and increased road fuel duty and will continue to fall because of the introduction of catalytic converters for new petrol cars.

Indicator n6:
Black smoke emissions

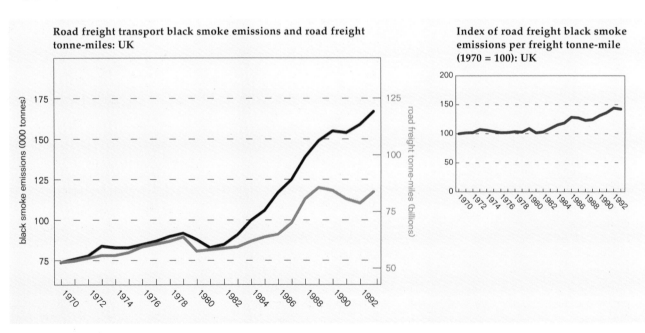

n Air

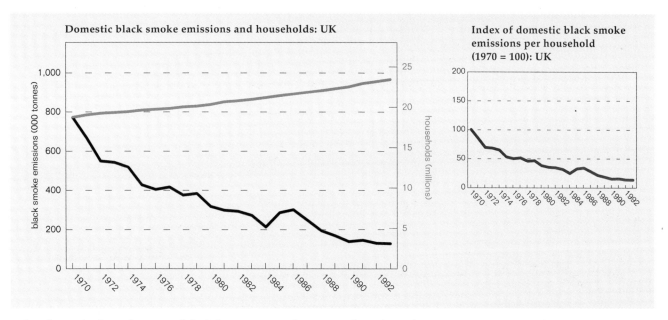

Domestic black smoke emissions and households: UK

Index of domestic black smoke emissions per household (1970 = 100): UK

Smoke emissions from road freight transport have continued to rise as a consequence of the growth in diesel vehicles. Domestic smoke emissions have fallen dramatically with the switch away from coal for home heating.

Indicator n7: Lead emissions

Lead emissions from cars have declined substantially as a result of a reduction in the lead content of petrol. Unleaded petrol accounted for 65 per cent of total petrol consumption by the end of 1995.

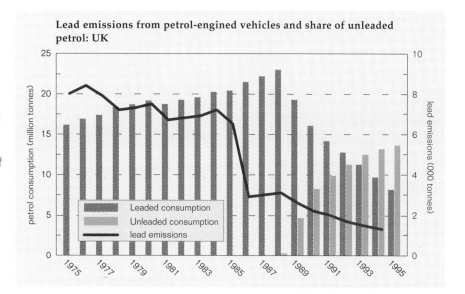

Lead emissions from petrol-engined vehicles and share of unleaded petrol: UK

Leaded consumption
Unleaded consumption
lead emissions

n Air

The main human activities giving rise to pollutants which adversely affect air quality are road transport, power generation, industrial combustion processes and domestic heating. Electricity generation from fossil-fuelled power stations is the major source of sulphur dioxide accounting for 66 per cent of total emissions in 1993. It also accounts for 24 per cent of nitrogen oxide emissions. Road transport is the main source of nitrogen oxides, black smoke, carbon monoxide and volatile

organic compound emissions accounting for 49 per cent, 51 per cent, 91 per cent and 38 per cent of total emissions respectively in 1993. The majority of carbon monoxide and volatile organic compound emissions from road transport are from passenger vehicles; most black smoke emissions from road transport are from freight vehicles. The contribution of nitrogen oxide emissions from passenger transport and freight transport is more equal. Industrial processes and solvent

use account for 55 per cent of volatile organic compound emissions. Domestic heating, particularly from coal-burning, accounts for 29 per cent of total black smoke emissions in 1993. Road transport is also a major source of lead emissions.

Indicator m2 on power station emissions of sulphur dioxide and nitrogen oxides and Indicator m3 on road transport emissions of nitrogen oxides are included in the section on *Acid deposition.*

Indicator n4 gives the trends since 1970 of volatile organic compound emissions from road passenger transport in relation to road passenger transport traffic, and from industry related to the sector's contribution to GDP.

Volatile organic compound emissions from road passenger transport have increased steadily, rising by around 85 per cent between 1970 and 1990. Since then, emissions have declined as a result of tighter emission standards and increased road fuel duty, and because of a substantial increase in the number of diesel cars which emit less volatile organic compounds than non-catalyst equipped petrol-fuelled cars. Emissions will continue to fall following, in 1993, the fitting of catalytic converters to all new petrol cars. About one quarter of petrol cars were fitted with catalytic converters by the end of 1994. By the year 2000, approaching 70 per cent will be fitted and by the year 2005 well over 95 per cent of petrol cars will have catalysts. The ratio of road passenger transport emissions to road passenger-miles has remained fairly constant since 1970, although the ratio started to decline in 1993. Volatile organic compound emissions from road freight transport are relatively small, at about one-tenth of the emissions from road passenger transport.

Volatile organic compound emissions from industry have gradually increased over the last two decades and are 12 per cent higher in 1993 than in 1970. Industry's contribution to GDP has grown steadily by 33 per cent over the same period, punctuated by fluctuations in the economic cycle, with peaks in 1973, 1979 and 1990 and troughs in 1975, 1981 and 1992. The ratio of industrial VOC emissions to industrial output is 16 per cent lower in 1993 than it was in 1970.

The UNECE VOC Protocol sets a target for total VOC emissions of a 30 per cent reduction by 1999 from a 1988 baseline. By 1993, the UK had achieved a 7 per cent decrease in emissions compared with 1988 levels.

Indicator n5 gives annual carbon monoxide emissions from road passenger transport since 1970, road passenger-miles and the ratio between the two series.

The trend in carbon monoxide emissions from road passenger transport has been similar to that of volatile organic compounds, with emissions in the late 1980s over double the level in 1970. Since then, emissions have declined as a result of tighter emission standards and increased road fuel duty and because of a substantial increase in the number of diesel cars which emit less carbon monoxide than non-catalyst equipped petrol-fuelled cars. Emissions will continue to fall following, in 1993, the fitting of catalytic converters to all new petrol cars. Until recently, the growth in emissions has outstripped the growth in road passenger traffic, with the result that emissions per passenger-mile have increased gradually since 1970, although recently the ratio has started to decline. Carbon monoxide emissions from road freight transport are relatively small, at about 4 per cent of the emissions from road passenger transport.

Indicator n6 shows the trends since 1970 in black smoke emissions from road freight transport compared with goods moved, and black smoke emissions from the domestic sector in relation to the number of households.

Emissions are at present not cast in terms of PM_{10} but in terms of "black smoke". "Black smoke" is defined by the measurement method BS 1747 Part 2 which tends to collect finer particles than PM_{10}. Black smoke allows for the different soiling capacities of smoke particles from different sources. Black smoke emissions from road freight transport have more than doubled since 1970 and, unlike other pollutants, there is no evidence as yet of a downturn in the trend, although improved vehicle standards should bring about future improvements. The ratio of emissions to goods moved in 1993 was 40 per cent higher than it was in 1970. Black smoke emissions from road passenger transport are relatively small, at about 7 per cent of the emissions from road freight transport. Over the period 1970 to 1993, black smoke emissions from domestic sources have fallen dramatically as a result of the switch from coal to less polluting energy sources for heating. Emissions in 1993 were less than a fifth of those in 1970. The number of households has increased by a quarter over the period resulting in a very steep decline in emissions per household.

Indicator n7 shows the trends since 1975 in lead emissions from petrol-engined vehicles and the market share of unleaded petrol.

Lead emissions from petrol-engined road vehicles fell after the reductions in the lead content in petrol from 0.45 to 0.40 grams per litre in 1981 and the further reduction to 0.15 grams per litre in 1985. Since 1985, lead emissions have continued to fall, despite the increase in total petrol consumption, because of the introduction of unleaded petrol. Virtually all petrol stations in the UK now sell unleaded petrol compared with only around 10 per cent as recently as late 1988. Assisted by the duty differential between leaded and unleaded petrol, the uptake of unleaded petrol has increased from virtually zero in 1987 to nearly 63 per cent of total petrol consumption in 1995. By the end of 1995, this share had increased to 65 per cent.

Expenditure on air pollution abatement

Indicator n8:

Expenditure on air pollution abatement

Annual UK expenditure on air pollution abatement is estimated to be around £1.5 billion with around £1.0 billion incurred by private enterprise.

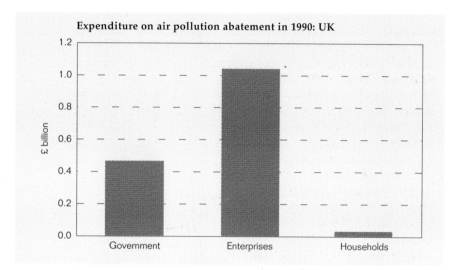

One of the key sustainable development issues is to consider the balance between environmental protection and economic growth. It is therefore important not just to quantify the extent of air pollution and how it is changing, but also the burdens borne by businesses, consumers and government in order to prevent or ameliorate pollution, whether through voluntary action or in response to mandatory controls. This enables consideration of value for money and priorities between different areas of pollution control. Problems arise in identifying and quantifying pollution abatement expenditure - these are discussed under Indicator a8 in the section on *The economy*

Indicator n8 shows the estimated expenditure in the UK on air pollution abatement in 1990.

Expenditure on air pollution abatement is mainly incurred by enterprises but data are not generally available for individual companies on a consistent basis. Expenditure estimates for 1990 have been made, based on the market for air pollution control equipment in the various industrial sectors and taking account of the main environmental pressures for expenditure on air pollution control. This analysis indicates an annual capital expenditure by enterprises of approximately £540 million and includes expenditure on flue gas desulphurisation at power stations. Annual operating costs have been estimated at around £500 million, resulting in a total expenditure estimate for enterprise at around £1,040 million, excluding expenditure on vehicle exhausts. It is considered that this estimate is accurate to ±20 per cent. In addition to expenditure by enterprises, Government expenditure, including that by local authority environmental health departments, attributed to air pollution abatement has been estimated at around £470 million in 1990. Household expenditure on fitting cars with catalytic converters in 1990 was estimated at £30 million.

Future indicator development:

The DoE is conducting a pilot survey of business spending on the environment, to establish the practicality of obtaining more accurate estimates of air pollution abatement expenditure, together with estimates of how much pollution is abated, and provide a basis for monitoring expenditure trends over time.

n Air

p Freshwater quality

The key sustainable development objectives are to sustain and improve water quality and the aquatic environment. Other objectives included under these broad aims are to manage the discharge of waste water, to control pollution, to ensure adequate water resources of sufficient quality are available for abstraction for treatment as drinking water, and to facilitate the recreational use of water where appropriate. Indicators relevant to these objectives include chemical and biological measures of freshwater quality, concentrations of important pollutants, water pollution incidents, and expenditure on water supply and treatment. Acidification of freshwater is covered by Indicator m1 in the section on *Acid deposition.*

River quality

Indicator p1:
River quality - chemical and biological

Most UK rivers are of "good or fair" chemical quality and "good or moderate" biological quality. Those in Scotland tend to be of the highest quality, but in England and Wales, and Northern Ireland there have been significant improvements in chemical quality in the 1990s.

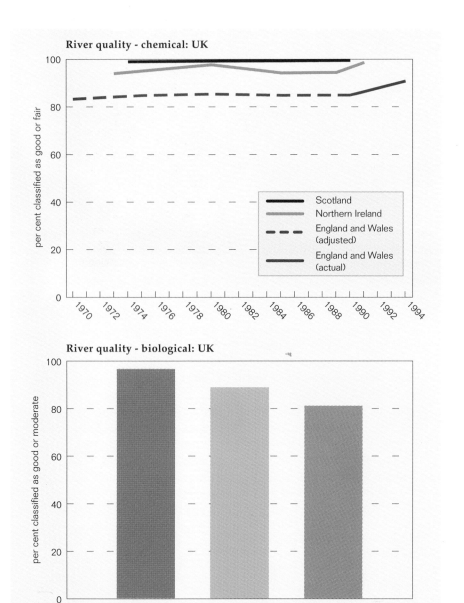

The quality of rivers and canals in the UK is influenced by a variety of factors - discharges from sewage works and industrial installations, pollution incidents and deposition, leaching and run-off from rural and contaminated land, as well as levels of rainfall and water abstraction. Regular chemical and biological surveys provide a general indication of the quality of rivers and canals across the UK.

Indicator p1 shows trends in the proportion of river and canal lengths in the UK classified in the top two chemical grades and the proportion classified in the top two biological grades in 1990.

General chemical water quality is assessed primarily on the basis of three determinands: dissolved oxygen, biochemical oxygen demand, and ammonia. These are used because they are good, simple, generally applicable indicators of the extent to which

water is affected by waste-water discharges, and run-off and drainage from farms. In England, Wales, and Northern Ireland, the top two chemical grades represent "good or fair" water quality; in Scotland they represent "unpolluted or fairly good" water quality. While figures are not directly comparable between the countries, they do provide national trends over the last 20 years or so. In addition, the top two grades broadly correspond to those lengths of river which support at least reasonably good coarse fisheries, have moderate or high amenity value, and are generally appropriate for abstraction for treatment as drinking water.

Most of UK rivers are of "good or fair" (or "unpolluted or fairly good" in Scotland) chemical quality. Quality in Scotland has remained high over the last two decades, while in England and Wales, and Northern Ireland there were net improvements in chemical quality in the 1970s, followed by minor declines in the 1980s and significant improvements in the 1990s. Whilst the 1990 baseline was influenced to some extent by the effects of low rainfall, the

improvements in water quality since the start of the decade are attributable primarily to the positive impact of the investment programme of the water industry and pollution control measures.

To provide a broader picture of the "health" of rivers, biological testing was also carried out in 1990, using gradings that are directly comparable across the UK. Biological testing assesses the extent to which particular groups of species of small animals, (ie invertebrates), are present in the river, and compares this with what could be expected to be present in an unpolluted river given the natural features of the particular location. Most UK rivers are of "good or moderate" biological quality. In Scotland, 97 per cent of river and canal lengths were classified as such in 1990, compared with 89 per cent in Northern Ireland and 81 per cent in England and Wales.

Future indicator development:

New biological grading systems may be employed for future surveys.

Nutrients in water

Indicator p2:
Nitrates in rivers and groundwater

Rivers in the eastern lowlands of GB generally have higher nitrate levels than western lowland rivers, which in turn have higher levels than upland rivers. Nitrate levels in a selected group of 17 groundwater sites experiencing elevated levels have risen between 1980 and 1993.

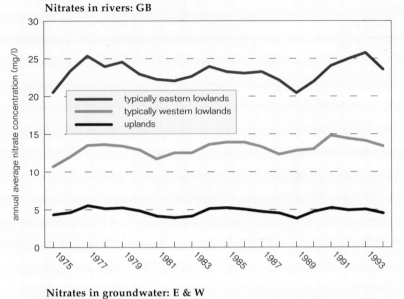

Nitrates in rivers: GB

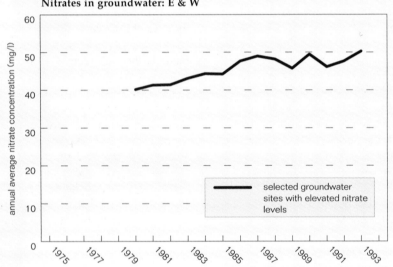

Nitrates in groundwater: E & W

Indicator p3:
Phosphorus in rivers

Rivers in the eastern lowlands of GB generally have higher phosphorus levels than western lowland rivers, which in turn have higher levels than upland rivers. Since 1989, phosphorus levels have fallen in lowland rivers.

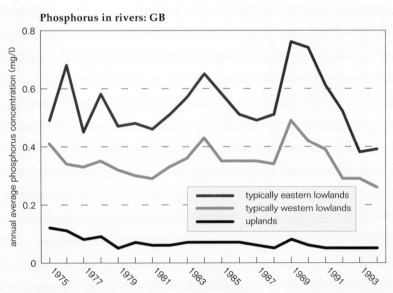

Phosphorus in rivers: GB

p Freshwater quality

The presence of various nutrients in excessive quantities in water, combined with particular weather conditions, can lead to eutrophication (excessive algal growth). This can cause long-term ecosystem disruption by oxygen depletion, which adversely affects fish, and by-production of toxins, which are potentially poisonous to other animals. The nutrients in the UK which generally lead to this are nitrate in marine or coastal waters and phosphorus in freshwater.

The majority of UK waters are free from eutrophication. However, there is concern about nitrate leaching to freshwater as some of this nitrate will eventually reach the sea, where in some places this could lead to eutrophication, and also because high nitrate levels in drinking water may present a risk to human health. There is a precautionary EC standard of 50 milligrams of nitrate per litre for water abstracted for public supply. Groundwater pollution is potentially more problematical because, once polluted, it may take many years before nitrate levels fall, even when the source of the pollution has been reduced. The main source of nitrate in UK freshwater is leaching from agricultural land, although treated sewage discharges are also a factor for rivers. There is also concern about phosphorus inputs, which can lead to eutrophication of freshwater; the main sources are outputs from sewage treatment works and diffuse pollution from agriculture. The proportions from these two sources vary greatly across the country.

Nitrogen inputs to agriculture are covered by Indicator s5 in the *Land cover and landscape* section. Nutrient discharges into coastal waters are covered by Indicator q5 in the *Marine* section.

Indicator p2 shows annual average nitrate concentrations in GB rivers by landscape category, and the combined annual average nitrate concentration of 17 selected groundwater sites in England and Wales experiencing elevated nitrate levels.

Nitrate levels at tidal limits of the 162 major GB rivers have been monitored since 1975 as part of the Harmonised Monitoring Scheme (HMS). Average concentrations at these sites reflect levels at lower reaches of the rivers, but are not necessarily representative of levels found further upstream or in rivers further inland. Rivers typical of eastern lowland landscapes generally have higher levels (averaging 24 mg of nitrate per litre in 1994) than rivers typical of western lowlands (13 mg/l) and uplands (5 mg/l). In both lowland landscapes, average levels were higher in the early 1990s than in the 1970s and 1980s, but there is some evidence of recent declines.

Selective information on nitrate levels in groundwater sites, ie underground aquifers, is available for England and Wales for about 200 boreholes used for public water supply abstraction which experience levels close to or above 50 mg/l. These sites are not representative of all aquifers either in their immediate region or in England and Wales as a whole. There was a generally rising trend in levels at many of these sites between 1980 and 1993. The combined average for a selected group of 17 of these sites increased from 40 mg/l in 1980 to 50 mg/l in 1993. There is little correspondence between the yearly fluctuations in levels in rivers and in these particular groundwater sites because of the time taken for nutrients to leach through the soil and sub-soil.

Indicator p3 shows annual average phosphorus concentrations in GB rivers by landscape category.

Phosphorus levels in GB rivers have also been monitored since 1975 as part of the HMS. Eastern lowland rivers generally have higher levels (averaging 0.4 mg per litre in 1994) than western lowland rivers (0.3 mg/l) and upland rivers (less than 0.1 mg/l). Average levels have fluctuated in eastern and western lowlands up to 1989, since when they have fallen. This fall is thought to be largely attributable to substituted use of phosphate-free washing powders/liquids.

Future indicator development:

The future establishment of a national network of groundwater monitoring sites will aid the development of a general indicator of groundwater nitrate levels based on a greater number of more representative groundwater sites.

p Freshwater quality

Dangerous substances in water

Indicators p4:
Pesticides in rivers and groundwater

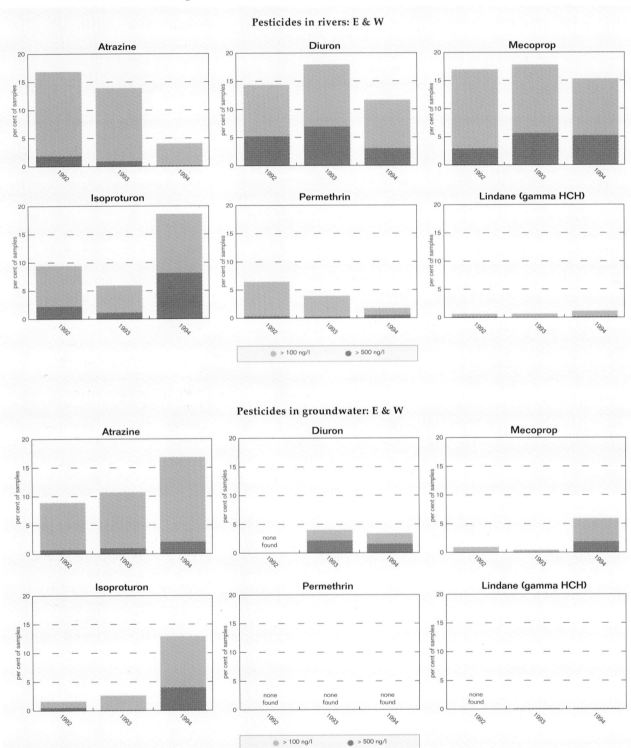

Most pesticides detected in freshwater are found in very small quantities, and are well below any existing or proposed Environmental Quality Standards (EQSs). Quantities of pesticides found in groundwater tend to be lower than in rivers.

p Freshwater quality

The UK has developed the "Red List" of the most dangerous substances in water, including pesticides and heavy metals, scientifically selected for their persistent toxic and bioaccumulative characteristics.

Pesticides are important to modern agriculture and also have significant non-agricultural uses to control pests, weeds, and diseases. However, they can have an adverse effect on the aquatic environment, and, if present in significant quantities in water abstracted for public supply, treatment to remove them is necessary. There are currently about 450 active ingredients approved for use as pesticides in the UK; about 340 of these are used as agricultural pesticides. The majority of pesticides detected most frequently in water are herbicides used for non-agriculture purposes.

Pesticide usage is covered by Indicator s6 in the *Land cover and landscape* section. Levels of a number of heavy metals found in UK waters are covered by Indicator q2 in the section on *Marine*.

Indicator p4 shows the proportion of river and groundwater samples in England and Wales exceeding 100 ng/l and 500 ng/l for 6 selected pesticides.

This indicator shows recent changes in concentrations of 6 commonly used pesticides. Comparable national figures prior to 1992 are not available. Concentrations of pesticides in the aquatic environment are generally very low, and may fall below the detection limit of current analytical techniques. Where they have been detected, they are normally well within EQSs introduced under the EC Dangerous Substances Directives. Thus, it is difficult to illustrate any changes over time in terms of these standards. For this reason, two arbitrary levels of 100 ng/l and 500 ng/l (based on the values specified in the EC Drinking Water Directive) have been used. The proportion of samples above these levels has been presented to illustrate both the relative frequencies in which these 6 pesticides are found, and also any changes in levels over the last 3 years.

The majority of pesticides most frequently detected in freshwater are herbicides used for non-agriculture purposes, eg atrazine and simazine which were approved for such uses up until 1993, and diuron which is currently approved. In order to be effective, many herbicides are water soluble and relatively persistent. There is thus a pollution risk associated with applying herbicides to verges and hard surfaces, such as roads and railways, where run-off can occur readily. Only 2 agricultural pesticides, mecoprop and isoproturon, regularly appear in the 10 pesticides most frequently found in rivers, although many agricultural pesticides are detected at low concentrations in surface waters at certain times of the year.

There is some indication of a decline in the levels of atrazine in rivers, following the ban on its non-agricultural use from September 1993. However, there also appears to have been an initial rise in the levels of diuron, the herbicide which was possibly used as an alternative to atrazine, although levels fell back again in 1994 following campaigns from the manufacturer, water companies and the National Rivers Authority (NRA). Mecoprop is the most commonly found agricultural pesticide in rivers; levels have remained fairly steady between 1992 and 1994. Isoproturon levels fell in 1993, mainly due to a particularly wet autumn and winter in 1992/93 which resulted in less isoproturon being applied than usual, but increased in 1994. Permethrin arises primarily from point sources and the reduction in concentrations over the last three years is a result of better treatment technology for industrial discharges.

'In general, even smaller quantities of pesticides are found in groundwater than in rivers. The pesticide most frequently detected in groundwater is atrazine, which appears to have increased from 1992 to 1994, despite the ban in 1993. This is probably to be expected as groundwaters take longer to recover than surface waters. Isoproturon levels also increased over this period.

p Freshwater quality

page 105

Pollution

Indicator p5:
Pollution incidents

The total number of substantiated water pollution incidents in England classified either as major or significant rose between 1991 and 1992, but has fallen since then. In 1994, sewage, industry, and agriculture accounted for about 30 per cent, 25 per cent, and 15 per cent respectively of major and significant incidents.

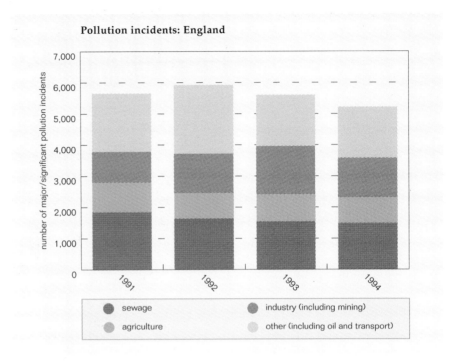

Pollution incidents: England

number of major/significant pollution incidents

- ● sewage
- ● agriculture
- ● industry (including mining)
- ● other (including oil and transport)

The NRA, Scottish River Purification Authorities, and the Department of the Environment for Northern Ireland monitor aspects of water quality in England and Wales, Scotland, and Northern Ireland respectively. Consents are issued to control point source discharges to water at a level consistent with the achievement of quality objectives for the waters concerned and their users. However, occasionally consents are breached or other incidents occur at points where no consent has been issued which lead to pollution, eg accidental spillages and storm overflows. Local inland water quality can be adversely affected by a variety of pollution incidents, with most incidents caused either by sewage, industry, or agriculture.

The relevant authorities take action to minimise the environmental impact of incidents by containing the pollution and countering any effects. They investigate the source and cause of the pollution, and notify any users of the water concerned. They can also bring prosecutions for incidents and have powers to carry out preventative or remedial operations to deal with

pollution, and to recover costs incurred from those responsible. From April 1996 the Environment Agencies will be able to require polluters to take such action at their own expense.

Indicator p5 shows major and significant substantiated water pollution incidents in England by source since 1991.

This indicator provides an illustration of water pollution control for the NRA regions in England (comparable data for Wales, Scotland, and Northern Ireland are not currently available). The total number of reported and substantiated incidents in England has increased over the last decade, but this is believed to be attributable largely to increased rates of reporting by the public of minor incidents, which form about three quarters of all substantiated incidents. Increased reporting rates may be associated with heightened public concern about pollution and encouragement by the NRA of the

public to report incidents, eg through publicity, 24-hour reporting lines, etc. Major and significant incidents are thought to be less likely to be influenced by a change in reporting rates, and thus the combined number of major and significant incidents may provide a more meaningful indication of actual trends in pollution incidents.

Overall, the number of major and significant incidents rose between 1991 and 1992, but has fallen in the two years since then. In 1994, sewage accounted for nearly 30 per cent of major and significant incidents, while industry accounted for nearly 25 per cent and agriculture for about 15 per cent. The remaining incidents result from other sources, including oil and transport. The number of incidents caused by sewage fell over the period 1991 to 1994, while those caused by industry rose until 1993 before falling in 1994, and those caused by agriculture remained about the same.

Indicator p6:
Pollution prevention and control

An increasing proportion of discharge consents to sewage treatment works operated by Water Companies are meeting compliance standards; 94 per cent of consents in England and Wales were complied with in 1993. Compliance rates for trade discharges and private sewage discharges are lower, 71 per cent and 51 per cent respectively.

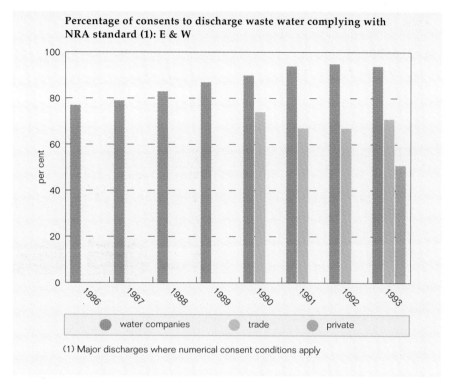

Percentage of consents to discharge waste water complying with NRA standard (1): E & W

Legend: water companies, trade, private

(1) Major discharges where numerical consent conditions apply

To improve the quality of waters by controlling pollution, the NRA sets standards or consents for the discharge of waste water. There are over 95,000 discharges in England and Wales which have consents, many of which are small. These are discharges from point sources, ie fixed outfalls such as sewage works, pipes and drains, because it is only these discharges which can be controlled by consents.

Around a third of consented discharges are sufficiently important to require numeric conditions to limit the amount of pollution in the effluent by setting limits on the concentration or load of substances in the effluent and on the discharge flow. For other discharges, non-numeric or descriptive consents apply, which involve alternative assessments such as type of treatment required, polluting effects to be avoided, or rate of flow. Not all numeric discharges are monitored. This indicator is concerned with compliance with monitored numeric consents by sewage treatment works operated by the water and sewerage undertakers, trade discharges

(which will include site drainage as well as discharges from industrial processes) and privately operated sewage treatment works (in some cases these may be little more than septic tanks).

Discharges of domestic sewage are generally subject to a compliance regime based on "95-percentile" standards (which means that a small number of samples may exceed limits in any 12-month period) although in some cases absolute standards (exceedance of which on a single occasion constitutes a breach) may also be set (particularly for dangerous substances). Absolute standards are set for many trade discharges because of the nature of the substances being discharged. Relatively lower compliance rates may apply to discharges subject to absolute limits. Therefore, some caution has to be exercised in making comparisons between different types of discharges as well as in comparing data for different years, particularly because of changes in the extent of monitoring and sampling.

Indicator p6 shows the percentage of monitored consents to discharge waste water into inland and coastal waters in England and Wales which meet the standards (numeric consents) set by the NRA.

An increasing proportion of discharge consents to sewage treatment works operated by Water Companies meet the standard set by the NRA. The compliance rate increased from 77 to 94 per cent between 1986 and 1993. Compliance with consents for trade discharges was 71 per cent in 1993, and the rate has fluctuated around this level since 1990. Just over a half of private sewage discharges monitored (51 per cent) were compliant in 1993.

p Freshwater quality

Water treatment

Indicator p7:
Expenditure on water
abstraction, treatment and
distribution

*Annual operational costs of
water resource and treatment
remained at about 7 pence per
cubic metre over the last three
years in England and Wales (at
1994/95 prices). Annual capital
expenditure of treatment of
drinking water rose to just over
10 pence per cubic metre
supplied in both 1992/93 and
1993/94, but declined to 8
pence in 1994/95.*

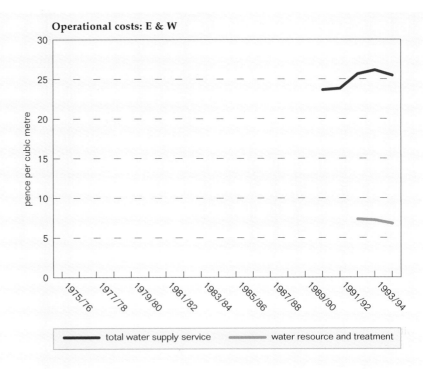

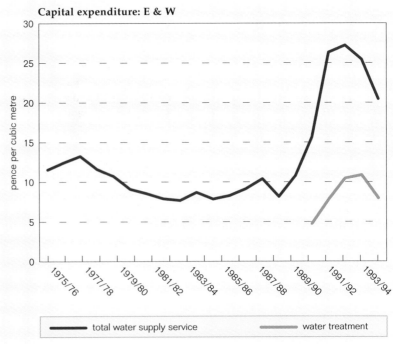

p Freshwater quality

One of the key sustainable development issues relating to drinking water quality is to ensure that adequate freshwater resources of sufficient quality are available for abstraction for treatment as drinking water. A secure supply of clean water is essential for both human health and quality of life. The issues surrounding the supply and quality of drinking water are extremely complex. Different water sources provide water of widely varying quality, and so the necessary treatment can vary from simple disinfection to multistage treatment. The cost of water treatment may thus reflect to some extent the quality of this source water, but also a wide range of other factors such as the efficiency with which particular pollutants can be treated, drinking water standards, etc.

In the UK, public water supplies are of a very high quality. In recent years quality has improved as a result of legislation introducing a new regulatory framework and the increased effort to comply with these standards. Over 99 per cent of nearly 4 million samples taken by water suppliers in GB in 1994 complied with statutory drinking water quality standards. The cost of treatment of water supplied for public consumption increased sharply in the early 1990s to meet the new standards. A key sustainable development issue is therefore balancing how much it is worth paying, or how much can be afforded, for further improvement to drinking water quality. At some point in the future a further tightening of standards may become too expensive and the improvements may not be justified.

Chemical and biological river quality is covered by Indicator p1 in this section.

Indicator p7 shows operational costs and capital expenditure on the public water supply in England and Wales, including costs of treatment in recent years.

The trends shown by this indicator need to be interpreted with considerable caution, particularly the trends for capital expenditure, because expenditure and operating costs on treatment depend on a complex variety of factors. The sharp increase in capital expenditure after 1989 followed the privatisation of the water industry, and largely reflects the additional treatment needed to comply with the standards. The trend can be expected to become more stable in the future.

During the 1990s, operational costs of water service (at 1994/95 prices) have risen slightly from 24 pence to 26 pence per cubic metre supplied. Within this total the costs of resource and water treatment have remained at about 7 pence per cubic metre over the last three years. Separate operational costs for treatment alone are not readily available. On average, about 60 cubic metres of water are supplied per head of population each year (ie 160 litres per day).

Capital expenditure on the supply of public water service (at 1994/95 prices) has increased from 8 - 11 pence per cubic metre supplied during the 1980s to about 25 pence in the early 1990s, falling back to 21 pence in 1994/95. This reflects the considerable investment made by water companies since the early 1990s. Within this overall total, the capital cost of treatment of drinking water rose to just over 10 pence per cubic metre supplied in both 1992/93 and 1993/94, but declined to 8 pence in 1994/95.

Future indicator development:

An alternative approach would be to use an appropriate broad measure of the quality of water available, prior to treatment, for abstraction for public supply.

p Freshwater quality

Indicator p8:
Expenditure on sewage treatment

Annual operational costs of sewage treatment have remained at about £7 per head of population over the last three years in England and Wales (at 1994/95 prices). Annual capital expenditure of sewage treatment rose from £5-£6 per head during most of the 1980s to a peak of nearly £20 per head in 1991/92 and has declined since to £13-£14 in the last two years.

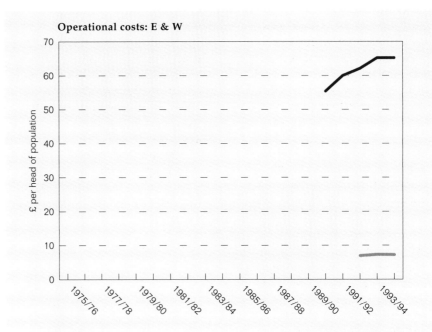

Operational costs: E & W

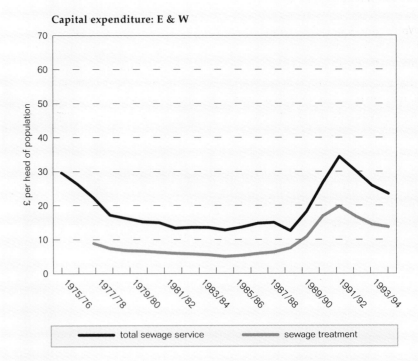

Capital expenditure: E & W

total sewage service   sewage treatment

p Freshwater quality

The key sustainable development issues relating to waste water treatment (including sewage and industrial effluent) are to maintain and, as necessary, improve the quality of waters receiving waste water effluent discharges, to promote the natural environment and biodiversity, and to ensure adequate water resources are available for particular uses. The polluting load of the effluent, and hence water quality in the area of the discharge, will depend on the level of treatment provided.

A major programme of investment is under way on sewage treatment works, sewerage collection systems and pipelines into coastal waters and the sea, funded by Water Service Companies in England and Wales, the Regional and Island Councils in Scotland, and DoE Northern Ireland.

These investment programmes are in response to current government initiatives to treat all significant sewage discharges into coastal waters, and to end sewage sludge disposal at sea, and in response to the EC Directive on urban waste water treatment which was adopted by member states in 1991. The Directive sets minimum standards of treatment for municipal waste water and a timetable for implementation of these standards in stages up to 2005.

Indicator p8 shows operational costs and capital expenditure on sewage services in England and Wales, including costs of sewage treatment

Such an indicator might be presented in terms of costs per cubic metres of sewage treated, but estimates of the total sewage treated are not available on a consistent basis before 1992/93, so all figures have been expressed as costs per head of population.

During the 1990s, operational costs of sewage service (at 1994/95 prices) have risen from £55 to £65 per head of population in England and Wales. Within this total the costs of sewage treatment have remained at about £7 per head of population. Capital expenditure on sewage (at 1994/95 prices) increased sharply from less than £15 per head of resident population during the 1980s to a peak of £34 in 1991/92 and has declined since to £23 in 1994/95, but is predicted to rise to an average of £28 per head per year between 1995 and 2005. This reflects the considerable investment made by Water Companies since the early 1990s. Within this overall total the capital cost of sewage treatment rose from £5-£6 per head during most of the 1980s to nearly £20 per head in 1991/92 and has declined since to £13-£14 in each of the last two years.

p Freshwater quality

q Marine

The key sustainable development issue for the coastal and marine environment is to prevent pollution from human activities especially those which result in the discharge of effluent reaching the sea via rivers, estuaries and directly from the coast, by maintaining and improving current controls on man-made inputs, particularly those containing substances which are toxic, persistent and liable to bioaccumulate. The indicators relevant to this issue are estuarial water quality, inputs of contaminants, contaminant concentrations in water and in fish, bathing water quality, and oil spills and operational discharges of oil.

Indicator q1:
Estuarial water quality

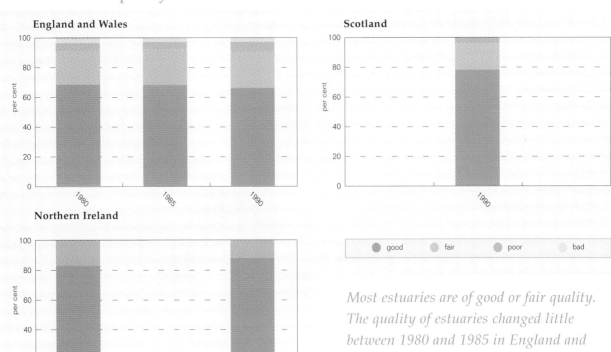

Most estuaries are of good or fair quality. The quality of estuaries changed little between 1980 and 1985 in England and Wales but there was some net deterioration between 1985 and 1990.

An assessment of the quality of estuaries is based on four classes, Good, Fair, Poor, Bad, which take into account biological, aesthetic and chemical quality of the water and the minimum dissolved oxygen content. The classification system is based on an assessment by experts where points are awarded if certain criteria are met and the overall points count determines the quality class. There are plans to change the classification system using a more objective and comprehensive General Quality Assessment.

Indicator q1 shows trends in the quality of estuaries and the proportions of estuaries falling in different quality classes.

Most estuarial lengths are of good or fair quality; 92 per cent in England and Wales, 96 per cent in Scotland and 88 per cent in Northern Ireland. The quality of estuaries changed little between 1980 and 1985 In England and

Wales, but there was some net deterioration between 1985 and 1990; estuarial length classified as good reduced from 68 per cent in 1985 to 66 per cent in 1990 and there was a corresponding increase in the poor class from 5 to 7 per cent. In Northern Ireland the quality of estuaries has remained unchanged since 1985, after allowing for the increase in estuarial length due to the inclusion of the Larne and Strangford Loughs in the survey.

Indicator q2:
Concentrations of key pollutants

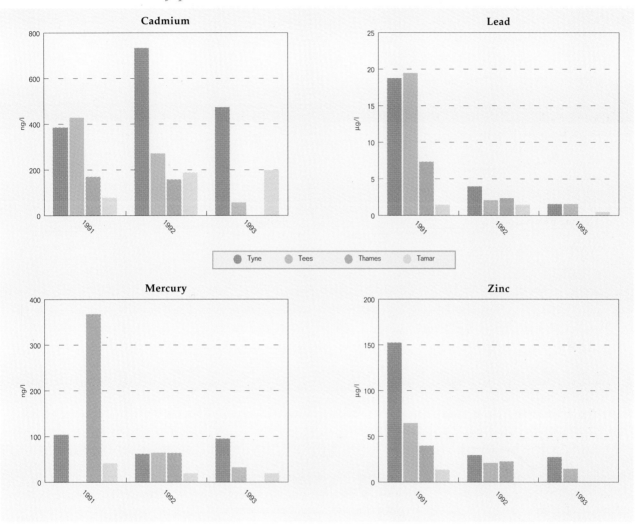

Concentrations of dissolved metals in estuaries have fallen over the last three years. The number of sample exceedences of Environmental Quality Standards reduced to three in 1993.

Concentrations of metals and other contaminants result from effluent discharged into rivers from sewage treatment works and from industry. Some areas will also tend to have relatively high concentrations of certain metals as a result of natural geological factors. Environmental Quality Standards (EQSs) have been set for metals of concern in estuaries, expressed in terms of annual means at each sample site. These are, cadmium 5µg/l, lead 25µg/l, mercury 0.5µg/l and zinc 40µg/l. The indicator shows

average values for selected estuaries by taking the mean of average values for each sampling point in the estuary and are not therefore directly comparable with the EQSs. They do indicate, however, general concentrations relative to the standards.

Indicator q2 shows trends in concentrations of heavy metals in selected estuaries since 1991.

The estuaries included are meant to be broadly illustrative of general trends in concentrations but there will be local variations from estuary to estuary. Concentrations have generally fallen over the last three years, particularly lead and zinc, and average levels for estuaries are well below EQSs. There were a few exceedences at individual sampling points in estuaries around the UK prior to 1993 for chromium, copper, lead, mercury, nickel and zinc, but only three in 1993, for cadmium and copper.

q Marine

Indicator q3:
Contaminants in fish

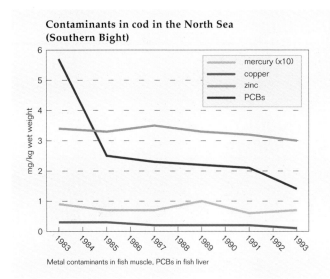

Contaminants in cod in the North Sea (Southern Bight)

mg/kg wet weight

mercury (x10)
copper
zinc
PCBs

Metal contaminants in fish muscle, PCBs in fish liver

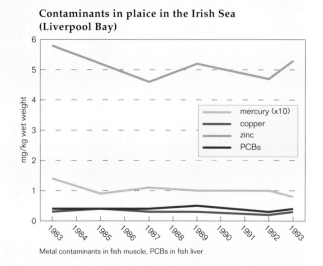

Contaminants in plaice in the Irish Sea (Liverpool Bay)

mg/kg wet weight

mercury (x10)
copper
zinc
PCBs

Metal contaminants in fish muscle, PCBs in fish liver

Concentrations in contaminants have been relatively stable over the last decade in the areas considered to be at higher risk, except for polychlorinated biphenyls (PCBs) in North Sea cod, where concentrations have fallen sharply. Concentrations are well within recommended guideline values.

q Marine

Discharges of contaminants such as heavy metals and PCBs into the sea either directly, or via inputs to rivers and to the atmosphere can accumulate in fish and shell fish causing potentially harmful concentrations which may affect marine life and human heath. In most marine waters around the UK however, concentrations tend to be low and well within recommended guideline values.

Indicator q3 shows trends in contaminants in fish in the North Sea (Southern Bight) and in the Irish Sea (Liverpool Bay), since 1983.

The contaminants shown are mercury, copper, zinc and PCBs. Cadmium and lead are excluded since concentrations tend to be extremely low, falling below the limit of detection. The marine waters covered by the indicators (Liverpool Bay and Southern Bight) are where there are relatively higher risks of contamination. Guideline values ("lower", "medium" and "upper" concentrations) for mercury and PCB's have been issued by the Oslo and Paris Commission. For mercury these are <0.1, 0.1-0.3, >0.3mg/kg wet weight in fish flesh, and for PCBs in cod liver <2.0, 2.0-5.0, >5.0mg/kg wet weight. There are also Food Standard Committee recommendations and guidelines for the levels of copper and zinc in foods, ie < 20mg/kg wet weight

(a recommendation) and <50mg/kg wet weight (a guideline) for copper and zinc respectively.

Concentrations of contaminants have been relatively stable over the last decade in Liverpool Bay and Southern Bight, where there are relatively higher risks of contamination, except for PCBs in cod in Southern Bight where levels have fallen sharply. Most of this reduction occurred in the early to mid 1980s. Mercury and PCBs concentrations are now in the low to medium ranges of the Oslo and Paris Commission guidelines values, (PCBs were in the upper category in Southern Bight in the early 1980s). Copper and zinc concentrations are well below recommended/guideline values for contaminants in food.

Indicator q4:
Bathing water quality

Since 1988 there has been a considerable improvement in the quality of bathing waters. In 1995, 89 per cent of bathing waters complied with the Directive's mandatory coliform standards. This trend is expected to continue as further investments are made in improving the sewerage system.

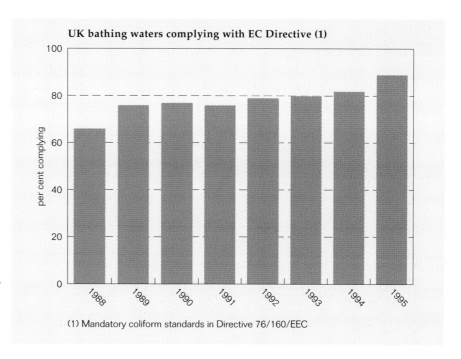

UK bathing waters complying with EC Directive (1)

per cent complying

(1) Mandatory coliform standards in Directive 76/160/EEC

Bathing water quality may be affected by discharges from sewage treatment works and storm overflows and also by rivers. The main concern is to avoid contamination of bathing waters by sewage. An indicator of such contamination is the concentration of total and faecal coliforms in samples of bathing waters and these microbiological parameters are among the parameters tested under the EC Bathing Waters Directive. The majority of UK bathing waters currently comply with the EC mandatory coliform standards. An extensive investment programme is under way to bring up to standard those currently at significant risk of failing to comply. The programme includes improved levels of sewage treatments and improvements to outfall arrangements and storm overflows.

Indicator q4 shows the trend in the percentage of bathing waters complying with EC mandatory coliform standards.

There has been a substantial improvement in the proportion of bathing waters meeting the EC Directive's mandatory coliform standards since 1988 and in 1995 89 per cent of bathing waters complied. Further improvements are expected as the compliance programme is completed and further investments are made with the aim of treating all significant discharges of sewage to estuaries and coastal waters by the end of 2005 in line with the timetable for implementation of the Urban Waste Water Treatment Directive.

q Marine

Indicator q5:
Inputs of contaminants

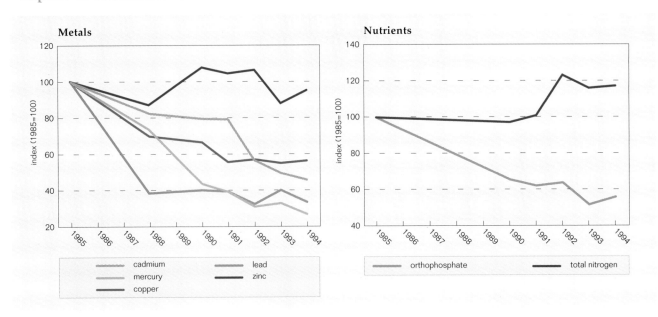

Inputs of cadmium, mercury, copper, lead and orthophosphate declined substantially between 1985 and 1994. Inputs of total nitrogen remained relatively constant until 1992 when inputs increased, levelling off subsequently in 1993 and 1994. Inputs of zinc have fluctuated from year to year since 1985.

Effluent containing metals, nutrients, organic compounds and other contaminants reach the sea via discharges into rivers, or directly from pipeline discharges into coastal and estuarial waters. Such inputs can come from point sources which are controlled by discharge consents or from diffuse sources where controls operate on the general activity giving rise to these inputs. The pollutant impact of discharges depends on the amount discharged and whether the contaminants are toxic, persistent and liable to bioaccumulate. There are international agreements to monitor and control discharges (the Paris Convention, North Sea Conference Declarations and EC Directives) and standards and targets have been set to reduce input loads of the most dangerous substances.

Indicator q5 shows trends in direct and riverine inputs of contaminants to UK coastal waters since 1985.

Input loads may vary considerably from year to year because of natural variations such as rainfall and it is the overall trend which is significant. The values given in the indicator are maximum estimates; where sample values used to calculate input loads are below the limit of detection it is assumed that the actual value is at the limit of detection.

Inputs of mercury, lead, cadmium and copper have declined substantially between 1985 and 1994 (a 73 per cent reduction in mercury inputs, 66 per cent lead, 54 per cent cadmium, and 44 per cent copper). Inputs of total nitrogen remained relatively constant until 1992 when inputs increased, levelling off subsequently in 1993 and 1994. Inputs of zinc have fluctuated from year to year; inputs in 1994 are 5 per cent below 1985 levels.

q Marine

Indicator q6:
Oil spills and operational discharges

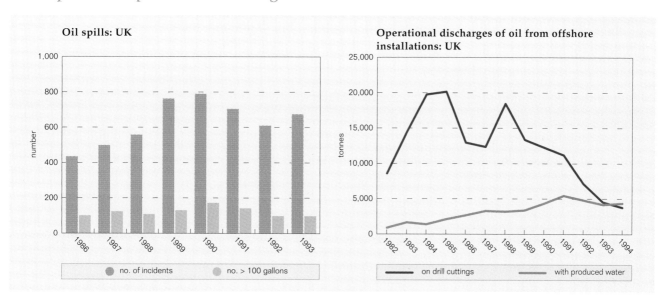

Oil spills: UK

Operational discharges of oil from offshore installations: UK

After rising sharply in the late 1980s, the number of oil spills from shipping and offshore installations declined compared with the peak in 1990; 99 incidents were relatively large with spills of over 100 gallons. Operational discharges of oil from drill cuttings on offshore installations have been falling since 1988.

Oil can damage marine ecosystems, endanger marine life and pollute beaches and coastlines. It has toxic effects, which can kill or damage marine organisms and physical effects, on seabirds for example, where it can damage plumage resulting in the loss of water repellent properties and reduced thermal insulation and buoyancy. Oil pollution may be caused by accidental or illegal spillage from ships, and spills from offshore installations. Most oil spills are small and in many cases the oil is dispersed naturally, but there are a number of more substantial spillages from ships which require cleaning up.

Oil pollution may also result from operational discharges during exploration and production of oil and gas offshore, either from discharged produced water (oil-contaminated water that is extracted and then discharged from the production process) or from drill cuttings using

oil-based drilling mud. Although the total amounts of oil discharged are relatively large, the oil is considerably diluted (the average oil content of discharged water in 1993 was 0.0029 per cent).

The Paris Commission determines the maximum permitted levels of operational discharges of oil from offshore installations and the International Convention for the Prevention of Pollution from Ships limits operational discharges of oil from ships (MARPOL, Annex a)

Indicator q6 shows the trend in the number of incidents of accidental or illegal spillage of oil from ships and offshore installations in UK coastal waters, and operational discharges of oil from offshore installations.

The number of oil spill incidents reached a peak in 1990, declining thereafter compared with the 1990 level. The number of large incidents (spills of over 100 gallons) has also declined since 1990. There were 99 such incidents in 1993. Operational discharges from offshore installations have fallen since the mid 1980s due to reductions in discharges of oil from drill cuttings. Oil discharged with produced water has declined relative to the peak in 1991, partly as a result of tighter operational requirements. It is anticipated, however, that quantities of produced water, and hence oil discharged in the treated produced water effluent, will increase in the short to medium term as more oilfields in the UK sector approach the end of their working lives.

q Marine

r Wildlife and habitats

The key sustainable development objectives for wildlife are to conserve as far as reasonably possible the wide variety of wildlife species and habitats in the UK, and to ensure that commercially exploited species are managed in a sustainable way.

We value wildlife for its own sake, and because it is part of our natural capital resource which we aim to preserve for future generations. In the context of indicators, however, wildlife can also provide an indication of the state of the environment and changes occurring in it. Such indicators can give a broader assessment than the measurement of individual aspects of environmental quality, eg the presence of different aquatic invertebrates in a river can give a biological measure of the total impact of a wide range of factors in that particular environment. Such indicators have to be treated with caution because a variety of natural factors (eg the weather) also impact on wildlife. Nevertheless, taken together with more specific measures given in other sections of the report, wildlife indicators can

give a useful pointer to important changes over time.

This points to a set of indicators which measures:

● changes in *UK biodiversity*, and our response to these changes;

● the extent and quality of *key habitats* which are important in a national or international context because, for example, they are rare or at risk or contain important species;

● the extent and quality of other *broader habitats in the wider countryside*;

● *habitat fragmentation*;

● *landscape features* which are significant for wildlife such as hedgerows and small ponds; and

● populations of *important species groups* which tell us something about the wider environment.

The current set of indicators tends to deal with the state of wildlife and the environment, but future development might include new indicators of pressure and response. The Sustainable Development Strategy identified the principal causes of the losses of the number and range of plant and animal species in the UK over the last 50 years as urban development, transport developments, forestry expansion, and intensification of agricultural production. Other factors such as acidification and pollution will also have had an impact. These pressures are covered in other sections of the report, particularly in the *Land use*, *Land cover and landscape*, *Forestry*, and *Freshwater quality* sections.

UK Biodiversity

Indicator r1:
Native species at risk

Between about 10 and 20 per cent of native GB species are considered "threatened". Similar proportions of invertebrates and plants are "nationally scarce".

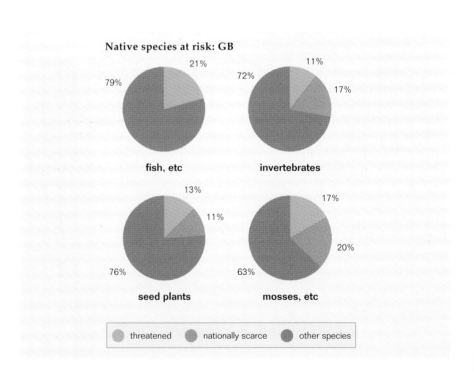

Native species at risk: GB

fish, etc — 79% / 21%

invertebrates — 72% / 11% / 17%

seed plants — 76% / 13% / 11%

mosses, etc — 63% / 17% / 20%

● threatened ● nationally scarce ● other species

Conservation of the UK's biodiversity is an important policy priority. The Government published its Biodiversity Action Plan in January 1994 in response to Article 6 of the Convention on Biodiversity. The Biodiversity Steering Group, set up under the UK's Plan, published in December 1995 a set of proposed specific, costed targets and action plans for 116 *priority species* and 14 *key habitats* of conservation importance. The habitat plans cover about 2 per cent of the UK land area. The Government's response will follow in early 1996. Other plans will be prepared over the next three years for an additional 286 priority species and 24 key habitats. The agreed targets and action plans will form the basis for conservation action in the UK for the immediate and foreseeable future.

Indicator r1 shows estimated proportions of GB native species under threat or nationally scarce.

This indicator provides a broad-brush measure of the extent and status of biodiversity in GB. Comparable information is not available for the UK as a whole. The indicator gives the proportions of four groups of species that are considered to be "threatened" (ie endangered, vulnerable, or rare based on criteria devised by the International Union for the Conservation of Nature (IUCN)) and, where available, the proportions which are "nationally scarce" (ie species recorded as present in only 16 -100 ten km squares in GB). "Threatened"

(ie Red Data Listed) and "nationally scarce" species are used in evaluating the conservation importance of sites and their presence is one of the criteria used to select Sites of Special Scientific Interest (SSSIs). Comparable information for mammals and birds at risk is not available since IUCN threat status for these species is assessed on an international basis and not for GB populations separately.

While many species native to GB are relatively common, between about 10 and 20 per cent of native species are considered threatened. Over a third of the 2,700 native species of mosses, liverworts, and lichens are threatened or nationally scarce. The comparable proportions for seed plants, ferns, and related plants (about 2,300 species in total) and for invertebrates (about 15,000 species in those groups covered by the Red Data Books) are each about a quarter.

Figures here have to be interpreted with caution. Some species will always be rare simply because the extent of their habitat is naturally very small or because GB is at the geographical limit of their natural range.

Future indicator development:

Further indicators could be developed based on the progress towards meeting agreed Biodiversity Action Plan targets for the 400 or so priority species. Although this will not in itself measure biodiversity directly, it will measure the success of the specific Government policies to preserve and enhance biodiversity.

Key habitats

The Biodiversity Steering Group has identified 38 key habitats which are important because, for example, the UK has international obligations, or the habitats are at risk or rare, or they contain important species. Together, these habitats account for about 5 per cent of the UK land area. As mentioned earlier specific, costed targets and action plans have been or will be developed for each of these key habitats.

Many of the sites within these key habitats are covered by SSSIs. Others are covered by management agreements under the two major farmland conservation schemes, ie Environmentally Sensitive Areas (ESA) and Countryside Stewardship schemes.

Trends in the extent of designated and protected areas is covered by Indicator s2, loss and damage to SSSIs is covered by Indicator s3, and environmentally managed land is covered by Indicator s8 in the *Land cover and landscape* section.

Future indicator development:

A monitoring programme is being established under the Biodiversity Action Plan to measure changes in both the extent of key habitats and their quality, in terms of the populations of characteristic flora and fauna found in them. Over time it should be possible to develop broad, aggregated indicators based on this monitoring which will show how we are performing in protecting and enhancing these areas.

r Wildlife and habitats

Broader habitats in the wider countryside

As well as being concerned with key habitats, indicators are also needed to measure the quality of other, broader habitats. For example indicators are needed for the two most common types of land cover, namely farmland (which accounts for about 76 per cent of the UK land area) and woodland (about 10 per cent). They could also be useful for other broad habitats such as coastal areas and wetlands. The quality of these areas can also be characterised by the flora and fauna which are present there. Here we give examples of indicators of birds and plants that are typical of some broader habitat types. Where possible figures are also given for the extent of these habitats.

Indicator r2:
Breeding birds

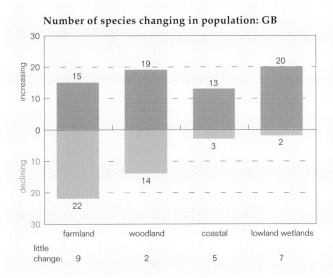

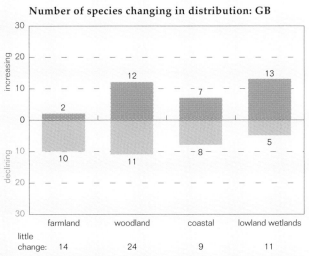

Over the last twenty years there have been substantial changes in population sizes and geographical distributions of many British breeding birds. In woodland, coastal, and wetland habitats more species experienced an increase in numbers than a loss. However, this trend was reversed for farmland birds where 22 species experienced a decline in population size and 10 a decline in geographical distribution.

Birds provide several advantages as representative indicators of the broad state of wildlife and the countryside. They are wide-ranging in habitat distribution and tend to be at or near the top of the food chain. Their mobility and the relatively long life expectancies of some species can result in the integration of environmental effects over large areas and long time spans. In addition, birds are generally well studied and monitored and reasonably reliable data on population and geographical distribution are available over time. Under the EC Birds Directive, the UK has a commitment to protect all species of naturally occurring wild birds in the UK and to preserve a sufficient diversity of habitats in order to maintain populations at an ecologically sound level. All bird species naturally occurring in the wild are protected under the Wildlife and Countryside Act 1981.

Indicator r2 shows the numbers of GB breeding bird species increasing and declining in population size and geographical distribution, by broad habitat type.

r Wildlife and habitats

Almost a half (ie 22 species) of farmland species have declined in *population size* over the last twenty years. Species such as the linnet, skylark, and corn bunting each decreased in population by over a half during this period. Within farmland habitats the numbers of species declining was higher in cultivated land (about 60 per cent of species) than in grazing land (40 per cent). A similar pattern is seen in the numbers of farmland species declining in *geographical distribution*, with around 40 per cent (ie 10 species) showing decreases in their geographical extent. Nevertheless, around 30 per cent of farmland species have increased in population, eg the populations of jackdaw, magpie, and stock dove all more than doubled.

For woodland, coastal, and lowland wetland birds more species have increased than decreased in population, with about 70 per cent of lowland wetland species, 60 per cent of coastal species, and 50 per cent of woodland species increasing. The pattern for numbers of species changing in geographical distribution is similar, with more species experiencing increases in these habitats than those in farmland habitats.

Indicator r3: Plant diversity in semi-improved grassland

There was a significant loss of plant diversity in semi-improved grasslands in GB lowlands between 1978 and 1990, in both "arable" and "pastural" landscapes. This particularly affected plants associated with unimproved meadows.

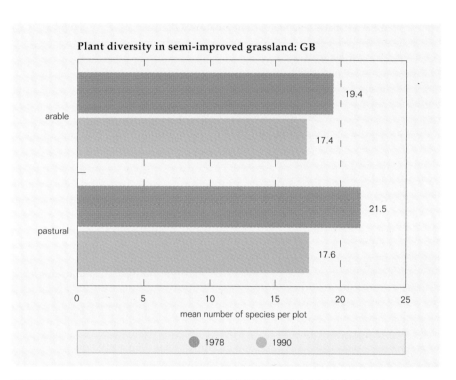

Plant diversity in semi-improved grassland: GB

arable — 19.4 / 17.4
pastural — 21.5 / 17.6

mean number of species per plot

● 1978 ● 1990

Indicator r4: Area of chalk grassland

Within semi-improved grasslands there was a substantial decrease in the total area of chalk grassland in England, particularly in Wiltshire, between the 1960s and 1980s.

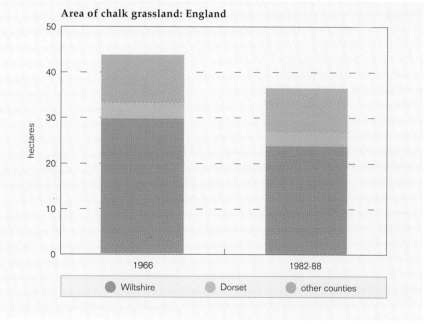

Area of chalk grassland: England

hectares

1966   1982-88

● Wiltshire   ● Dorset   ● other counties

r Wildlife and habitats

r Wildlife and habitats

Semi-natural grassland is a good quality habitat found in the wider countryside in the UK, some of which may have originated naturally before human clearance of shrubs and trees, but most of which owes its existence to prehistoric farmers. There are many different types of grassland which support a diverse range of plants and animals in lowland areas. The wildlife in these areas is best sustained by traditional, low-intensity management, eg as hay meadows and grazing pastures. The application of fertilisers or herbicides (ie grassland "improvement") can eliminate all but a few common, tolerant species.

Indicator r3 shows changes in the number of different plant species found in semi-improved grassland (used as a proxy for semi-natural grassland) in GB.

Data from the 1978 and 1990 Countryside Surveys show the mean number of all identified species found in survey plots of semi-improved grassland. These data have been used as a proxy for semi-natural grassland, which forms only a part of the semi-improved grassland category. In 1990 lowland semi-improved grassland covered an estimated 13 per cent of the total area of GB. Between 1978 and 1990 there was a statistically

significant reduction in plant diversity in semi-improved grasslands both in "arable" and "pastural" landscapes, reflecting a shift towards more intensively managed vegetation types. The most pronounced declines were of plants associated with unimproved meadows, including some rarer grassland species.

The Countryside Surveys illustrate the general picture for semi-natural grassland. However, within this broad habitat group there are a variety of very different types of grasslands, many of which are found in relatively small areas of the country and are of particular conservation importance. One example of such grasslands is calcareous grassland which is recognised as a resource of great ecological interest and value for nature conservation. Such grassland is scattered throughout GB on soils derived from chalk and limestone, but is estimated to cover less than 50,000 ha (or 0.2 per cent) of the total land area. A number of such areas are now targeted for maintenance and enhancement by the two major farmland conservation schemes (ESAs and Countryside Stewardship). Environmentally managed land under ESA and Countryside Stewardship schemes is covered by Indicator s8 in the *Land cover and landscape* section.

Chalk downland was probably the first area of GB occupied by humans. Between the 12th and 18th centuries it provided some of the

main grazing areas upon which the wool trade depended. However, during the 1800s extensive areas were ploughed to grow corn, and grassland improvement and arable ploughing continued into the 1900s. Chalk grassland in Dorset, for example, has declined from about 117,000 ha in 1793 to 13,000 ha in 1815, and about 3,000 ha in the 1990s. Similar declines have occurred elsewhere and few large areas of chalk grassland now remain, the most extensive being on Salisbury Plain and Porton Down in Wiltshire.

Indicator r4 shows changes in the area of chalk grassland (an important example of semi-natural grassland) in counties in England.

The overall area of chalk grassland continued to decrease in England, particularly in Wiltshire, between the first national survey in 1966 and subsequent surveys in the 1980s. About 60 per cent of the grassland lost during the period had been ploughed and 32 per cent was invaded by scrub following cessation of grazing. About a third of the remaining calcareous grassland on chalk is located within SSSIs.

Future indicator development:

Focused surveys (eg English Nature's grassland inventories) may be used to provide a better means of understanding grassland change.

Indicator r5:
Plant diversity in hedgerows

About a half of all GB hedges are found in lowland "pastural" landscapes. Between 1978 and 1990 there was a significant loss of plant species in hedgerows in these landscapes, particularly of plants associated with meadow and chalk grasslands.

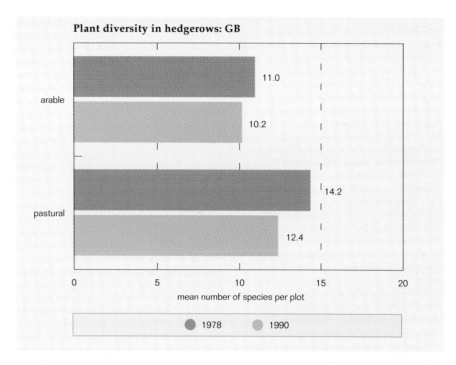

Plant diversity in hedgerows: GB

arable — 11.0 / 10.2

pastural — 14.2 / 12.4

mean number of species per plot

● 1978   ● 1990

Hedgerows and other field boundaries are an important part of the UK landscape. Hedges, verges, and stream-banks contain many plants which are absent or rare in the surrounding land, and therefore form important reservoirs of plant biodiversity. This is particularly true in "arable" landscapes, where more plant species tend to be found in linear features than in the open countryside, eg fields. Linear features may also be important as a source of locally native seed as it may be possible for species-rich habitats to regenerate from these seed banks in the future. Further loss of the best quality hedgerows, and the meadow species they often contain, may limit the scope to conserve biodiversity in lowland areas.

Length of hedgerows is covered by Indicator s7 in the *Land cover and landscape* section.

Indicator r5 shows changes in the number of different plant species found in hedgerows in GB.

The data used have come from the 1978 and 1990 Countryside Surveys, and consist of the mean number of all identified species found in survey plots of hedgerows. A third of all field boundaries in GB contain hedges; most are in England and half are in lowland "pastural" landscapes. Hedges are less common in "marginal upland" landscapes, and almost absent from "true uplands". Indicator r5 complements Indicator s7, which shows that there have been substantial declines in the net length of hedgerows over the last 10 years. The remaining hedges continue to hold a high species diversity, although there was a statistically significant loss of species between 1978 and 1990 for hedge plots in "pastural" landscapes, particularly of plants associated with meadow and chalk grasslands. The changes in the different types of species suggest that the decline reflects an overall shift to more intensively managed vegetation. There was no change in the woody species composition of hedge plots and no significant change in the species richness of hedges in lowland "arable" landscapes, although there was a shift towards plants more characteristic of arable fields.

Future indicator development:

Future development work may refer to the monitoring of the length of 'species-rich' hedgerows.

The Countryside Survey data has not been utilised for *woodlands* because of the wide variety of types of woodlands (eg broadleaved, coniferous, ancient, etc) and the relatively small sample sizes involved. Woodland issues and other measures are covered in the *Forestry* section (Indicators h1 to h5).

The wildlife value of *marine* areas is particularly important for the UK. Some relevant indicators on the state of the marine environment are included in the *Fish resources* and *Marine* sections of this report. However, a comprehensive set of marine wildlife indicators has not yet been developed, and further work is needed in this area.

Suitable indicators may also be developed covering wildlife in the *urban environment* and other habitats such as *heather moorlands*. Other indicators might focus on "characteristic" or representative species of habitats, and might also include data from the Biological Records Centre.

r Wildlife and habitats

Habitat fragmentation

The size and lack of isolation, as well as the quality, of individual habitat sites are important for sustaining biodiversity. In general, large areas of a given habitat support more species than small areas. Population numbers of some species can become fragile in small sites. If a site also becomes more isolated or unconnected to other fragments, then the potential to recover its species complement from other sites following a catastrophic event (eg summer droughts) may be reduced, and species could disappear, degrading the quality of the habitat. Sites may also become simply too small to support viable populations of certain plants and animals. Fragmentation can thus pose a threat not only to the extent, but also to the quality and biodiversity of many habitats (eg grasslands, ancient woods, heaths, etc).

Fragmentation can result from development, road building, and agricultural changes, etc. Some measures of habitat fragments or parcels are available, although not over time or on a consistent basis across the country.

Indicator r6:
Habitat fragmentation

Over the last twenty years chalk grassland in Dorset has become more fragmented, ie sites have become smaller and more isolated.

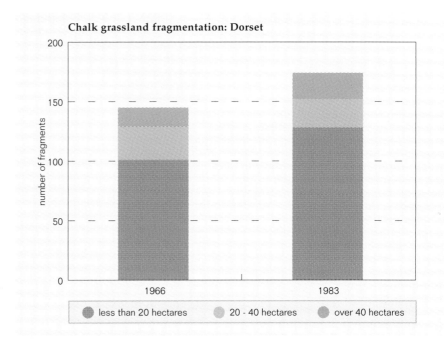

Chalk grassland fragmentation: Dorset

number of fragments

- ● less than 20 hectares
- ● 20 - 40 hectares
- ● over 40 hectares

Indicator r6 shows changes in the numbers and size of chalk grassland sites in Dorset.

While there is little or no national data on the process of fragmentation over time, some local data are available for specific habitats. Indicator r6 is included by way of illustration of fragmentation of calcareous grassland on chalk in Dorset. Indicator r4 showed a general decline in the extent of calcareous grassland on chalk in England as a whole, and in Dorset in particular, between the 1960s and 1980s. In Dorset, this decline has been accompanied by greater fragmentation of such grasslands over the same period. More recent survey data suggests a continued fragmentation into the 1990s, although the data are not strictly comparable with earlier surveys.

Future indicator development:

Fragmentation is an important issue for a number of other habitats, eg woodlands, heathlands, etc. Work currently being done to monitor changes in parcel size may be used for future national indicators for different habitats.

r Wildlife and habitats

Landscape features

Certain features in the landscape are important for wildlife. These include hedgerows, individual trees, small coppices, and small ponds and streams. Some examples are provided here of indicators of these features. Other examples are covered in other sections, eg hedgerow length is covered under Indicator s7 in the section on *Land* *cover and landscape*, and plant biodiversity within hedgerows is covered by Indicator r5 earlier in this section.

Indicator r7: Lakes and ponds

The number of lakes and ponds in GB fell from about 470,000 to 330,000 between 1945 and 1990. From 1984 to 1990, ponds (which make up more than 90 per cent of all static inland water bodies) declined in number by at least 6 per cent.

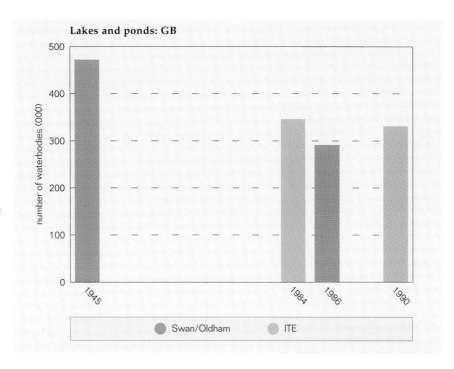

Lakes and ponds have value as wildlife habitats, landscape features, and recreational amenities. Ponds are important because they are widespread and provide aquatic habitats in otherwise terrestrial environments. They thus form additional havens of biodiversity in these environments, as many plants and animals live in the water or at the water edge, or use them in one stage of their life cycle.

Ponds were once a vital feature of many farms, used for watering livestock, but changing farming practices have made ponds largely redundant and many have disappeared. However, since the late 1980s a number of measures have been taken which may eventually arrest this decline. These include changes to the Common Agricultural Policy, and the introduction of more environmental land management schemes.

Environmentally managed land is covered by Indicator s8 in the *Land cover and landscape* section.

Indicator r7 shows estimates of the numbers of lakes and ponds in GB between 1945 and 1990.

This indicator illustrates trends in the numbers of lakes and ponds in GB since 1945. Estimates are available from two sources. Swan & Oldham collated data on the distribution of static water bodies in 1945 and 1986, while the Institute of Terrestrial Ecology (ITE) surveyed water bodies as part of the Countryside Surveys in 1984 and 1990. The number, rather than the area, of water bodies has been selected for this indicator because areas would be dominated by larger lakes, etc which have different ecological characteristics to ponds.

Results between the two surveys are not directly comparable, but, broadly speaking, the number of static inland water bodies in GB declined from about 470,000 in 1945 to about 330,000 in 1990. The total number of water bodies was estimated to have fallen between 4 and 9 per cent between the two ITE surveys in 1984 and 1990; part of this reduction arose from permanent loss following the drought in 1990. Ponds (which have been assumed to correspond to smaller water bodies of less than 0.2 hectares in area) comprised more than 90 per cent of all water bodies in both ITE surveys, and were estimated to have fallen in number by at least 6 per cent between 1984 and 1990.

r Wildlife and habitats

Indicator r8:
Plant diversity in streamsides

The number of plant species in stream banks decreased throughout GB between 1978 and 1990. These losses were significant in "pastural" and "true upland" landscapes.

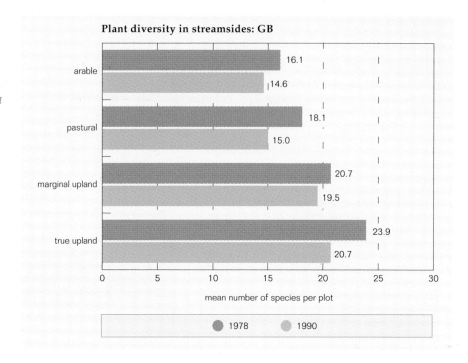

Plant diversity in streamsides: GB

arable: 16.1 (1978), 14.6 (1990)
pastural: 18.1 (1978), 15.0 (1990)
marginal upland: 20.7 (1978), 19.5 (1990)
true upland: 23.9 (1978), 20.7 (1990)

mean number of species per plot

● 1978   ● 1990

Like hedges (see indicator r5), stream banks contain many plant species which are absent or rare in the surrounding landscape, and they therefore form an important reservoir of plant biodiversity. Stream banks also form an integral part of the aquatic environment, with many animals dependent on both the quality of the stream's water and the environmental quality of its banks. They also form important corridors between different habitat sites.

Indicator p1 in the *Freshwater quality* section shows that most rivers in the UK are of "good or moderate" biological quality. Evidence from the 1990 Countryside Survey shows a very similar pattern for streams and other smaller watercourses. Streams in "true upland" and "marginal upland" landscapes were, on average, of higher biological quality than streams in the lowlands (ie "arable" and "pastural"

landscapes). The average numbers of plant species on stream banks in these upland landscapes were also higher than the comparable numbers in the lowlands.

Water quality within channels does not necessarily reflect the quality of the bankside habitats, eg straightening and re-cutting the channel may remove all vegetation without changing the water quality.

Indicator r8 shows changes in numbers of plant species found in streamsides.

The mean number of plant species in stream banks decreased throughout GB between 1978 and 1990. These losses were significant in "pastural" and "true upland" landscapes. Stream banks comprising of moorland grass and grazed pasture became less common, and there was an increase in overgrown grassland.

Throughout the lowlands, species typical of wet meadows and moist woodlands became less common. Some of these declines may have been in response to drought conditions prevalent in southern Britain in 1990. However, similar changes were also recorded in the uplands which were not affected by the drought. Furthermore, most of the species losses were long-lived perennials which were unlikely to be lost as a result of seasonal drying.

Future indicator development:

As for indicators covering habitats, future development might focus on "characteristic" or representative species of streamsides and may also include the quality and extent of particular types of key streamside habitats.

Important species groups

While species are important in their own right, and broad indicators of species conservation are covered above, some species groups can also provide useful indicators of changes in the wider countryside. Species of birds and plants typical of particular habitat types are presented in indicators r2, r3, r5, and r8 earlier in this section. Other species which may be quite significant, and for which data sets are available, include mammals (see indicator r9), dragonflies (r10), butterflies (r11), and moths.

Indicator r9:
Mammal populations

Over a third of British species of mammals are believed to have declined in population size over the last 30 years (most of these being species of rodents or bats) and about a quarter are believed to have increased (most of these being carnivores or deer, and half being non-native species).

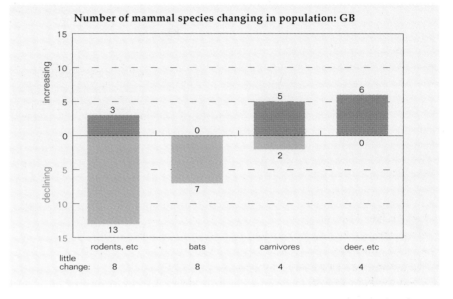

Number of mammal species changing in population: GB

Mammals are a useful group of species for monitoring biodiversity, because they are widespread, easy to identify, present in large numbers, and include species that might potentially serve as good indicators of a variety of changes in the countryside. For example, some mammals such as deer and rabbits (which are increasing in population) have a significant impact through their grazing on plant diversity and hence influence habitat quality and other species within their ecosystem. Other mammals such as the mountain hare, yellow-necked mouse, and the common dormouse (which may be declining in numbers) may form good indicators at different scales of habitat fragmentation. Others such as the hedgehog, brown hare, harvest mouse, stoat, and weasel (which may also be all declining) may be good monitors of the wider countryside, particularly arable land.

There are 61 species of land-based mammals currently breeding in GB. These include 39 native species, 21 introductions and feral species which have had persistent breeding populations in the wild for at least fifteen years, and 1 migrant species (ie, Nathusius' pipistrelle bat). Many of our mammals are protected under both the Wildlife and Countryside Act 1981 and the EC Habitats and Species Directive 1992, eg all bat species, the common dormouse, pine marten, otter, and wildcat. British populations of a number of species form a significant proportion of the total European populations, eg the brown hare, rabbit, field vole, otter, badger, and red, sika, and fallow deer.

Indicator r9 shows the numbers of mammal species increasing and numbers declining in population over the last 30 years in GB.

One disadvantage of using mammals as biological indicators is that for many species there are very few national population data. However, a recent review of British mammals carried out for JNCC (Harris et al, 1995) attempted to summarise the available information and knowledge for each species, and to assess their population changes over the last 30 years.

About a half of GB's 39 species of smaller mammals (eg rodents, insectivores, and bats) are believed to have declined in population over the last 30 years. The populations for most of the remaining smaller species have been stable, and only three are believed to have increased (ie, the rabbit, grey squirrel, and fat dormouse); none of these latter three species are native to GB.

In contrast, just over a half of GB's 22 larger mammals (eg carnivores and deer) increased in population. Most of the rest were thought to be relatively stable and only two native carnivorous species are believed to have declined (ie, the stoat and weasel). The two most common deer in GB (ie, the Roe and Red deer) are native species, whilst the remaining five species of deer are all introductions; the populations of three of these introduced species (eg the Chinese muntjac) are increasing.

Future indicator development:

Indicators for mammals might be further developed and refined; mammals could be split into different groups outlined above (eg a group of grazers such as deer and rabbits which can have large impacts on their ecosystems). However, such development will largely depend on the availability of information and the implementation of monitoring programmes for bats and other mammals.

Indicator r10: Dragonfly distributions

Just over a half of GB dragonfly species declined in geographical distribution between the period up to 1975 and 1975-88, while about a quarter of species increased. Species in lowland "arable" landscapes were the most adversely affected, while those in uplands were less affected.

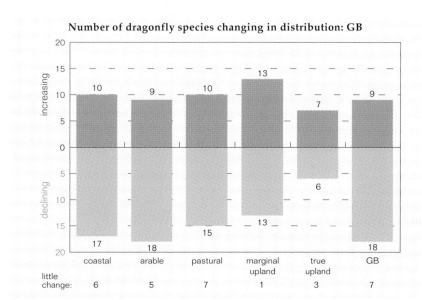

Number of dragonfly species changing in distribution: GB

	coastal	arable	pastural	marginal upland	true upland	GB
increasing	10	9	10	13	7	9
declining	17	18	15	13	6	18
little change:	6	5	7	1	3	7

r Wildlife and habitats

Dragonflies breed in a variety of aquatic habitats in GB, including rivers, streams and ditches, lakes and ponds, and bogs, heaths and moorlands. They are reliant on the water from which they emerge, and on habitats surrounding the water which provide feeding areas. Some species are highly specialised to a single or narrow range of habitats, while others are tolerant of a wide variety of habitat types and water quality. Dragonfly populations can be adversely affected by both loss of habitats (eg the loss of ponds, the lowering of water levels in rivers and wetlands, etc) and habitat degradation (eg through water pollution, adverse management of marginal vegetation, etc). Different species vary in their sensitivity to pollution, which means that it may be possible to gauge the health of an aquatic habitat by the species of dragonflies present.

Many National Nature Reserves, Sites of Special Scientific Interest, and reserves of the RSPB, the Wildlife Trusts, and the National Trusts offer protected sites for British dragonfly species. All species are represented on at least one protected site, and most occur on several reserves. Some newly created habitats (eg new ponds dug by farmers or renovated old ponds, and flooded disused gravel pits) now also play host to several dragonfly species.

Trends in the extent of designated and protected areas is covered by Indicator s2 in the *Land cover and landscape* section.

Indicator r10 shows the proportion of GB dragonfly species whose geographical distribution has changed, by landscape type, between the period up to 1975 and 1975-88.

National data on dragonfly populations are not available, so data for changes in geographical distribution from the Biological Record Centre (BRC) have been presented. Between the period up to 1975 and 1975-1988 the geographical distribution of around a half of British dragonfly species declined, while about a quarter of species increased. In general, the more highly habitat-specific species declined, and the more generalist species increased in geographical distribution. All landscape types experienced similar distributional changes, although landscapes classified by the Institute of Terrestrial Ecology as "arable" (ie, typically eastern lowlands) were most adversely affected, while landscapes classified as "true upland" were less affected.

While these figures do not relate to population numbers, where there are more species decreasing than increasing their geographical distribution, it is probable that this is indicative of dragonfly populations in that landscape type also being adversely affected. The pattern of geographic change mirrors the results of intensive local surveys and detailed site studies, which provide more information on actual populations.

Indicator r11:
Butterfly distributions

Just over a half of GB butterfly species declined in geographical distribution between the period up to 1970 and 1970-82, while nearly a third of species increased. Species in all landscape types experienced very similar distributional changes.

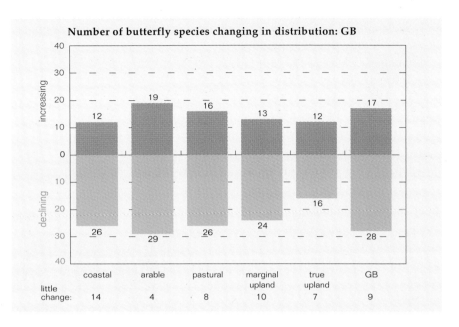

Number of butterfly species changing in distribution: GB

	coastal	arable	pastural	marginal upland	true upland	GB
little change:	14	4	8	10	7	9

Figures for butterfly species can be used to reflect the health and quality of some land-based habitats, just as dragonflies can be used for aquatic habitats. Butterfly populations can be adversely affected by both loss of habitats and habitat degradation, and are also very sensitive to the climate. Like dragonflies, some species of butterfly are highly specialised to a particular habitat or are sensitive to changes in habitat management and agricultural practices, while others are tolerant of a wide range of variation in habitat type and quality. Different species vary in their sensitivity to pollution, which means that it may be possible to gauge the health of some habitats (eg chalk grassland) by the species of butterflies present.

There are 54 species of butterfly native to GB and 3 further common immigrants (eg the red admiral) which sometimes breed successfully in this country. Many National Nature Reserves, Sites of Special Scientific Interest, and reserves of the RSPB, the Wildlife Trusts, and the National Trusts, offer protected sites for British butterfly species.

Trends in the extent of designated and protected areas is covered by Indicator s2 in the *Land cover and landscape* section.

Indicator r11 shows the proportion of GB butterfly species whose geographical distribution has changed, by landscape type, between the period up to 1970 and 1970-82.

Data for changes in geographical distribution from the Biological Record Centre (BRC) have been presented in a similar format to that for dragonflies in indicator r10, although the periods of comparison are different. Between the period up to 1970 and 1970-1982 the geographical distribution of around a half of British butterfly species declined, while nearly a third of species increased. In general, the more highly habitat-specific species declined, and the more generalist species increased in geographical distribution.

All landscape types experienced very similar distributional changes. While these figures do not relate to population numbers, it is probable that they are indicative of butterfly populations in each landscape type also being adversely affected.

Future indicator development:

Population figures for 29 of the 57 British species of butterfly are available from the Butterfly Monitoring Scheme (BMS). Analyses of population trends for 19 of these species has suggested that the populations for the majority (16 species) neither increased nor decreased significantly between 1976 and 1989. This picture appears more encouraging than that illustrated by the earlier geographic distribution data above. However, these species may not be representative of all GB butterfly species and the BMS sites are biassed towards south-east England and to nature reserves and other protected or managed sites. The coverage of BMS sites is being reviewed. Future indicator work or refinement might include population trends for butterflies based on the BMS and use these either as a replacement or in addition to the BRC's geographical distribution data.

Further indicators could also be developed for other groups of species, eg trends in moth populations using the Rothamsted Insect Survey light trap network.

r Wildlife and habitats

S Land cover and landscape

A key sustainable development issue is to balance the protection of the countryside's landscape and habitats of value for wildlife with the maintenance of an efficient supply of good quality food and other products. The indicators relevant to this objective are changes in rural land cover, in particular for agricultural land which is the dominant cover, the extent of designated and protected areas in the UK, damage to designated and protected areas, agricultural productivity, nitrogen and pesticide inputs, the loss of linear landscape features, and agri-environment land management schemes.

Indicator s1:
Rural land cover

Arable and improved grassland cover predominate in lowland landscapes while heath/ moorland and other semi-natural cover predominate in the uplands. Between 1984 and 1990, there were small net reductions in the area of arable land, improved grassland and heath/moorland cover in lowland landscapes partly because of increased urbanisation and afforestation. There was relatively little net change in upland landscapes; some improved grassland was converted to arable and there was a net loss of other semi-natural cover types, such as bracken.

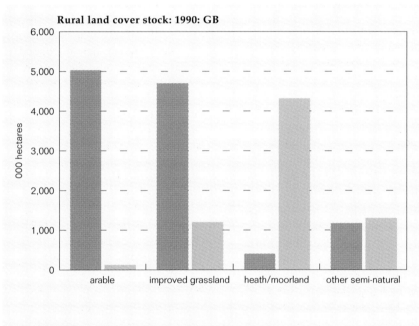

Rural land cover stock: 1990: GB

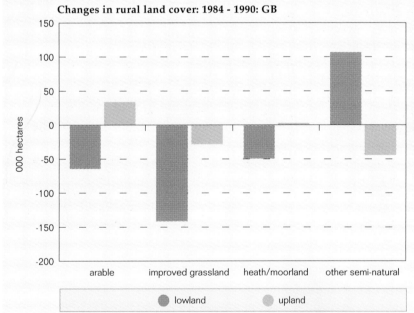

Changes in rural land cover: 1984 - 1990: GB

● lowland   ● upland

s Land cover and landscape

Agricultural land dominates the rural landscape of the UK. Changes in agricultural practices have the potential to cause positive environmental effects, such as the maintenance of valued landscapes and habitats by environmentally-friendly farming practices, as well as negative ones, such as the loss of hedgerows and walls. The drive for increased food production since the mid-1940s has resulted in an intensification of production and environmental pressures on landscapes and habitats, in particular semi-natural habitats such as ancient meadows, heaths and wetlands. Reform of the Common Agricultural Policy (CAP) in 1992, however, together with increased environmental awareness, has reduced some of the incentives to intensify production and has encouraged the improved management of rural land.

There are also voluntary incentive schemes such as the Environmentally Sensitive Areas (see Indicator s8) and Nitrate Sensitive Areas Schemes and compulsory rules designed to maximise the environmental benefits of set-aside land. Farmers are also offered free advice, for example, on farm waste and conservation, as well as environmental management of set-aside land to benefit wildlife.

Alongside agriculture, urbanisation and afforestation are the other main drivers of change in rural land cover in the UK. Indicators for these issues are presented in the *Land use* and *Forestry* sections.

Indicator s1 shows the stock of rural land (excluding forestry) in GB in 1990 and changes in stock for broad categories between 1984 and 1990.

Between 1984 and 1990, the area of arable land in lowland landscapes fell by 1 per cent mainly caused by losses to woodland, urban and semi-natural land cover types which were partly offset by the conversion of improved grasslands to cropped areas. There was also a change in the balance between crop types on arable land, with large increases recorded for wheat and oil-seed rape, and for non-cropped arable land owing to set-aside. These increases were partly offset by a large decline in the area covered by barley. The area of improved grassland fell by 3 per cent in lowland landscapes between 1984 and 1990 and by just over 2 per cent in upland landscapes with losses to arable, woodland, urban and semi-natural land cover types.

There were also some major changes between 1984 and 1990 in the balance of grassland types within managed grassland, with a large expansion of weedy grasslands and declines for well-managed grass. The small surviving area of heath and moorland in lowland landscapes in GB decreased further between 1984 and 1990, mainly as a result of afforestation. However, there was little net change in area for the great majority of heath and moorland in upland landscapes. The area of "other semi-natural land"

cover types in lowland landscapes increased by 10 per cent over the same period, with gains observed for non-agriculturally improved grass, unmanaged tall grassland, and felled woodland, but fell by 3 per cent for upland landscapes. The changes reported for semi-natural and heath/moorland cover types were generally small in relation to total stock. However, these figures are expressed in net terms which represent the balance between losses and gains and, for some land cover types, the creation of new habitats cannot compensate for the loss of older habitats. Some further measures of change in habitat quality are given in the section on *Wildlife and habitats*.

Since 1990, the UK has introduced measures, as part of the 1992 CAP Reforms, to encourage environmental management of set-aside. These measures have had a beneficial impact on agricultural land management and the rural landscape. In particular, the voluntary set-aside scheme, introduced in 1988, was superseded in 1992 by the Arable Area Payments Scheme (AAPS) which includes a compulsory set-aside requirement except for the smallest farmers. Farmers are not eligible for payments under the AAPS for land which on 31 December 1991 was under permanent crops, permanent grass, woodland or non-agricultural use. This acts as a disincentive to those farmers who claim under the Scheme (the vast majority of arable farmers) to plough up permanent pasture for arable crops. In 1995, there were some 640,000 hectares of arable land in set-aside in GB.

s Land cover and landscape

Indicator s2:
Designated and protected areas

Number and area of Sites of Special Scientific Interest: UK

NB: Known as Areas of Special Scientific Interest (ASSIs) in Northern Ireland. Data for ASSIs included from 1987 onwards

Area of National and Local Nature Reserves: UK

NNR LNR

LNRs are for GB only

Number and area of Ramsar sites: UK

Number and area of special protection areas: UK

Areas of Outstanding Natural Beauty: E & W; NI

s Land cover and landscape

There have been large increases over the last decade in the extent of designated and protected areas in the UK.

Landscapes and habitats in the UK, and a number of plant and animal species, have been influenced by human activities over the centuries. In recent decades, urban and transport development, together with agricultural intensification, have led to the deterioration or loss of some areas of land with landscape or habitat value. National and international legislation aims to protect the areas which are of special interest or outstanding quality and a number of different types of designations have been introduced for this purpose. These areas do not receive unlimited protection, rather in each case every attempt is made to strike a balance between the importance of the site for biodiversity conservation and other economic, social and health needs. Therefore, in many protected areas, limited development and economic activity continues to take place. In many cases, continuation of the latter is essential for the maintenance of the character of the landscape.

Indicator s2 shows trends in the extent of designated and protected areas in the UK.

National Parks, Areas of Outstanding Natural Beauty (AONBs) in England, Wales and Northern Ireland, and National Scenic Areas (NSAs) in Scotland are the major areas designated for their landscape importance. The

National Parks in England and Wales, together with the Norfolk and Suffolk Broads, cover some 1.4 million hectares. AONBs in England, Wales and Northern Ireland cover some 2.4 million hectares, while in Scotland, NSAs cover just over 1 million hectares.

A number of areas are also protected for their value as wildlife habitat, especially for endangered species. National Nature Reserves (NNRs), Sites of Special Scientific Interest (SSSIs) in GB and Areas of Special Scientific Interest (ASSIs) in Northern Ireland have been established under national legislation. These national designations underpin the sites protected in order to meet international obligations, such as Special Protection Areas for Birds (SPAs) and Special Areas for Conservation (SACs) under the EC Birds and Habitats Directives. Areas and sites are designated on the basis of scientific evidence of the importance of the habitat or species and the richness of biodiversity to be found there. This evidence is reviewed over time to assess whether the nature conservation interest is being properly maintained.

The area of SSSIs in GB increased by over a third between 1984 and 1995 from 1.4 million hectares to 2 million hectares, while the area of ASSIs in Northern Ireland increased 100-fold from 500 hectares to nearly 50,000 over the same period.

National Nature Reserves and Local Nature Reserves covered over 200,000 hectares in 1995 compared with around 90,000 hectares in 1984. Over the same period, the area covered by internationally designated Ramsar sites increased to 300,000 hectares from 69,000 hectares. Special Protection Areas for Birds covered nearly 330,000 hectares in 1995 compared with only 18,000 hectares in 1984.

Future indicator development:

The extent of designated areas provides only a partial picture of how well the UK is protecting its important landscapes and habitats. Some measure of the quality and health of these areas is needed to assess whether the situation is getting better or worse. The indicator on damage to SSSIs is a partial attempt at achieving this. In order to measure quality, a clearer idea is needed of the value of the site and the objectives for managing it successfully. Only then can a meaningful assessment be made of whether the UK is being successful in achieving its objectives (see indicators in the *Wildlife and habitats* section). The Joint Nature Conservation Committee have adopted common standards for monitoring SSSIs which will in future give an assessment of the quality of the nature conservation interest on each site, and will be reported upon by the statutory conservation agencies.

s Land cover and landscape

Indicator s3:
Damage to designated
and protected areas

*The area of SSSIs in GB
damaged to some degree by
development and other
economic activities has fallen
sharply since the early 1990s.*

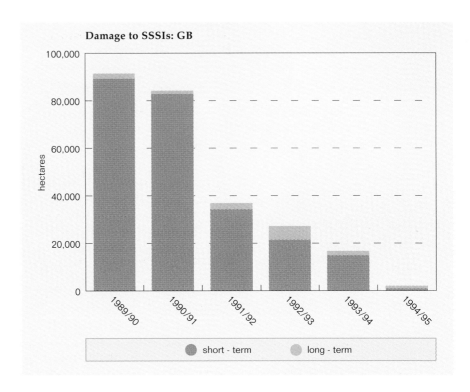

Damage to SSSIs: GB

hectares

● short - term   ● long - term

The level of protection afforded to the protected and designated areas shown in Indicator s2 varies between different types of designation. For all these areas a balance is struck between the importance of the sites for conservation purposes and the need to allow development and other economic activities such as agriculture and forestry to take place. The countryside agencies - English Nature, Scottish Natural Heritage and the Countryside Council for Wales - collect information on damage to such sites, in particular damage to SSSIs.

Indicator s3 shows the area of SSSIs damaged by a range of activities.

Figures on damage to SSSIs should be treated with caution. The data concentrate on single events such as the building of a road or the drainage of a field; they are much less effective at indicating the

deterioration in the nature conservation interest through long-term air pollution or unsympathetic land management, such as overgrazing in the uplands.

Damage to SSSIs from single events occurs at a small minority of sites. Most of the reported damage has been short-term from which sites recover; only a small fraction of damage has resulted in loss of all or part of the SSSI. There have been 2 cases of full loss of SSSI sites since 1989/90. The first occurred in 1989/90, resulting in the loss of a 7 hectare site, the second occurred in 1991/92 and resulted in the loss of a 5 hectare site. 6 SSSIs, covering 105 hectares, suffered partial loss in 1989/90, compared with 10 SSSIs (covering 13 hectares) in 1990/91, 6 SSSIs (covering 19 hectares) in 1991/92, 7 SSSIs (covering 17 hectares) in 1992/93, 11 SSSIs (covering 38 hectares) in 1993/94 and 14 SSSIs covering 242 hectares in 1994/95.

The area of SSSIs affected by long-term damage fell from 2,300 hectares in 1989/90 to around 1,450 hectares in 1990/91, then rose to around 2,650 hectares in 1991/92 and 5,800 hectares in 1992/93. Around 1,900 hectares were affected by long-term damage in 1993/94 and some 1,250 hectares (0.05 per cent of the total SSSI area) in 1994/95. The main causes of long-term damage include agricultural activities and inappropriate management.

The area of SSSIs affected by short-term damage decreased from 89,000 hectares in 1989/90 to 34,000 hectares in 1991/92, 15,000 hectares in 1993/94 and nearly 1,000 hectares (0.05 per cent of the total SSSI area) in 1994/95. Agricultural activities were the largest single cause of short-term damage in each year, except for 1994/95 when miscellaneous activities, eg pollution, unauthorised tipping and burning, were the single largest cause.

Indicator s4:
Agricultural productivity

Over the last 50 years agricultural productivity in the UK has almost quadrupled.

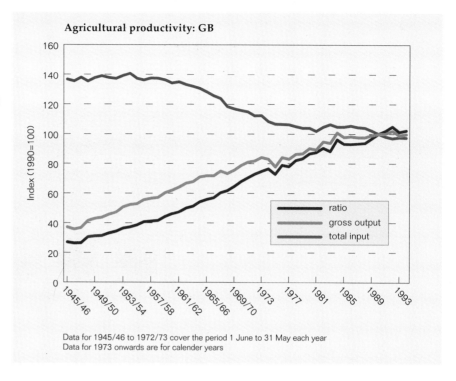

Agricultural productivity: GB

Index (1990=100)

ratio
gross output
total input

Data for 1945/46 to 1972/73 cover the period 1 June to 31 May each year
Data for 1973 onwards are for calender years

Agriculture occupies 76 per cent of the land area of the UK and contributes 1.4 per cent to UK GDP (around £7 billion). The agricultural sector employs directly over $^1/_2$ million people and, while this is only around 2 per cent of the workforce, it is of considerable importance in some rural areas. The UK produces 40 per cent of its consumption of food and feed, with the remainder met from imports; Details of trade in imports and exports of food and feed, beverages and tobacco are given in the *Overseas trade section.*

Efficient use of rural land, in particular arable land and grassland, is therefore important for maintaining a healthy, economic and social balance in rural areas and for ensuring an adequate supply of good quality food. However, as consumers expect to be able to buy an ever-wider choice of foods (not just exotic foods, but out of season products as well), self-sufficiency in agriculture is unlikely and is not, in any case, an objective of policy.

Indicator s4 shows agricultural inputs and outputs since the mid-1940s and agricultural productivity as measured by the ratio of inputs to outputs.

Agricultural productivity (the ratio of gross output to total input) increased more or less continuously between 1945 and 1994 and by almost $2^3/_4$ percent a year on average. The rate of increase has been slower over the second half of the period, at nearly 2 per cent, compared with $3^1/_2$ per cent in the first half.

Gross output rose steadily between 1945 and 1992, by around 2 per cent a year on average. The rate of increase in output was again greater in the first half, of the period at nearly 3 per cent per year than in the second half when it averaged only 1 per cent per year. Agricultural output has been restricted in the most recent years as a result of

supply controls imposed by the 1992 CAP reforms.

Total inputs declined by around 0.7 per cent a year on average between 1945 and 1994. The rate of decrease was variable over the period but averaged 0.7 per cent in both halves.

Since the mid-1980s, gross output has been more or less stable with total inputs declining, and productivity increasing, by about 1 per cent a year.

s *Land cover and landscape*

Indicator s5:
Nitrogen usage

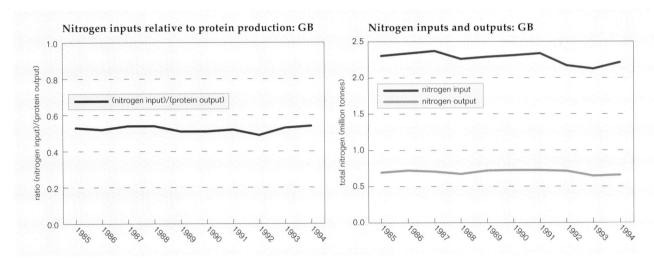

Nitrogen inputs relative to protein production: GB

Nitrogen inputs and outputs: GB

Nitrogen inputs to agricultural soils relative to protein production have been generally constant over the last decade. Inputs of nitrogen to agricultural soils increased from 1945 up to the mid-1980s. Over the last 10 years inputs and outputs of nitrogen remained broadly stable until the early 1990s. Since then, both have fallen slightly.

Nitrogen is vital for the growing of crops and rearing of livestock for food. It is contained in mineral fertiliser, organic wastes such as manures and slurries, and animal feed. Atmospheric nitrogen is also fixed in the soil by legumes. However, because crops and animals are naturally inefficient at utilising it, only a proportion of the nitrogen applied to agriculture ends up in food and other products. The quantity, timing, and method of application also affects the efficiency with which nitrogen is taken up by crops and animals.

Nitrogen that is not consumed in agricultural products is transformed in soil, air, and water in the "nitrogen cycle", a complex process influenced by many interacting factors. Some forms of nitrogen can have adverse effects on the environment (eg excess nitrate in freshwater) whilst others are benign (eg nitrogen gas, which makes up 80 per cent of the atmosphere). Protein is required by humans and animals to sustain life and is contained in crops and

livestock products. It is comprised largely of carbon, hydrogen, oxygen and nitrogen. However, protein production is mostly driven by nitrogen availability.

Indicator s5 shows agricultural outputs compared with nitrogen inputs to soils

Agricultural outputs of protein are related to crop yields and to the quantities of milk, meat, and other animal products that are produced each year. Yields vary from year to year depending on factors such as the weather, improved crop varieties and animal breeds, fertiliser inputs, feedstuffs and pesticides, as well as economic drivers (eg CAP subsidies and world commodity prices).

The first part of the indicator shows the ratio of UK inputs of nitrogen to agricultural soils over outputs in terms of protein. The protein outputs are derived by multiplying nitrogen outputs by 6.25 (which is

the conventional factor that relates the nitrogen and protein contents of organic material). This indicator follows a key principle of sustainable development philosophy in that it includes both the economic benefit (ie the production of protein for consumption by humans) and the environmental risk arising from different forms of nitrogen used in agriculture. The ratio illustrates the efficiency with which agriculture uses nitrogen to produce protein. The higher the ratio, the more nitrogen is used to produce a given amount of protein. Ideally, one would seek to maximise outputs while minimising inputs - both for economic and environmental reasons. Over the last decade, nitrogen inputs relative to protein production have been generally constant.

The second part of this indicator shows the crude input and output data from which the ratio is derived. Since 1945, the drive for increased production resulted in large increases in both inputs and outputs. Inputs reached a peak in the mid-1980s. Over the last 10 years, inputs and outputs of nitrogen remained broadly stable until the early 1990s; since then both levels have fallen. The gap between nitrogen inputs and outputs illustrates the quantity of nitrogen cycling through agricultural soils with the potential to cause pollution. The

inefficiency of plants and animals in utilising nitrogen limits the extent to which this gap can be reduced; part of the nitrogen in this is dealt with harmlessly in the nitrogen cycle. Over the last 10 years the gap has fluctuated but the trend has been for the gap to narrow as both inputs and outputs have declined.

Nitrate concentrations in GB rivers are shown in Indicator p2 in the *Freshwater quality* section and nitrate inputs to UK coastal waters are given in Indicator q5 in the *Marine* section.

Indicator s6: Pesticide usage

The overall quantity of pesticides used on cereal crops reached a peak in the early 1980s but has since declined. Within this total the quantity of herbicides , in particular, has fallen sharply. In contrast the quantity of fungicides and plant growth regulators used was higher in the 1990s than in the previous two decades.

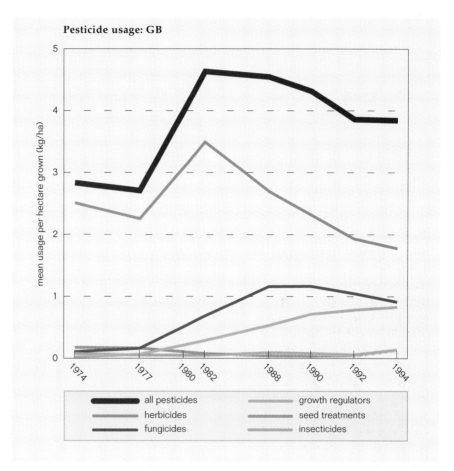

Pesticide usage: GB

mean usage per hectare grown (kg/ha)

Legend:
- all pesticides
- herbicides
- fungicides
- growth regulators
- seed treatments
- insecticides

Pesticides are important to modern agriculture and also have significant non-agricultural uses to control pests, weeds, and diseases. However, they can have an adverse effect on the environment, by impacting on non-target species of plants, insects and aquatic life, and by contaminating water abstracted for public supply.

Government policy is to encourage the minimisation of pesticide use through a strict approvals process, Codes of Practice on Use, and appropriate research and

development. In this context minimisation means that the amounts of pesticides used should be limited to the minimum necessary for the effective control of pests compatible with the protection of human health and the environment.

The levels of selected pesticides found in rivers and groundwater are covered by Indicator p4 in the *Freshwater quality* section.

Indicator s6 shows the average amount of active ingredient applied per hectare of cereals for different types of pesticides.

About 340 different chemicals are used as active ingredients in agricultural pesticides and formulated into some 3,400 different products. This indicator can thus give only a broad guide to trends in pesticide inputs to

s Land cover and landscape

agriculture. Cereals are the predominant UK crop, and pesticides applied to cereals currently account for 34 per cent of pesticide usage. The trends for cereals are typical of the situation with most other crops.

The quantity of herbicides used on cereals increased markedly up to the early 1980s, but has since declined. This decline is attributable, in part, to the development of more biologically-active pesticides, which has meant that lower quantities of these herbicides need to be applied. The quantity of fungicides and plant growth regulators used was higher in the 1990s than in the previous two decades. The tonnage of insecticides used over the last 20 years was considerably lower than the quantities used of these other 3 types of pesticides. The amount of each pesticide applied depends on many factors, including weather, the type of crop and its resistance to disease, the efficacy of the pesticide, and the level of pest and disease pressure.

Future indicator development:

The development of more precise indicators on the overall impact of pesticides is difficult owing to the wide variety of chemicals and products used. Each product poses a different level of risk to different components of the environment, and "global" indicators of risk are bound to be imperfect in some respect. Tonnage is not a good measure of the environmental impact of pesticides, particularly as no account is taken of their varying toxicities. If usage data are modified to take account of toxicity then a more complex picture emerges.

A decline in the overall mammalian toxicity of the pesticides applied is seen, but, in recent years, an increase in the potential toxicity of certain groups of pesticides to the aquatic environment has occurred. In the case of insecticides, this is associated with a switch from organo-phosphates to synthetic pyrethroids. In order to monitor the progress of the Government's pesticide minimisation policy,

indicators are being further researched in an attempt to measure more accurately the environmental risk posed by the use of pesticides. The results of this work will be used in the future as a better indicator. In general, the level of pesticide use is related to the value of agricultural production. Future work will include development of an indicator of agricultural output to set alongside indicators of the environmental impact of pesticides.

Many of the pesticides which are most commonly detected in water are of non-agricultural origin. Surveys of the use of non-agricultural pesticides were conducted in 1972 and of non-agricultural herbicides in 1989, but the results are not comparable. A further survey on the use of non-agricultural pesticides will be carried out in 1996, so in the future it may also be possible to develop an indicator of pesticides used on non-agricultural land.

s Land cover and landscape

Indicator s7:
Length of landscape linear features

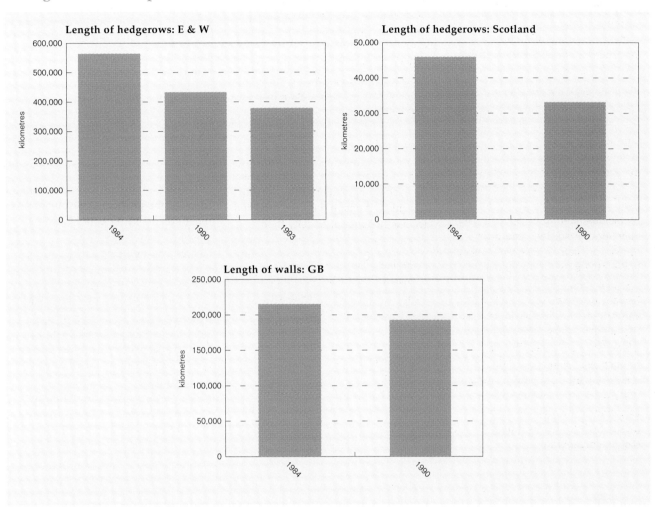

Both hedgerows and walls declined in the 1980s. Evidence from the latest survey for England and Wales suggests that hedgerows are still in decline, with many becoming derelict through neglect although more hedges are now being planted than uprooted.

Hedges and walls can be attractive landscape features of the countryside and are characteristic of many, but not all landscapes. In some cases, they are of historical importance and provide a valuable habitat for wildlife. Linear features can also act as important barriers against soil erosion in those very localised areas where erosion is a problem. In certain cases, hedgerows have been removed to facilitate more efficient use of farm machinery. More commonly, however, hedgerows and walls have suffered from lack of maintenance because of the costs involved and the fact that these boundary features are not always relevant to modern farming methods. Some of the loss of hedgerows caused by removal and neglect has been offset by new planting and restoration.

Indicator s7 shows the loss of hedgerows and walls in GB since 1984.

Hedgerow lengths in GB decreased by an estimated 150,000 km (25,000 km per year) between 1984 and 1990, of which an estimated 130,000 km (22,000 km per year) was lost in England and Wales and some 20,000 km (around 3,000 km per year) was lost in Scotland. About a third (36 per cent) of the loss of hedgerows in Britain between 1984 and 1990 was caused by uprooting and the other two-thirds through management neglect (23 per cent) and conversion to other types of boundaries (41 per cent), in particular fences. These losses were to some extent compensated for by gains through new planting and restoration. Between 1990 and 1993, the net rate of loss of hedgerows in England and Wales slowed to around 18,000 km per year, with the majority of hedgerow loss resulting from management neglect. Over the same period, the rate of new planting exceeded the rate of outright hedgerow removal

by some 800 km per year. The length of walls in GB decreased from an estimated 215,000 km to 195,000 km between 1984 and 1990 (around 3,000 km per year).

The creation and proper management of hedgerows and stone walls is promoted through schemes such as Countryside Stewardship (see also Indicator s8).

In order to prevent the removal of *important* hedgerows in England and Wales, the Government has taken powers under Section 97 of the Environment Act 1995 to make regulations to protect them. It intends to introduce these regulations in 1996.

Indicator s8: Environmentally managed land

Agri-environment schemes are voluntary and designed to promote conservation by farmers of wildlife habitats and rural landscapes. The area in England covered by management agreements under the two major farmland conservation schemes (ESAs and Countryside Stewardship) more than trebled between 1990 and 1994. The area covered by such schemes is likely to continue to increase following the launch of new agri-environment measures in 1994 and 1995.

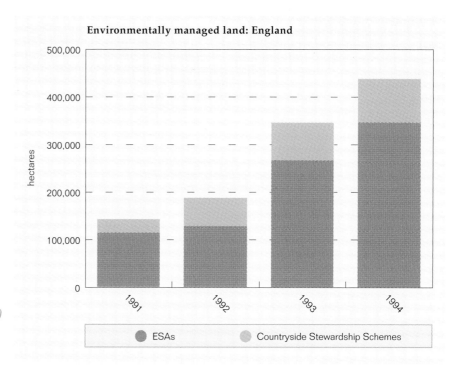

Environmentally managed land: England

Over the centuries, much of the rural landscape has been shaped by agriculture and continued management is essential to maintain the characteristics and quality which are so much a part of our natural heritage. However, many aspects of good land management are not readily quantifiable, particularly on a national scale. As a proxy, therefore, this indicator shows the extent of land covered by land management agreements, which are designed to ensure that land is managed in an environmentally friendly way, and to conserve or re-create valued landscapes and wildlife habitats, including the promotion of better management of

features such as hedgerows and traditional stone walls (see also indicator s7 on linear features).

The Environmentally Sensitive Areas (ESA) scheme operates in areas designated for their outstanding landscape or wildlife value which are threatened by changes in agricultural practices. The ESA scheme is complemented in England by the Countryside Stewardship scheme, which promotes the conservation of landscape types outside ESAs. The Rural White Paper, published in October 1995, announced the Government's intention to give priority to providing extra funding

s Land cover and landscape

for Countryside Stewardship enabling it to retain the full range of existing options and add two new options targeting traditional stone walls and banks and the remaining unimproved areas of old meadow and pastures on neutral and acid soils throughout lowland England.

Indicator s8 shows the areas of land under management agreements in the Environmentally Sensitive Areas and Countryside Stewardship Schemes.

By 1994, some 440,000 hectares of land in England - around 4 per cent of the total agricultural land area - was covered by management agreements under the ESA and Countryside Stewardship Schemes. The area under ESAs trebled between 1991 and 1994 from 114,000 hectares to 346,000 hectares. Over the same period, the area of land covered by the Countryside Stewardship scheme more than trebled from 28,000 hectares to 91,000 hectares.

As with the indicator on designated and protected areas (Indicator s2), the amount of environmentally

managed land alone does not give the full picture, since it does not measure the effectiveness or impact of the changes in terms of environmental quality. However, all agri-environment schemes are monitored and evaluated to assess the extent to which their various environmental objectives are being achieved, and the results of Indicator s8 should be viewed in the light of this information.

s *Land cover and landscape*

t Soil

A key objective of sustainable development is to protect soil as a limited resource for the production of food and other products, and as an ecosystem for vital organisms. The chosen indicators relevant to this objective are soil quality - concentrations of organic matter, acidity and concentrations of nutrients (phosphorus and potassium) in agricultural topsoils; and concentrations of heavy metals in agricultural topsoils.

Indicator t1:
Soil quality

Over the last 15 years, there has been a small increase in the proportion of agricultural topsoils found to have organic matter concentrations of <3.6 per cent and a corresponding decrease in the number of agricultural topsoils with organic matter concentrations of >7 per cent. The ploughing up of grasslands, the loss of ley/ arable rotations in some

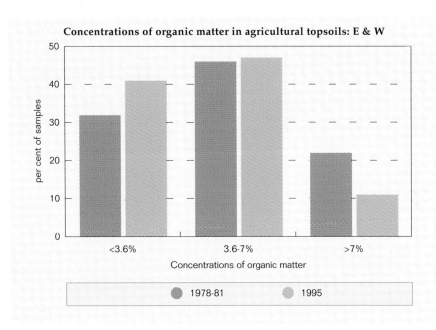

agricultural systems and other arable farming practices have reduced the organic matter content of some soils although there is not a single threshold of organic matter content below which soil structure inevitably deteriorates.

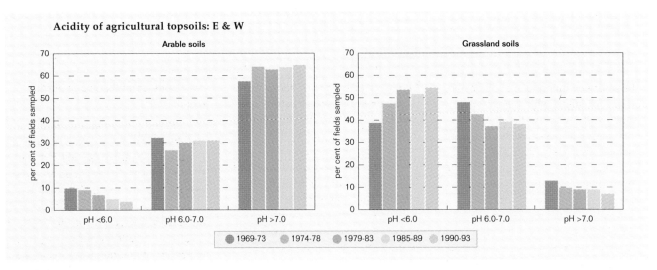

pH6-pH7 is the optimum range for arable soils. If soils become more acidic than pH6, the yields of some arable crops may be restricted. The proportion of fields below this threshold has declined since 1969. Over the same period, there has been some increase in the proportion of grassland soils below pH6. However, grassland is less sensitive to acidity and a pH below this threshold need not restrict grass growth.

Available nutrient concentrations in agricultural topsoils: E & W

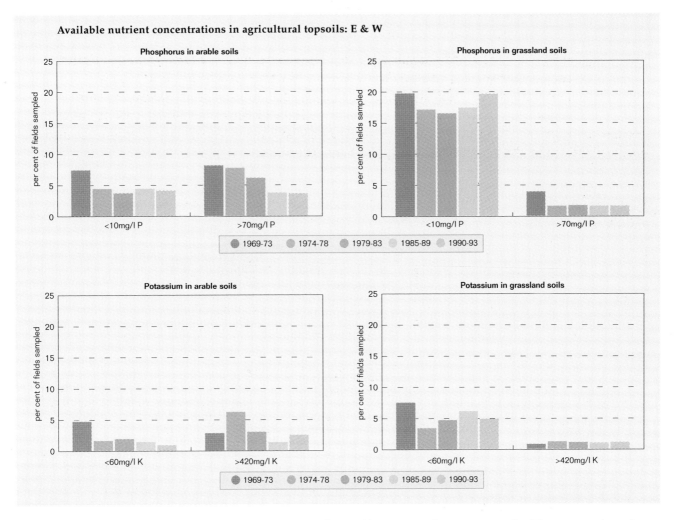

Available phosphorus concentrations below 10 mg/l in soils can restrict crop growth,. The proportion of arable soils below 10 mg/l has decreased since 1969. The proportion of arable soils above 70 mg/l also decreased over the same period. Potassium uptake is important for crop growth and growth can be restricted where available potassium concentrations are below 60 mg/l. Potassium concentrations in agricultural soils in England and Wales have been relatively stable since 1969, with no apparent long-term trends.

Loss of soil function is an important issue for sustainable development, since soil is essential for food and timber production and also provides habitats for many plant and animal species. It also has other important functions, including the ability to filter, transform and neutralise potentially polluting substances which can enter the soil from rainfall or as a result of human activities. It can act as an important reservoir for water, as a physical base for buildings and as a sink for carbon sequestrated from the atmosphere (see section on *Climate change*).

Organic matter is important for the development of soil structure and contributes to soil stability. Its adsorption properties help to regulate the movements of pollutants and contaminants in soils (see Indicator t2). Organic matter also plays an important role in the cycling and storage of plant nutrients, which are vital for food production, and low organic matter concentrations can increase the risk of erosion. Many soil organisms obtain their energy supply from the breakdown of organic matter. High organic matter concentrations can increase nitrate leaching and

emissions of methane and nitrous oxide.

Maintaining pH in arable soils at suitable levels is important for soil productivity and overall soil fertility. Productivity can be reduced as soils become acidic. The UK's climate tends to increase the acidification of soils by the leaching of nutrients. This is the result of rainfall exceeding evaporation and because of the natural acidity of rainfall, even when unpolluted.

In those areas where soils are not naturally calcareous, farmers protect their soils from acidification

t Soil

by regular additions of lime so as to maintain production potential. Highly acidic soils can also cause the mobilization of heavy metals which have accumulated naturally through the soil formation process or as a consequence of contamination, for example, as a result of atmospheric deposition of industrial emissions. Once mobilised, heavy metals can leach into, and contaminate, surface and groundwaters (see Indicator t2).

Crop growth is dependent upon the availability of plant nutrients such as phosphorus and potassium, therefore maintaining an adequate supply of these and other nutrients in soil is necessary to obtain optimum crop performance. Accumulation can occur where the application of fertilisers and manures is regularly greater than off-take in crops. Yields are likely to be restricted when soils are deficient in these major nutrients even where extra fertilisers are applied within the crop year.

Indicator t1 shows trends in concentrations of organic matter, acidity and concentrations of phosphorus and potassium in agricultural topsoils in England and Wales.

The ploughing up of grasslands, the loss of grass rotations in some agricultural systems and other arable farming practices have reduced organic matter concentrations in some soils in recent years. An analysis of 661 sites sampled under the National Soils Inventory in 1978-81 and again in 1995 shows that the proportion of samples with organic matter concentrations of <3.6 per cent increased from 32 per cent in 1978-81 to 41 per cent in 1995. The proportion of samples with organic matter concentration of >7 per cent fell from 22 per cent in 1978-81 to 11 per cent in 1995. The land-use regime at both sampling dates was either arable or short-term grass. Interpretation of these data are, however, difficult owing to the lack of knowledge of the land-use history between the sampling dates. The re-establishment of long-term leys, and the incorporation of organic matter can increase organic matter concentrations. It is expected that the introduction of agri-environment schemes (see Indicator s8 in the *Land cover and landscape section*) and, to a lesser extent the ban on straw burning should lead to enhanced organic matter concentrations over the long term, in particular where long-term grass leys are grown.

Soil acidity can restrict the growth of arable crops when the pH level falls below 6.0. Of soils sampled under the Representative Soil Sampling Scheme (RSSS), the proportion of arable soils in England and Wales with pH<6.0 fell from 10 per cent in 1969-73 to 4 per cent in 1990-93. Over the same period, the proportion of arable soils with an optimum pH of 6.0-7.0 remained broadly constant at just over 30 per cent, while the proportion of arable soils which were alkaline (ie pH>7.0) increased from 58 per cent to 65 per cent. The proportion of grassland soils with a pH of <6.0 increased from 39 per cent in 1969-73 to 55 per cent in 1990-93, however, a pH of <6.0 for grassland soils does not necessarily restrict grass growth.

Phosphorus is an important nutrient in soils and available concentrations below 10 mg/l can restrict crop growth. Under the RSSS, the proportion of arable soils sampled with phosphorus concentrations <10 mg/l decreased from 7 per cent in 1969-73 to 4 per cent in 1990-93, while the proportion of arable soils with concentrations above 70 mg/l also decreased from 8 per cent in 1969-73 to just below 4 per cent in 1990-93. For grassland soils, the proportion of soils below 10 mg/l remained fairly constant at between 15-20 per cent over the same period while the proportion above 70 mg/l fell from 4 per cent in 1969-73 to 2 per cent in 1990-93.

Potassium is also an important soil nutrient and concentrations below 60 mg/l can restrict crop growth. The proportion of arable soils with potassium concentrations of <60 mg/l was 1 per cent in 1990-93 compared with 5 per cent in 1969-73 while the proportion of grassland soils below this value fell from 8 per cent in 1969-73 to 5 per cent in 1990-93.

t Soil

Indicator t2:
Heavy metals in topsoils

Concentration of heavy metals in agricultural topsoil: E & W

Copper (mg/kg)

Below 12.6
12.6 - 18.1
18.1 - 24.9
24.9 - 43.3
Above 43.3

Cadmium (mg/kg)

Below 0.5
0.5 - 0.7
0.7 - 1.0
1.0 - 1.7
Above 1.7

Zinc (mg/kg)

Below 59
59 - 82
82 - 108
108 - 181
Above 181

Lead (mg/kg)

Below 28
28 - 40
40 - 66
66 - 123
Above 123

© SSLRC Cranfield & IACR 1996

t Soil

Enhanced concentrations of heavy metals in soils are mainly to be found in areas of present or past industrial activity.

Some soils can be naturally contaminated but human activities have increased metal concentrations in many others. Metal-based industries, fossil fuel burning, waste incineration, chemical industries and the use of leaded petrol have all contributed to an increase in the atmospheric deposition of heavy metals and are probably the largest sources of inputs to soils. The spreading of industrial wastes, sewage sludge and river dredgings on agricultural land is another source of heavy metal contamination. Sewage sludge is spread on around 1 per cent of total agricultural land, but the amount of sewage sludge applied to land is likely to increase when the dumping of wastes at sea ceases in 1998 because of the requirements of the EC Urban Waste Water Directive. Very high applications of inorganic fertiliser and animal manures can also increase heavy metal concentrations in soils. However, most of the pesticides that contain heavy metals have been withdrawn from use.

Once in soils, heavy metals are immobilised almost indefinitely as the natural removal rate is very low. Remedial treatment to reduce contamination levels are available but can be very expensive and therefore requires careful consideration of the potential benefits to be accrued from the costs that will be incurred. Tackling heavy metal contamination in soils therefore highlights the types of choices and issues we face within the context of sustainable development, although it should be recognised that this is a significant problem only in very localised areas.

Indicator t2 shows concentrations of some of the most important heavy metals in agricultural topsoils in England and Wales.

The maps for this indicator show that the range of values for each metal can be large, with the upper values above those recommended for the control of soil pollution. Elevated concentrations of heavy metals are mainly to be found in areas of present or past industrial activity, some of which goes back centuries eg lead mining in the Pennines. Some high values do, however, represent naturally occurring processes in soils. This can make it difficult to distinguish accurately between contaminants in soils derived from natural processes and those which result from human activities.

Future indicator development:

Soil is a complex environmental medium for which monitoring activities are not as extensive as for other environmental media, eg air and water. The most recent inventory of soils was undertaken for the National Soils Inventory (NSI) of England and Wales in 1979-81. Partial re-sampling of the NSI sites was undertaken in 1995 and results for organic matter are presented in Indicator t1. Further analyses of the re-sampled sites for other parameters, eg heavy metals, will be undertaken in 1996 and presented in the next Indicators publication.

The Royal Commission for Environmental Pollution (RCEP) has recently undertaken a study into environmental problems associated with soils. The RCEP's report, which is expected in 1996, may help to inform the further development of soil indicators.

The European Environment Agency in Copenhagen is to establish a European Topic Centre (ETC) for Soils in 1996. The ETC will be tasked with improving data on soil at the European level to assist policy making in the European Union and in Member States. Among the tasks of the ETC will be to develop suitable indicators for soil. The work of the ETC for Soils in this area should help to contribute to the future development of UK indicators.

t Soil

u Minerals extraction

A wide range of commercially important minerals are present and are worked in the UK. The geological extent of many of these mineral resources is large, but increasingly there are limitations on sources of supply which are free from environmental constraints. The key sustainable development objectives are to conserve minerals as far as possible while ensuring an adequate supply, to minimise waste production and to encourage efficient use of materials, to minimise environmental damage from minerals extraction, and to protect designated areas from development. Indicators relevant to these objectives are output of non-energy minerals, land worked for minerals and restored, and aggregates extracted from marine dredging. Consumption of fossil fuels is covered in the section on *Energy*.

Primary aggregates

Indicator u1:
Aggregates output

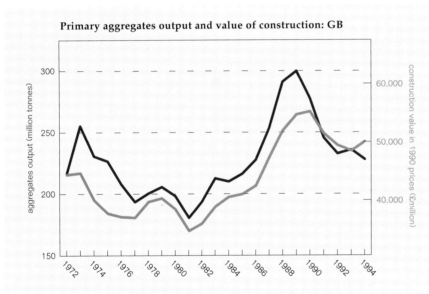

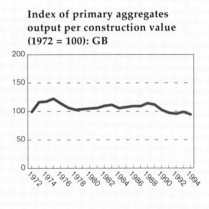

Annual output of primary aggregates (crushed rock, sand, gravel) has fluctuated since the early 1970s, although projections anticipate a growing need for aggregates in the next 20 years. Aggregates output per construction value has also fluctuated, falling from 1975 to 1978, increasing through the 1980s, and declining since 1988.

A wide range of minerals is worked in the UK. Principally this includes mineral use in construction (aggregates, chalk and limestone used in cement manufacture, clay, shale, and slate used for bricks, tiles, and roofing), fossil fuels (coal, oil, and gas), and other industrial minerals (eg specialist clays,

gypsum, salt, and silica). In quantity terms, the main minerals extracted in the UK are aggregates and fossil fuels.

The majority (90 per cent) of GB aggregates supplied is from primary materials; crushed rock constitutes about 56 per cent of the total, sand and gravel from land-based sources

about 30 per cent, and sand and gravel from marine dredging a further 4 per cent. In addition, a number of secondary materials are used as aggregates, including wastes such as colliery spoil and blast-furnace slag, and recycled materials such as demolition arisings. The principal uses of

u Minerals extraction

aggregates are for road construction, road maintenance, and new housing and housing maintenance (approximately one-third each). It is difficult to be precise about which minerals will continue to be classified as an economic resource in the long term, as this will depend on demand and new and different materials being developed as substitutes. However, it will become increasingly important to be aware of the nature, quantity, and location of mineral reserves as workable resources in environmentally acceptable areas become scarcer.

Indicator u1 compares total output of primary aggregates with the value of construction work in GB since 1972.

The pattern of output behaviour of primary aggregates is in sympathy with that of the economic cycle, which in turn affects investment programmes for infrastructure. Outputs fell from 256 to 181 million tonnes between 1973 and 1981, then rose to 300 million tonnes by 1989, before falling again to 228

million tonnes by 1994. Aggregates output per construction value has also fluctuated, falling sharply from 1975 to 1978, increasing gradually through the 1980s, and declining again since 1988 to its lowest level over the period in 1994. The recent decreases may be due to increases in re-use and recycling, together with the value of building work increasing due to high-tech finishes and components. Projections suggest that demand could be between 370 and 400 million tonnes per annum by 2011, 25 to 45 per cent higher than the 1989 peak level.

Indicator u2:
Aggregates from wastes

Only a very small proportion of wastes from construction are currently used as substitutes for primary aggregates.

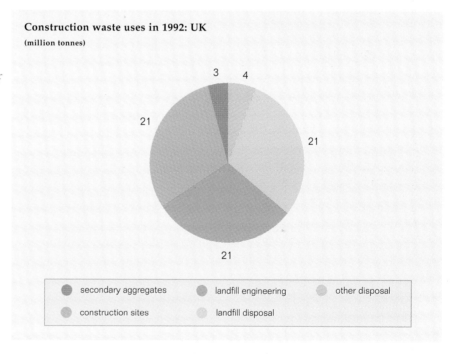

Construction waste uses in 1992: UK
(million tonnes)

- secondary aggregates
- construction sites
- landfill engineering
- landfill disposal
- other disposal

To minimise the adverse impacts of aggregates extraction in the future, the construction industry is being asked by the DoE to increase its use of secondary and recycled materials (eg from demolition rubble) by 100 per cent and reduce its dependence on land-won aggregates from 83 per cent in 1992 to 68 per cent by 2006.

Indicator u2 shows estimated proportions of construction wastes being used for different purposes in the UK in 1992.

There are no reliable figures on the proportion of total aggregates or construction aggregates that are derived from secondary or waste

materials. Recent work for the DoE estimates that construction wastes amount to approximately 70 million tonnes per annum. About 4 per cent of these are used in place of primary aggregates, and 30 per cent are used in an unprocessed form for levelling and infill at construction and demolition sites; 60 per cent goes to landfill sites, approximately half being used for temporary access and hardstanding.

u Minerals extraction

Land worked for minerals and restored

Indicator u3:
Mineral workings on land

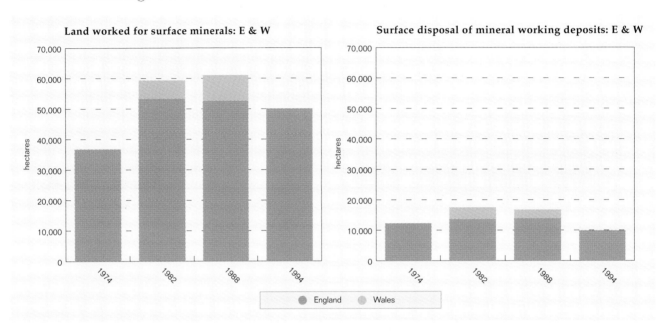

Land worked for surface minerals: E & W

Surface disposal of mineral working deposits: E & W

Legend: ● England ● Wales

60,000 hectares of land in England were being or had been worked for minerals but had not yet been restored in 1994. This was slightly less than in 1982 and 1988, but considerably more than in 1974. Land worked but not restored in Wales increased from 10,000 hectares in 1982 to 11,000 hectares in 1988.

u Minerals extraction

It is necessary to balance society's need for minerals that contribute to economic growth with the need to conserve resources and protect the environment. Minerals extraction may often impact on attractive countryside and on communities through noise, dust, visual impact, and traffic. Modern best practice is to avoid or mitigate long-term effects. Areas of land are given permission for minerals extraction and at any particular time mineral working activities will occupy a proportion of that land which has not yet been restored. For some types of workings, such as hard rock quarries, the same area of land may continue to be extracted for many years. For others, such as sand and gravel, there can be quicker progressive working and restoration.

Indicator u3 shows the amount of land which had been occupied by surface mineral workings and spoil disposal but not yet restored, in England 1974-94 and Wales 1982-88.

50,000 hectares of land in England were being or had been worked for surface minerals but had not yet been restored in 1994, representing 53 per cent of all land with permission for such working. The majority of the area was for the extraction of aggregates, particularly sand and gravel. A further 10,000 hectares were being or had been used for surface disposal of mineral working

deposits, largely spoil from deep-mined coal. The amount of land already worked or being worked for surface minerals fell slightly between 1982 and 1994, after an apparent increase between 1974 and 1982, possibly due to more complete survey data from 1982 onwards; land for spoil disposal increased slightly to 1988 before falling in 1994. In Wales, land for surface minerals increased between 1982 and 1988, while land for spoil disposal fell.

Indicator u4:
Land covered by restoration/aftercare conditions

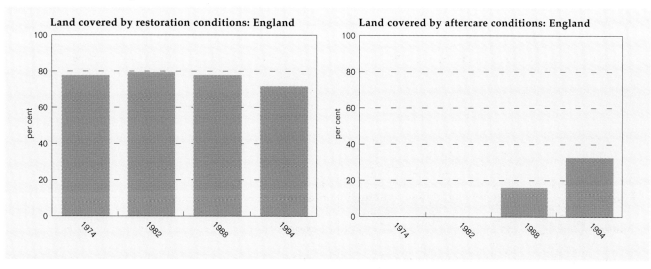

The proportion of land in England with permission for minerals extraction which is covered by some form of restoration conditions has remained between 70 and 80 per cent between 1974 and 1994, while the proportion with aftercare conditions has increased between 1988 and 1994 from 16 to 33 per cent.

Indicator u5:
Reclamation of mineral workings

On average, about 3,400 hectares each year were reclaimed from minerals workings in England between 1974 and 1994. About 400 hectares each year were reclaimed in Wales between 1974 and 1988.

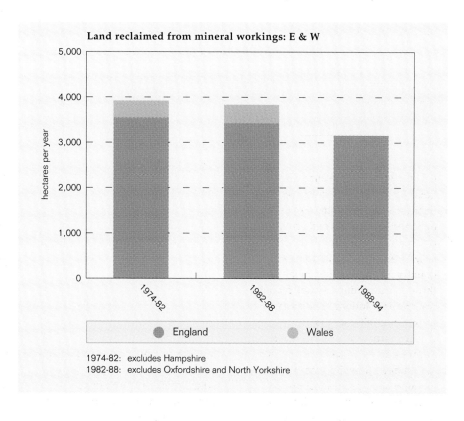

1974-82: excludes Hampshire
1982-88: excludes Oxfordshire and North Yorkshire

u Minerals extraction

It is desirable that land worked for minerals should be restored to beneficial use as soon as possible. Modern planning permissions require restoration and "aftercare" of sites following minerals extraction. Aftercare conditions, introduced in 1982, require the treatment of land for up to 5 years following the replacement of soil after mineral working has finished. Aftercare treatments include cultivation, application of fertilisers, etc, and have been shown to greatly improve the quality of land following minerals extraction.

Indicator u4 shows the proportion of land in England with permission for minerals extraction which is covered by restoration and aftercare conditions between 1974 and 1994.

Nearly 80 per cent of land in England with permission for minerals extraction was covered by restoration conditions between 1974 and 1988, but this proportion fell slightly in 1994. This fall may be due to the first-time inclusion, in the 1994 survey, of a number of sites granted permission for minerals extraction in the period 1943 to 1948 under Interim Development Orders. These sites were required to be registered by March 1992 but most are unlikely to have progressed as far as agreeing restoration and aftercare schemes. The effects of these and other similar requirements for updated planning controls for permissions granted between 1948 and 1982 should be seen in future surveys.

The proportion of land covered by aftercare conditions has more than doubled between 1988 and 1994 from 16 to 33 per cent. Increasingly, sites given permission for minerals extraction before 1982 will also be covered by aftercare conditions as old mineral permissions are reviewed and updated.

Indicator u5 reports the amount of land in England and Wales used for minerals working and spoil disposal which has been restored to beneficial use.

A total of 68,000 hectares of land was restored to beneficial use in England in the period 1974 to 1994; 28,000 between 1974 and 1982, 21,000 between 1982 and 1988, and 19,000 between 1988 and 1994. The annual rate of land reclamation slowed marginally over the whole period from 3,500 to 3,200 hectares per year. However, the rates of production and usage of some minerals (eg aggregates - see Indicator u1) fluctuated considerably over this period. Around 5,000 hectares were restored in Wales between 1974 and 1988, with the annual rate increasing slightly over the period. Around 80 per cent of land reclaimed comes from sand and gravel workings, open-cast coal workings, and deep-mined coal spoils. Over 50 per cent of the land reclaimed is used for agriculture, with a further 30 per cent for amenity uses. Anecdotal evidence suggests that the quality of reclamation achieved is continuing to improve.

u Minerals extraction

Aggregates extracted from marine dredging

Indicator u6:
Aggregates dredged from the sea

The area of the seabed around the UK licensed for dredging of aggregates has fluctuated around the 1,600 square kilometre mark since 1988.

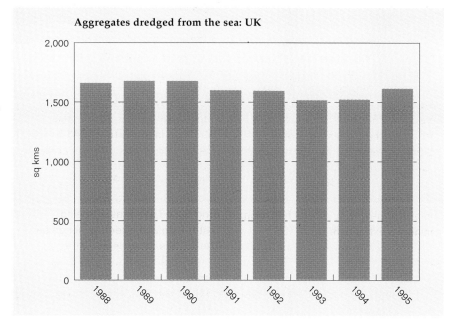

Aggregates dredged from the sea: UK

Marine extraction impacts on the marine environment in the immediate area of dredging and may affect local fishing operations. The sediment plume may also have a wider effect outside dredging areas. However, dredging takes place under strict conditions, including monitoring, to prevent coastal damage and to protect the marine environment.

Indicator u6 shows the area of the seabed around the UK covered by licences issued by the Crown Estate for marine extraction between 1988 and 1995.

There has been some variation in the area licensed for dredging since 1988. The early 1990s saw some small reduction as the Crown Estate reviewed its licences and excluded areas which were never dredged. Some new licences for dredging were granted in 1995. The area of the seabed around the UK licensed for dredging, around 1,600 square kilometres, although representing a tiny proportion (0.2 per cent) of the area of the UK continental shelf, is concentrated in a limited number of areas where dredging can impact adversely on local fishing, particularly those who operate using small boats with a limited range.

u Minerals extraction

ひ Waste

The key sustainable development objectives for waste and waste management are to minimise the amount of waste which is produced, to make best use of the waste which is produced and to minimise pollution from waste. The UK has defined a hierarchy of waste management options, which are in order of preference: reduction, reuse, recovery (materials recycling, composting, energy recovery), disposal. The objectives of waste management policy are to move waste management further up the waste hierarchy, while retaining the best practical environmental option, particularly in respect of hazardous waste.

A number of challenging and indicative targets for more sustainable waste management have been set in "Making Waste Work: A strategy for sustainable waste management in England and Wales". Similar strategies will be produced for Scotland and Northern Ireland by their new Environment Agencies. Indicators relevant to these objectives are therefore amounts of waste generated by various sectors, including special waste, amounts of waste recycled, amounts of waste from which energy is recovered, and final disposal of waste.

Indicator v1: Household waste

Household waste arisings have been relatively stable over the last ten years. This stability may be due to changes in the composition of household waste rather than any reduction in the consumption of raw materials and resources.

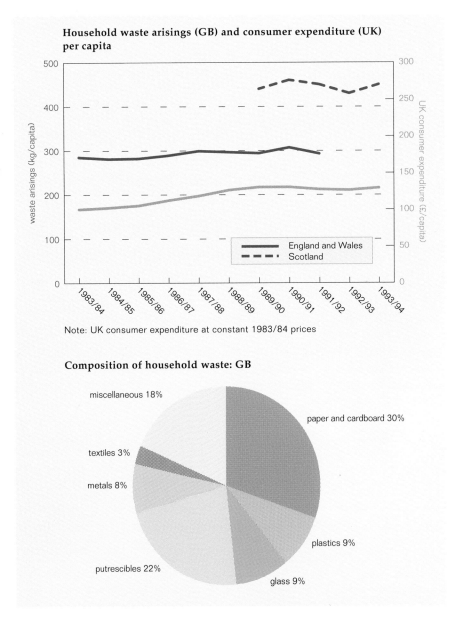

Household waste arisings (GB) and consumer expenditure (UK) per capita

Note: UK consumer expenditure at constant 1983/84 prices

Composition of household waste: GB

miscellaneous 18%

paper and cardboard 30%

textiles 3%

metals 8%

plastics 9%

putrescibles 22%

glass 9%

ひ Waste

Waste arising directly from households accounts for only around 4-5 per cent of the approximately 400 million tonnes of waste produced in the UK each year. However, it is important because sustainable development depends on positive action by individuals as well as by government or industry. Individuals can reduce waste not only directly, by recycling, reusing and composting where possible, but also through their actions as consumers, by buying long-life, re-usable, environmentally friendly products with minimal packaging. Household and similar wastes collected by local authorities also have a relatively high calorific value and are potentially a valuable source of energy. The Government has therefore set a target for the recovery of 40 per cent of municipal wastes in England and Wales by 2005.

Indicator v1 shows recent trends in household waste arisings per capita in England and Wales and Scotland, together with consumer expenditure per capita, and the composition of household waste.

The amount of household waste produced per head of the population in both England and Wales and Scotland has increased by only 2-3 per cent over the last ten years. By comparison household expenditure rose by 30 per cent over the same period. The much slower rise in per capita waste arisings may be due to increases in recycling, lightweighting of packaging and substitution of plastics for glass. In 1991/92, amounts arising amounted to 293 kg per head in England and Wales and 450 kg per head in Scotland. The considerably higher figures for Scotland are a result of local authorities including both waste arising directly from households and other similar wastes collected by them. Figures for England and Wales refer to collected waste only. Approximately 50 per cent of household waste is potentially recyclable. Around a third of household waste is paper and card of which about half is recyclable, a further 20 per cent is kitchen waste, consisting of organic matter which could be composted. A quarter is glass, metal or plastic.

Indicator v2:

Industrial and commercial waste

Industrial and commercial waste is estimated to amount to around 85 million tonnes per year. Trends are currently uncertain, but the composition of the waste stream is likely to be changing as a result of changes in the structure of industry.

Ideally, this indicator would show trends in amounts of waste arising from these sectors against some measure of output, such as that shown in Indicator a2 in *The economy* section. However, information on commercial and industrial waste arisings is not currently updated on a regular basis and is insufficiently precise to allow trends to be shown. It is tentatively estimated that industrial and commercial waste arisings amount to around 85 million tonnes per year in the UK. The composition of these waste streams is also unknown but is almost certainly changing as a result of the decline in traditional heavy manufacturing industries such as steel-making and shipbuilding, and the expansion of the electronics sector. Similarly, changes in the size, structure and working practices of the tertiary or service industries are changing the nature and importance of commercial wastes.

Commitments have been given in the Waste Strategy for England and Wales to improve the availability of data on industrial and commercial waste. A programme of work is being developed jointly within DOE and the new Environment Agency to take forward initiatives to improve data on waste arisings and disposal.

v Waste

Indicator v3:
Special waste

Special waste arisings account for less than 1 per cent of total waste arisings in the UK. Amounts can fluctuate considerably from year to year.

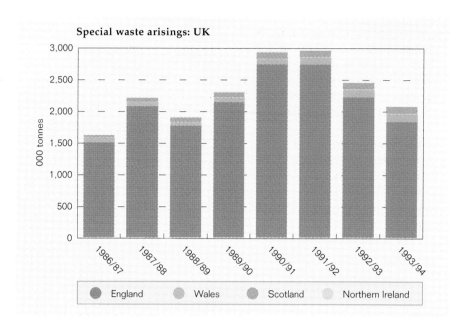

Special waste arisings: UK

Certain controlled wastes are defined in law as "special waste" because they consist of or contain substances which are "dangerous to life". Many of these substances may also pose a hazard to the environment if not carefully managed. Special wastes arise in the UK each year as by-products of industrial processes, or as spent and out-of-date chemicals from the business sector. A number of products found in ordinary household use, eg battery acids, and some household cleaners, would also be classed as special wastes when they are discarded.

The quantities of hazardous material in the household waste stream are thought to be small but the exact amounts are not known.

Indicator v3 shows the trends since 1986/87 in special waste arisings for constituent countries of the UK.

Approximately 2 to 2.5 million tonnes of special waste arise in the UK each year. This is less than 1 per cent of total waste arisings. Amounts fluctuate from year to year often as a result of large arisings of

contaminated soil from redevelopment. For example, the fall in waste arisings in England and Wales of almost one million tonnes between 1991/92 and 1993/94 is largely accounted for by a reduction in the amount of contaminated soil arising in Kent, with the completion of redevelopment at Chatham Docks. Figures for Northern Ireland, although small in comparison to England, have also fallen due to the completion of work to decommission industrial plant. These fluctuations make it difficult to identify clear trends in the quantity of special wastes arising.

Indicator v4:
Household waste recycling and composting

The proportion of household waste being recycled is still small. Considerable effort is needed on the part of local authorities, individual householders, industry and the voluntary sector, if the Government's target is to be met.

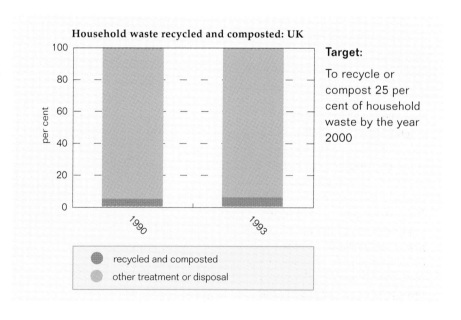

Household waste recycled and composted: UK

Target:

To recycle or compost 25 per cent of household waste by the year 2000

v Waste

One of the most obvious ways in which households can minimise the amount of waste which has to be disposed of is to recycle items such as paper, glass, plastics, metal and to compost kitchen and garden waste. This indicator, which measures the proportion of household waste recycled, is an important measure of the extent to which individuals are prepared to take action themselves to help the environment.

Indicator v4 shows the percentage of household waste in the UK which is recycled or composted together with the target for the year 2000.

50 per cent of household waste is potentially recyclable. Reliable trend information does not exist, but it is currently estimated that only around 5 per cent of household waste is recycled or composted in the UK, with around 90 per cent of waste arisings going to landfill and the remaining 5 per cent incinerated.

Indicator v5:
Materials recycling

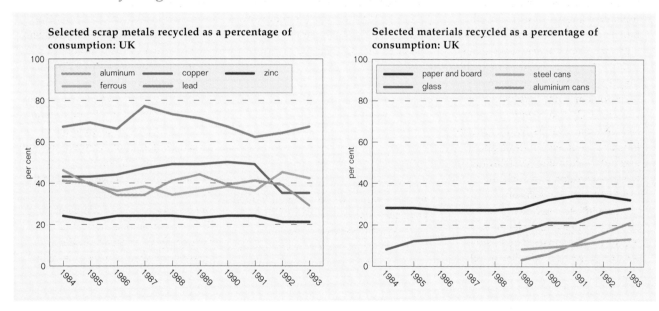

Selected scrap metals recycled as a percentage of consumption: UK

Selected materials recycled as a percentage of consumption: UK

Recycling of iron and other metals is well established and rates have changed little over the last ten years. Recycling of glass and metal cans has been increasing sharply since the second half of the 1980s.

Landfilling and incineration of wastes results in the loss of many tonnes of potentially reusable materials. Recycling of materials can contribute to the conservation of raw materials, reduce pollution from waste disposal and may contribute to reductions in energy use in and pollution from production processes where it replaces virgin materials. A number of industry groups have set targets for the recycling of their products, as part of the producer responsibility initiative.

Indicator v5 shows the amounts of selected scrap metals and other materials recycled since 1984 in the UK as a proportion of consumption.

The proportions of iron and other scrap metals recycled have hardly changed over the last ten years. In contrast, there have been marked increases in the amounts of glass, steel cans and aluminium cans recycled, mainly by households. The proportion of paper and board recycled has increased rather more slowly but stood at just over 30 per cent in 1993. Capacity for refining recycled materials and

v Waste

specifications for products manufactured can all constrain the levels of recycling achieved. For example, more ferrous metal is recovered in the UK than all other materials combined, but in the UK

the production of high quality steel limits the use of ferrous scrap, which is therefore exported to countries producing lower grade iron and steel products. Length of product life also influences the

availability of recycled materials.

Aggregates from wastes are covered under Indicator u2 in the *Minerals extraction* section.

Indicator v6:
Energy from waste

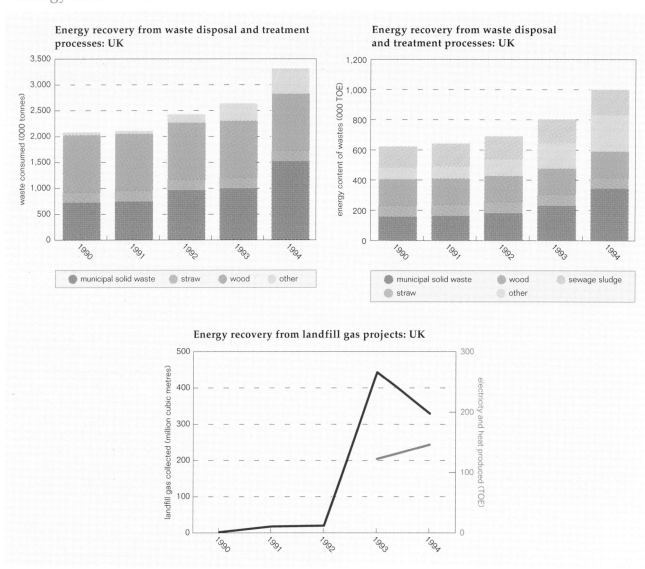

Energy recovery from waste disposal and treatment processes: UK

Energy recovery from waste disposal and treatment processes: UK

Energy recovery from landfill gas projects: UK

There have been sharp increases in the amount of energy recovered from wastes and from landfill gas under the non-fossil fuel obligation (NFFO) in England and Wales and the Scottish renewable obligation (SRO) arrangements. The amount of wastes producing energy via combustion or digestion remains small.

υ *Waste*

Where the environmental and economic costs of recycling are high, it may be better to recover energy from waste, either by burning it or by using the methane-rich gas which is generated as organic wastes decompose in landfill sites. Incineration of waste has a number of environmental advantages: it reduces emissions of methane which is a potent greenhouse gas, it reduces by up to 90 per cent the volume of waste which then has to be disposed of, and it converts waste into a material which is less biologically active and poses fewer potential risks for the environment. Using the gas produced in landfill sites reduces emissions of methane, a potent greenhouse gas, reduces local risks of explosion and enhances the restitution of landfill sites to other uses. The Government encourages waste to energy from both incineration and landfill by means of financial support through the non-fossil fuel obligation (NFFO) in England and Wales and the Scottish renewable obligation (SRO) in Scotland.

Indicator v6 shows since 1990 energy recovery from waste disposal and treatment processes and energy recovery from landfill gas projects.

Emissions of methane from landfill sites account for 46 per cent of total UK emissions of methane - around 2 million tonnes per year. It is estimated that in 1994, around 118,000 tonnes of this was recovered and used, generating an amount of electricity and heat equivalent to that produced by burning 146,000 tonnes of oil. Around 1.6 million tonnes of waste was incinerated with energy recovery in 1994.

Indicator v7:

Waste going to landfill

Landfill remains the predominant route for waste disposal in the UK and for some time yet will continue to account for the majority of UK waste disposal.

A wide range of waste types can be landfilled safely and landfill may remain the only option for some inert wastes and for wastes which are difficult to burn or recycle. However, landfill sites do have the potential to release pollutants into the water and soil, and generate significant quantities of methane which is a greenhouse gas. The Government's policy is therefore to reduce as far as possibly the amount of waste going to landfill. It has set a target for England and Wales of reducing the amount of controlled waste going to landfill to 60 per cent of arisings in 2005. It will also be introducing a landfill tax from 1 October 1996.

At present, about 124 million tonnes of controlled waste, excluding sewage sludge and dredged spoils, go directly to landfill annually. This is 70 per cent of all controlled waste going for final disposal and recovery. Controlled wastes, excluding sewage sludge and dredged spoils, account for about 40 per cent of all wastes arising in the UK.

υ Waste

W **Radioactivity**

The key objectives for sustainable development are to ensure radioactive wastes are not unnecessarily created, to ensure radioactive wastes are managed and treated in a manner which does not lead to excessive discharges or radiation doses to members of the UK population, and to ensure that wastes are safely disposed of at appropriate times and in appropriate ways. The indicators relevant to these objectives are average radiation dose to the UK population, discharges from nuclear installations relative to nuclear power generation and radioactive waste arisings and disposal.

Indicator w1:
Radiation exposure

Occupational exposure, radioactive discharges from nuclear installations and consumer products account for less than 1/2 per cent of the average individual dose of 2,600 μSv per year to the UK population from all radiation. Exposure from discharges accounted for less than 0.1 per cent of total exposure in 1991.

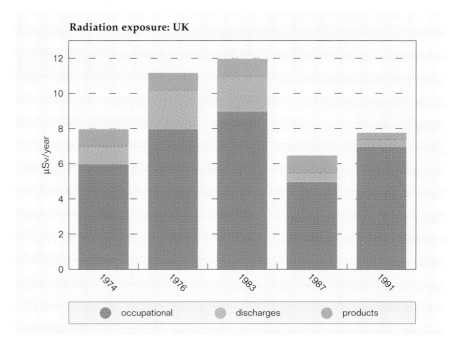

Radiation exposure: UK

μSv/year

● occupational   ● discharges   ● products

The radiation dose to individuals is an important indicator since there is an assumed linear relationship between dose received and the risk to humans of contracting cancers and other illnesses related to radiation exposure. In addition to the sources of exposure presented in Indicator w1, individuals are also exposed to artificial radiation from medical procedures and world-wide nuclear fall-out and to natural radiation, in particular radon. These sources are not covered in Indicator w1 (except for exposure of workers to radon) since they are not regarded as relevant within the context of sustainable development as set out in the UK's Strategy.

Indicator w1 shows the average radiation dose to members of the UK population from occupational exposure, discharges of radioactive wastes from nuclear installations and consumer products.

Around 85 per cent of the average radiation dose to UK individuals comes from natural sources, in particular radon, gamma and cosmic rays, but also through consumption of foodstuffs which contain various naturally occurring radionuclides. Man-made sources of radiation account for the remaining 15 per cent of population dose; medical

procedures, eg diagnostic X-rays account for most of the population dose from such sources.

The data for occupational exposure cover both workers in the nuclear industry and workers in other industries, eg radiographers and miners who are exposed to radon. Trends should be interpreted with care since the total dose has not been calculated on the same basis in each year. For example, the dose to workers in the nuclear industry halved between 1987-91 but this fall was more than offset by the inclusion for the first time in 1991 of exposure of workers to radon at above ground work places.

Discharges of radionuclides to the air and water by nuclear operators are strictly controlled. Exposure

w Radioactivity

from discharges of radioactive wastes increased in the late 1970s and early 1980s, but stricter discharge authorisation limits, based on improvements in technologies and working practices, resulted in population exposure to discharges falling in the late 1980s and early 1990s. In 1991, such discharges contributed less than 0.1 per cent of total radiation exposure in the UK and in subsequent years has further decreased.

In addition to assessing exposure of the average individual, a detailed environmental monitoring programme is carried out to ensure protection of those people living in the vicinity of nuclear sites. The programme is based on the "critical group" of people likely to be the most exposed; it is national policy that these people should not receive annual doses in excess of 1,000 μSv per year from discharges of radioactive wastes. In the early 1980s, doses to critical groups near

Sellafield were greater than 1,000 μSv per year, but this was within the then current limit of 5,000 μSv per year. Most of these doses resulted from the impact of atmospheric and liquid discharges.

There is another exposure pathway, direct shine, which is important for small groups of people living very close to some of the old Magnox stations. It has been estimated that the most exposed group of people living at one such location receive doses close to 1,000 μSv per year.

Indicator w2:
Discharges from nuclear installations and nuclear power generation

Between 1983 and 1993, nuclear power generation increased by 84 per cent. Over the same period, the toxicity of authorised discharges of radioactive waste to air and water fell by 7 per cent and 91 per cent respectively.

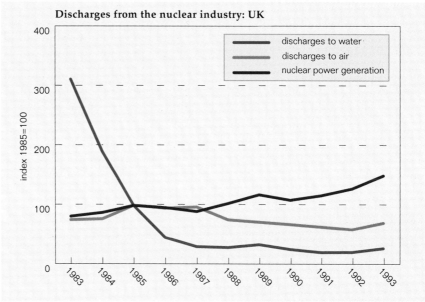

Discharges from the nuclear industry: UK

index 1985=100

Legend:
- discharges to water
- discharges to air
- nuclear power generation

Nuclear power provides economic benefits and is less environmentally damaging than fossil fuels in some respects - there are no discharges of sulphur dioxide and nitrogen oxides and only small emissions of carbon dioxide (the largest contributor to global warming). It does, however, generate radioactive wastes, some of which can be highly toxic, which are either stored (see Indicator w3) or, for the less toxic material, discharged under strict controls. Current UK policy on radioactive waste management is set out in the 1995 White Paper "Review of Radioactive Waste Management Policy - Final Conclusions" (Cm 2919).

Indicator w2 shows the amount of radioactivity discharged in relation to the amount of nuclear power generated.

The data for discharges cover discharges directly related to nuclear power generation and nuclear fuel reprocessing, both of which account for the bulk of radioactive discharges to the environment, and also discharges from defence establishments, eg Aldermaston. The data have been normalised to take account of the relative toxicities of different radionuclides that are discharged under authorisation.

In 1993, nuclear power generation was almost double the level in 1983 and accounted for some 27 per cent of all electricity generation in the UK (see Indicator e2 in the section on *Energy*). The reductions in radioactive discharges over the same period have been brought about mainly by more efficient working practices in the power generation and fuel reprocessing industries and increased emphasis on storing radioactive wastes as solids rather than discharging to the environment as liquid or gaseous wastes.

w Radioactivity

Indicator w3:
Radioactive waste arisings and disposal

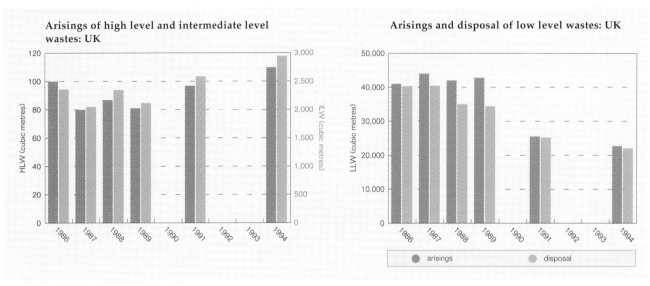

Arisings of high level and intermediate level wastes: UK

Arisings and disposal of low level wastes: UK

Arisings of high level wastes decreased by 20 per cent between 1986 and 1987 then increased by 38 per cent between 1987 and 1994, reflecting increased nuclear power generation and fuel reprocessing. Arisings of intermediate level wastes fell by 13 per cent between 1986 and 1987 then increased by 43 per cent between 1987 and 1994. Arisings and disposal of low level wastes almost halved between 1986 and 1994.

High and intermediate level radioactive wastes which are highly or moderately toxic, eg the primary concentrate from fuel reprocessing, are currently stored because they are unsuitable for disposal to the environment. Other less toxic wastes, such as nuclear workers clothing, are stored for short periods until they are disposed of in specially built shallow disposal facilities. Future arisings of solid wastes will result from the operation and decommissioning of existing nuclear installations and will need careful management to ensure damage is not caused to the environment and humans.

Indicator w3 shows the annual arisings and disposals of radioactive waste, measured in terms of volume.

Although small in volume, high level wastes contain over 95 per cent of all the radioactivity in wastes from nuclear establishments. Arisings in 1994 were estimated at 110 cubic metres compared with 97 cubic metres in 1991, 80 cubic metres in 1987 and 100 cubic metres in 1986. Intermediate level waste arisings were 2,950 cubic metres in 1994 compared with 2,590 cubic metres in 1991, 2,050 cubic metres in 1987 and 2,360 cubic metres in 1986. Low level waste arisings nearly halved from 41,100 cubic metres in 1986 to 22,800 cubic metres in 1994, whilst disposals also fell sharply from 40,400 to 22,100 cubic metres. These decreases were mainly a result of operators reducing wastes at source and to new methods such as volume compaction.

The UK is currently investigating, via UK Nirex Ltd, options for the safe disposal of intermediate level wastes (and some low level wastes unsuitable for near surface disposal) in a deep underground repository.

Future indicator development:

It would be preferable to include in Indicator w3 some measure of the radioactivity associated with stored solid wastes. Data on this are available from the radioactive waste inventories commissioned jointly by the Department and UK Nirex Ltd and covering all nuclear operators. However, further work is needed on interpreting the data to produce trends which are consistent and meaningful. It is expected that an indicator on activity levels in wastes will be covered in future Indicators publications.

w Radioactivity

Annex A

Analysis of indicators by cross-cutting issues

Sector/cross-cutting issues

Key sustainable development indicators	State/ Pressure/ Response	Health	Energy	Other industry and manufacturing	Transport	Agriculture	Construction	Leisure	Wildlife	Households and individuals
a The economy										
a1 Gross Domestic Product	S/P		x	x	x	x	x	x		x
a2 Structure of the economy	S/P			x				x		
a3 Expenditure components of GDP and personal savings	S/P									x
a4 Consumer expenditure	S/P									x
a5 Inflation	S/R									
a6 Employment	S/P									x
a7 Government borrowing and debt	S/R									
a8 Pollution abatement expenditure	P/R			x						
a9 Infant mortality	S	x								x
a10 Life expectancy	S	x								x
b Transport use										
b1 Car use and total passenger travel	P				x			x		x
b2 Short journeys	P									
b3 Real changes in the cost of transport	R									
b4 Freight traffic	P			x	x					
c Leisure and tourism										
c1 Leisure journeys	P				x					x
c2 Air travel	P									
d Overseas trade										
d1 UK imports and exports	P		x	x		x				
e Energy										
e1 Depletion of fossil fuels	S/P		x							
e2 Capacity of nuclear and renewable fuels	P/R		x							
e3 Primary and final energy consumption	P		x							
e4 Energy consumption and output	P		x							
e5 Industrial and commercial sector consumption	P		x	x						
e6 Road transport energy use	P		x		x					
e7 Residential energy use	P		x							x
e8 Fuel prices in real terms	R									
f Land use										
f1 Land covered by urban development	S/P					x	x		x	
f2 Household numbers	P									x
f3 Re-use of land in urban uses for development	R						x			
f4 Stock and reclamation of derelict land	R									
f5 Road building	P				x	x	x	x	x	
f6 Out-of-town retail floorspace	P									x
f7 Regular journeys	P				x					x
f8 Regeneration expenditure	R						x			
f9 Green spaces in urban areas	S							x	x	

Sector/cross-cutting issues

Key sustainable development indicators	State/ Pressure/ Response	Health	Energy	Other industry and manufacting	Transport	Agriculture	Construction	Leisure	Wildlife	Households and individuals
g Water resources										
g1 Licensed abstractions and effective rainfall	S/P								x	
g2 Low flow alleviation	S/P							x	x	
g3 Abstraction by use	P		x	x		x				x
g4 Abstractions for public water supply	P			x						x
g5 Demand and supply of public water	S/P									x
g6 Abstractions for spray irrigation	P					x				
h Forestry										
h1 Forest cover	S							x	x	
h2 Timber production	P			x			x		x	x
h3 Ancient semi-natural woodland	S								x	
h4 Tree health	S								x	
h5 Forest management	R								x	
j Fish resources										
j1 Fish stocks	S								x	
j2 Minimum Biological Acceptable Level (MBAL)	P/R								x	
j3 Fish catches	P								x	
k Climate change										
k1 Global greenhouse gas radiative forcing rate	P		x							
k2 Global temperature change	S									
k3 Emissions of greenhouse gases	P/R		x			x				
k4 Power station emissions of carbon dioxide	P		x							
l Ozone layer depletion										
l1 Calculated chlorine loading	S	x		x						
l2 Measured ozone depletion	S	x								
l3 Emissions of ozone-depleting substances	P	x		x						
l4 CFCs consumption	P			x						
m Acid deposition										
m1 Exceedences of provisional critical loads for acidity	S								x	
m2 Power station emissions of sulphur dioxide and nitrogen oxides	P	x	x							
m3 Road transport emissions of nitrogen oxides	P	x			x					
n Air										
n1 Ozone concentrations	S	x								
n2 Nitrogen dioxide concentrations	S	x								
n3 Particulate matter concentrations	S	x								
n4 Volatile organic compound emissions	P	x		x	x					
n5 Carbon monoxide emissions	P	x			x					
n6 Black smoke emissions	P	x			x					x
n7 Lead emissions	P	x			x					
n8 Expenditure on air pollution abatement	R									x
p Freshwater quality										
p1 River quality - chemical and biological	S	x							x	
p2 Nitrates in rivers and groundwater	S	x							x	
p3 Phosphorus in rivers	S			x					x	
p4 Pesticides in rivers and groundwater	S	x				x			x	
p5 Pollution incidents	P	x		x		x			x	
p6 Pollution prevention and control	P			x					x	
p7 Expenditure on water abstractions, treatment and distribution	P/R	x		x		x				x
p8 Expenditure on sewage treatment	R			x		x				x

Annex A

Sector/cross-cutting issues

Key sustainable development indicators	State/ Pressure/ Response	Health	Energy	Other industry and manufacturing	Transport	Agriculture	Construction	Leisure	Wildlife	Households and individuals
q Marine										
q1 Estuarial water quality	S								x	
q2 Concentrations of key pollutants	S								x	
q3 Contaminants in fish	S	x							x	
q4 Bathing water quality	S	x								x
q5 Inputs of contaminants	P			x					x	
q6 Oil spills and operational discharges	P		x						x	
r Wildlife and habitats										
r1 Native species at risk	S								x	
r2 Breeding birds	S					x			x	
r3 Plant diversity in semi-improved grassland	S					x			x	
r4 Area of chalk grassland	S					x			x	
r5 Plant diversity in hedgerows	S					x			x	
r6 Habitat fragmentation	S				x	x			x	
r7 Lakes and ponds	S					x			x	
r8 Plant diversity in streamsides	S					x			x	
r9 Mammal populations	S								x	
r10 Dragonfly distributions	S					x			x	
r11 Butterfly distributions	S					x			x	
s Land cover and landscape										
s1 Rural land cover	S					x			x	
s2 Designated and protected areas	S					x		x	x	x
s3 Damage to designated and protected areas	P							x	x	x
s4 Agricultural productivity	S					x				
s5 Nitrogen usage	P	x				x			x	
s6 Pesticide usage	P	x				x			x	
s7 Length of landscape linear features	S					x			x	x
s8 Environmentally managed land	R					x			x	
t Soil										
t1 Soil quality	S								x	
t2 Heavy metals in soils	S	x		x		x			x	
u Minerals extraction										
u1 Aggregates output	P						x			
u2 Aggregates from waste	R						x			
u3 Mineral workings on land	P		x	x			x		x	
u4 Land covered by restoration / aftercare conditions	R									
u5 Reclamation of mineral workings	R		x	x			x		x	
u6 Aggregates dredged from the sea	P									
v Waste										
v1 Household waste	P									x
v2 Industrial and commercial waste	P			x						
v3 Special waste	P	x		x						
v4 Household waste recycling and composting	R									x
v5 Materials recycling	R			x						
v6 Energy from waste	R		x							
v7 Waste going to landfill	P									
w Radioactivity										
w1 Radiation exposure	P	x	x							x
w2 Discharges from nuclear installations and nuclear power generation	P	x	x							
w3 Radioactive waste arisings and disposal	P	x	x						x	

Annex A

Annex B
Sources, references and details of measurement of individual indicators

a The economy

Indicator a1: Gross Domestic Product

Sources: CSO; OPCS.
References: *Economic Trends Annual Supplement 1996:* table 1.2 - HMSO, 1996.
Annual Abstract of Statistics 1995: table 2.1 - HMSO, 1995.

Gross Domestic Product (GDP) is the total of all economic activity taking place in the UK before providing for depreciation. The measure used here is GDP at constant (1990) market prices. This has been divided by the total population to give GDP per head.

Indicator a2: Structure of the economy

Source: CSO.
Reference: *United Kingdom National Accounts 1995:* table 2.2 - HMSO, 1995 [ISBN 0-11-620710-8].

The gross output of each major industry sector is the basis for showing its percentage contribution to the output measurement of GDP. For information on the environmental industry see *Towards a Statistical Profile of the UK Environmental Industry* in Statistical News - HMSO, summer 1995.

Indicator a3: Expenditure components of GDP and personal savings

Source: CSO.
Reference: *Economic Trends Annual Supplement 1996:* tables 1.3 and 1.6 - HMSO, 1996.

Consumers' expenditure covers all personal expenditure on goods, durable and non-durable, and services, including the value of income in kind, imputed rents for owner-occupied dwellings and the purchase of second-hand goods less the proceeds of sales of used goods.

Expenditure by Government includes that of central and local government. Investment comprises expenditure on the replacement of and additions to existing fixed assets, which include dwellings, other new buildings and works, vehicles, plant and machinery. Net transactions in land and existing buildings are also included. The balancing items are changes in levels of stocks and work in progress and the difference between imports and exports of goods and services.

Personal saving is derived from the difference between personal income and expenditure.

Indicator a4: Consumer expenditure

Sources: CSO; OPCS.
References: *Economic Trends Annual Supplement 1996:* table 1.3 - HMSO, 1996.
Annual Abstract of Statistics 1995: table 2.1 - HMSO, 1995.

Consumers' expenditure - see text for Indicator a3 - is expressed at 1990 prices. It has been divided by the total population to give expenditure per head.

Indicator a5: Inflation

Source: CSO.
Reference: *Economic Trends, December 1995:* table 3.1 - HMSO, 1995.
[Similar publications were produced by HMSO for earlier periods]

Inflation is defined here as the annual percentage change in the retail price index excluding mortgage interest payments. This is known as RPIX.

Indicator a6: Employment

Sources: CSO; OPCS.
References: *Employment Gazette Historical Supplement,* October 1994: table 1.12.
Labour Force Survey Quarterly Bulletin, December 1995.
Population Trends, Winter 1995: table 6 - HMSO, 1995.
[Similar publications were produced by HMSO for earlier periods]

The number of employees in employment in each industry sector are obtained from regular surveys of employers. The surveys obtain a count of civilian jobs of employees paid by an employer who runs a PAYE scheme. Participants of employment and training schemes are included if they have a contract of employment. Members of HM Forces, homeworkers and private domestic servants are excluded. Individuals holding 2 jobs with different employers will be counted twice. The number of self-employed are currently obtained from the Labour Force Survey.

Working age runs from the minimum school leaving age to the beginning of state retirement age. Thus, the population consists of men aged 16 to 64 and women aged 16 to 59.

The measure of unemployment used is claimant unemployment. This includes all those available for work who claim benefits at Employment Service Offices. It therefore includes those who claim Unemployment benefit, Income Support or National Insurance Credits. The unemployment rate is the number of claimant unemployed as a percentage of the estimated total workforce (defined as the sum of unemployed claimants, employees in employment, self-employed, HM Forces and participants in Government training programmes) at mid-year.

Indicator a7: Government borrowing and debt

Sources: CSO; Bank of England.
References: *Economic Trends Annual Supplement 1996:* table 5.5 - HMSO, 1996.
Bank of England Statistical Abstract 1995 Part 1: table 17.1 - Bank of England, 1995.

The Public Sector Borrowing Requirement (PSBR) is the amount borrowed by the Government during the financial year to cover the gap between its income and spending; it includes the requirements of central and local government and public corporations. The national debt comprises the total liabilities of the National Loans Fund. This includes the nominal value of all issued stocks. The measure used here, the net debt of the public sector, equals the market holdings of the national debt *plus* any other holdings of central government debt *less* the public sector's holdings of liquid assets. [Further details are given in November issues of the *Bank of England Quarterly Bulletin.*]

Indicator a8: Pollution abatement expenditure

Expenditure on environmental protection is difficult to define and quantify. It is often an integral part of expenditure on goods and services; increasingly, environmental impacts are taken into account in the design and processes used to manufacture goods. This is often referred to as "clean technology". It is easier to identify the so-called "end of pipe" technology, where additional pollution control systems are added to the production process. At present in the UK, most of the expenditure is believed to be of this latter type. Environmental expenditure can also cover a number of other activities. In addition to pollution abatement/control, it includes expenditure on conservation, education and training, research and development, management of natural resources, improvement of amenities and general administrative expenditure. Expenditure may be by central government, local government, businesses, individuals and non-profit making organisations.

Indicator a9: Infant mortality

Source: OPCS.
References: *Annual Abstract of Statistics 1995:* table 2.18 - HMSO, 1995.
Population Trends, Winter 1995: table 8 - HMSO, 1995.

The rate of infant mortality is expressed as the ratio of the number of deaths of infants less than 1 year old (excluding still births) per 1000 live births.

Indicator a10: Life expectancy

Source: OPCS.
References: *Social Trends 25:* table 7.2 - HMSO, 1995.
Population Trends, Winter 1995: table 12 - HMSO, 1995.

The measure used is, at birth, the average number of years that men and women can be expected to live, based on the current rates of mortality at each age. There has always been a difference in men's and women's life expectancies, but this difference has narrowed in recent years.

b   Transport use

Indicator b1:   Car use and total passenger travel

Source: DOT.

Reference: *Transport Statistics Great Britain 1995:* table 9.1 - HMSO, 1995 [ISBN 0-11-551716-2].

Figures are estimated from a range of sources relevant to the mode of transport, eg bus, coach and rail receipts, road lengths and - from the *National Travel Surveys* - number of passengers per vehicle. Figures of total travel in passenger miles have been divided by the total population to give figures which are more readily related to individuals' own travel patterns. The figure for car-use includes cars, taxis and light vans.

Indicator b2:   Short journeys

Source: DOT.

Reference: *National Travel Survey 1992/94:* table 2.7 - HMSO, 1995.

DOT collects information in their *National Travel Surveys* for GB on the use of the various transport modes; this enables comparisons of the relative importance of each mode to be made over time. The main identifiable modes documented are cars, taxis, light vans, motor cycles, pedal cycles, buses and coaches (local and other) and rail. Some information on walking is also included.

Indicator b3:   Real changes in the cost of transport

Source: CSO.

Reference: *Transport Statistics Great Britain 1995:* table 1.23a - HMSO, 1995 [ISBN 0-11-551716-2].

Components used were bus and rail fares, total motoring and petrol/oil. Figures were converted to real increases using the "all items RPI".

Indicator b4:   Freight traffic

Source: DOT.

Reference: *Transport Statistics Great Britain 1995:* table 9.3 - HMSO, 1995 [ISBN 0-11-551716-2].

The indicator shows, for road and rail traffic, the tonneage of freight lifted and its movement expressed in tonne-miles.

c   Leisure and tourism

Indicator c1:   Leisure journeys

Source: DOT.

Reference: *National Travel Survey 1992/94:* table 2.12 - HMSO, 1995.

Information collected by DOT in its *National Travel Surveys* includes identifying the purpose of each journey. This indicator shows for each type of journey which may be regarded as a leisure trip - holidays, visiting friends, day trips or participating in sports and entertainment events - the distance travelled per person per year.

Indicator c2:   Air travel

Source: International Passenger Survey

Reference: *Transport Statistics Great Britain 1995:* table 1.7 - HMSO, 1995 [ISBN 0-11-551716-2].

Figures exclude visits to the Irish Republic by UK residents and visits to the UK by Irish Republic residents; figures include North American visitors to the UK via the Irish Republic; figures exclude passengers changing planes at UK airports.

d   Overseas trade

Indicator d1:   UK imports and exports

Food, beverages and tobacco; other basic materials (including fuels); manufactured goods

Source: DTI.

Reference: *Monthly Review of External Trade Statistics:* tables B1, B6, C1 and C6 - CSO, 1995

Figures on UK imports and exports have been derived by converting data to £ billion at constant 1990 values using volume indices.

Annex B

Wood and wood products

Source: FC.
References: *Forest Industry Yearbook 1995* - Forestry Industry Council of Great Britain, 1995.
                  Forestry Commission Facts and Figures 1994/95 - FC, 1995.
                  Digest of Statistics 1975/76 - FC, December 1976.
                  [Similar publications were produced by the Forestry Industry Council of Great Britain and FC for earlier years]

Figures have been presented in £ billion, calculated from the volumes traded (measured in *Wood Raw Material Equivalent* - WRME) converted to 1990 values using the average 1990 values per m³ WRME separately for imports and exports.

Leisure travel; other services

Source: CSO.
Reference: *UK Balance of Payments, 1995:* tables 1.3 and 3.5 - HMSO, 1995.

Figures on UK imports and exports have been derived by converting data to £ billion at constant 1990 values using volume indices. "Other services" is all services except for "leisure travel".

Hazardous waste

Sources: DOE; SO; DOE(NI).
Reference: *Digest of Environmental Statistics No.17:* tables 7.8 to 7.11 - HMSO, 1995 [ISBN 0-11-753104-9].

Information on imports to and exports from the UK is derived from the consignment notes which were required to accompany all international movements of hazardous wastes under the *Transfrontier Shipment of Hazardous Wastes Regulation 1988*. Hazardous waste is defined as special waste under the terms of the *Control of Pollution (Special Waste) Regulations 1980*, unless it is deemed "special" solely because it consists of or contains any of the following substances: acids and alkalis arising from uses other than surface treatment and finishing of metals, barium compounds, inorganic sulphur compounds (except thiocyanates), nickel and nickel compounds, organic solvents, phosphorus and its compounds, silver, vanadium, zinc compounds or is a medicinal product.

e   **Energy**

Indicator e1:   Depletion of fossil fuels

Source: DTI.
References: *Digest of United Kingdom Energy Statistics 1995:* table A2 - HMSO, 1995 [ISBN 0-11-515368-3].
                  The Energy Report 1995: tables 5.1 and 5.2 - HMSO, 1995.

Resource depletion rates since 1970 are cast in terms of the proven and probable reserves remaining as estimated in 1994, rather than known reserves at the time. For oil and gas, past reserves have been calculated by taking current reserves estimates and adding successive year's extraction figures. Currently, reserves are estimated at around 1.5 billion tonnes of oil and 1,500 billion cubic metres of natural gas, but these estimates continue to increase each year as more reserves are confirmed. Figures for coal reserves are less easy to obtain. The remaining reserves at existing deep mines and opencast sites plus the proven reserves in potential opencast sites at the end of 1994 are estimated at 1 billion tonnes. This represents the economically viable reserves at the time. The depletion rate in 1994 was about 5 per cent. Data on this basis for earlier years are not available; it is therefore not possible to present a time series of coal reserves depletion. The UK is known to possess substantial additional resources of coal, though these are not at present economic to develop.

Indicator e2:   Capacity of nuclear and renewable fuels

Source: DTI.
Reference: *Digest of United Kingdom Energy Statistics 1995:* table 50 - HMSO, 1995 [ISBN 0-11-515368-3].

The capacity of nuclear power stations shown for each year represents the generating capacity of all generating companies at the end of March the following year. Since 1990, the Energy Technology Support Unit has been undertaking an ongoing study on behalf of the DTI to develop and maintain an inventory of all renewable energy sources in the UK. These include: active solar heating, photovoltaics, onshore wind power, wave power, large and small scale hydro, biofuels and geothermal aquifers. Natural flow hydro is the source of most of the electricity generated from renewable sources, with much of the remainder coming from biofuels.

Indicator e3:   Primary and final energy consumption

Source: DTI.
Reference: *Digest of United Kingdom Energy Statistics 1995:* tables A4 and A5 - HMSO, 1995 [ISBN 0-11-515368-3].

Primary energy consumption represents the total UK consumption of coal, petroleum, natural gas, nuclear, natural flow hydro and renewable fuels, including consumption for conversion into electricity and other secondary fuels. Final energy consumption of primary and secondary fuels excludes the fuel industry's own use and conversion, transmission and distribution losses, although it includes conversion losses by final users. In both cases, data on individual fuels in original units of measurement are converted to a common energy unit, the tonne of oil equivalent, using calorific values and conversion factors appropriate to each fuel. Trends in primary energy consumption are compared with those of final energy consumption.

Indicator e4:   Energy consumption and output

Sources: DTI; CSO.
References: *Digest of United Kingdom Energy Statistics 1995:* table A5 - HMSO, 1995 [ISBN 0-11-515368-3].
     Economic Trends Annual Supplement 1996: table 1.2 - HMSO, 1996.

The left-hand chart shows trends in total primary energy consumption from all fuel sources, expressed in million tonnes of oil equivalent, and trends in GDP at 1990 prices. The scales for these 2 series have been designed to start off at the same point in 1970 to convey, thereafter, relative rates of change. The right-hand chart shows the "energy ratio", ie energy consumption per unit of GDP, indexed to a value of 100 in 1970. These comparisons give an indication of the extent to which growth in GDP has outstripped the rates of growth in energy consumption, reflecting lower energy requirements per unit of output.

Indicator e5:   Industrial and commercial sector consumption

Source: DTI.
Reference: *Digest of United Kingdom Energy Statistics 1995:* tables 6 and A5 - HMSO, 1995.

Trends in industrial and service sector energy consumption from all fuel sources, expressed in million tonnes of oil equivalent, are compared with these sectors' contributions to GDP. The service sector includes commercial and public sector premises, ie offices, shops and warehouses. The scales for these 2 series in the left-hand chart have been designed to start off at the same point in 1970 to convey, thereafter, relative rates of change. The right-hand chart shows the ratio between the 2 series, indexed to a value of 100 in 1970.

Indicator e6:   Road transport energy use

Source: DTI; DOT.
References: *Digest of United Kingdom Energy Statistics 1995:* table A5 - HMSO, 1995 [ISBN 0-11-515368-3].
     Transport Statistics Great Britain 1995: tables 2.1 and 8.4 - HMSO, 1995 [ISBN 0-11-551716-2].

The estimated consumption of motor spirit and derv in tonnes of oil equivalent has been analysed into usage by passenger and goods vehicles. For the years 1970-81 the apportionments are published in *Transport Statistics* annual volumes; for the years 1982-94 the estimated apportionments of consumption of fuel type by vehicle type have been calculated from the percentages published in *Transport Statistics* annual volumes. The resulting tonnages have then been converted to tonnes of oil equivalent using average gross calorific values published in the *Digest of United Kingdom Energy Statistics 1995*: table A18. Although vehicle performance varies with type of fuel and type of vehicle, no adjustments for these variations have been made in the calculations. Thus the comparisons of petroleum tonnages are made directly with passenger-miles travelled and with goods tonne-miles moved. The scales for these 2 series in the left-hand charts have been designed to start off at the same point in 1970 to convey, thereafter, relative rates of change. The right-hand charts shows the ratio between the 2 series, indexed to a value of 100 in 1970. The data on transport energy consumption is for the UK, whereas the data on passenger and freight traffic published in *Transport Statistics* are for GB. Equivalent data back to 1970 for Northern Ireland are not readily available but this should not invalidate the relative trends shown in the charts.

Indicator e7:   Residential energy use

Sources: DTI; DOE.
References: *Digest of United Kingdom Energy Statistics 1995:* table A5 - HMSO, 1995 [ISBN 0-11-515368-3].
     Projections of Households in England to 2016 - HMSO, 1995.

A further category of energy users is those in domestic residential premises. Here the comparisons of energy consumption are made with the number of households. The scales for these 2 series in the left-hand chart have been designed to start off at the same point in 1970 to convey, thereafter, relative rates of change. The right-hand chart shows average household electricity, gas and other energy (solid fuels and oil) use in terms of kilowatt-hours.

Indicator e8:   Fuel prices in real terms

Source: CSO.
Reference: *Digest of United Kingdom Energy Statistics 1995:* table A14 - HMSO, 1995 [ISBN 0-11-515368-3].

The 2 fuel components of the Retail Prices Index are fuels used in the home (coal and other solid fuels, gas, electricity, heating oils and other petroleum products) and petrol and motor oil. The other fuel component from the Producer Price Index is fuels purchased by the manufacturing industry. The fuel price indices have been rebased to 1974=100 and deflated to show the changes in real terms, ie after adjustment for inflation.

Annex B

f   Land use

Indicator f1:   Land covered by urban development

Source: DOE.

Reference: Bibby, P. and Shepherd, J. (South East Regional Research Laboratory) *Urbanization in England: Projections 1991-2016* - HMSO, 1996 (to be published).

Land in urban uses comprises all land, wherever it occurs, which is used for housing, transport, utilities, industry, commerce, community services or is vacant urban land. It is defined by reference to the function of individual parcels of land, rather than location, and thus includes land which lies outside settlements, but which is used for any of the above purposes. Land use change statistics, ie hectares of land changing from one classified use to another, have been combined with housing completions data to produce an estimate for the number of hectares of land required to accommodate 1,000 dwellings and the associated infrastructure such as transport, employment, retail and leisure. This measure has then been applied to the projected growth in the number of households. The resulting "urbanization" projections provide estimates of the growth in land in urban uses which may be necessary to accommodate the projected increase in households.

Land Use Change Statistics are recorded for the DOE by Ordnance Survey (OS) as part of its map revision process. Housing completions data are collected by the DOE, and provide a simple and direct measure of housing change. Household projections are based on Office of Population Censuses and Survey (OPCS) population projections, including changes in the age structure of the population, and Government Actuary's Department (GAD) marital status projections. Projections for England are based on the 1992 mid-year population projections. The projections for the area of England in urban uses were developed through a research project undertaken for the DOE. The results have been published in *Urbanization in England: Projections 1991-2016*.

Indicator f2:   Household numbers

Sources: DOE; SO; WO; DOE(NI).

References: *Projections of Households in England to 2016* - HMSO, 1995.

A household is defined as a person living alone, or a group of people who share common housekeeping or a living room. Household formation data for 1971, 1981 and 1991 have been derived from the population censuses undertaken in these years by OPCS. Data on household formation are also available for years between censuses and have been derived from information collected by CSO under the Labour Force Survey. The 1991 figure for households includes an estimate to account for the number of households not recorded in the 1991 census owing to the under-count of population.

Household projections are based on OPCS population projections, including changes in the age structure of the population, and GAD status projections. Projections for England and Wales are based on the 1992 mid-year population projections. Projections for Scotland are based on 1989 mid-year population estimates. The projections data are trend-based and illustrate what would happen if past trends in household formation were to continue in the future. They are not policy-based forecasts and therefore do not provide a picture of what the Government expects or intends to happen. The projections are heavily dependent on the population projections and the assumptions embodied in them on internal and international migration. They depend also on marital status projections, including cohabitation. Projections of numbers of households therefore cannot be regarded as precise predictions for future years and uncertainties increase the further into the future the projections are made.

Indicator f3:   Re-use of land in urban uses for development

Source: DOE.

Reference: *DOE Statistical Bulletin; Land Use Change In England No.10* - HMSO, 1995.

The DOE has obtained land use change statistics from OS since 1985. Details of changes in land use are recorded by OS as part of its map revision work in England. New uses and previous uses of land observed by OS surveyors are each assigned to 1 of 24 use categories. These categories can be assembled into 10 groups, which in turn can be aggregated into 2 broad divisions: urban and rural. Land in urban uses comprises all land which is used for housing, transport, utilities, industry, commerce, community services, or is vacant urban land.

The changes recorded by OS in any one year depend on resources and their deployment on map revision surveys. The main consequence of OS map revision policy is that physical development, such as new houses or industrial building, tends to be recorded relatively sooner than changes between other uses, such as agriculture and forestry. Land use changes will not necessarily be recorded in the same year in which they occur. Thus for each land use change the approximate year of change has to be judged by the OS surveyors.

The information relates only to map changes recorded by OS between 1985 and 1994 in England for which the year of change is judged to have been the years shown on the chart. For data received between 1989 and 1992, only the dates of change judged to have occurred in the preceding 5 years are recorded to the nearest year. Dates of changes which occurred more than 5 years previous to the surveys were recorded in quinquennial bands to the nearest 5 years.

Indicator f4:   Stock and reclamation of derelict land

Source: DOE.
Reference: *Survey of Derelict Land in England, 1993* - HMSO, 1995.

The *Derelict Land Surveys* of 1982, 1988 and 1993 assessed the stock of derelict land in England, how much of this stock justified reclamation and how much land had been reclaimed between surveys. In addition, the 1988 and 1993 surveys gathered data on the beneficial uses to which reclaimed land had been put. Information was collected from local authorities. The definition of derelict land used in all the surveys was "land so damaged by industrial or other development that it is incapable of beneficial use without treatment".

Indicator f5:   Road building

See source, reference and text for Indicator f3.

Indicator f6:   Out-of-town retail floorspace

Source: Oxford Institute of Retail Management, Templeton College.
Reference: Unpublished.

The data have been derived from a comprehensive survey of out-of-town retail developments of 5,000 m² (50,000 sq ft) or over. Research into new developments involves a combination of field surveys, retailers' branch lists, company reports and press cuttings, supported by information from local authority planning departments.

Indicator f7:   Regular journeys

Source: DOT.
Reference: *National Travel Survey 1992/94:* table 2.12 - HMSO, 1995.

The data have been derived from the *National Travel Surveys* for GB undertaken by DOT continually since 1988. Analyses are produced covering 3-year periods since 1988 in order to provide a large enough sample for cross-sectional analysis. The surveys provide estimates on the number of journeys and the total distance travelled by type of vehicle and by journey purpose.

Indicator f8:   Regeneration expenditure

Source: DOE.
Reference: *DOE Annual Report 1995, The Government's Expenditure Plans 1995-96 to 1997-98* - HMSO, 1995.

The expenditure programmes covered include all those incorporated in the Single Regeneration Budget (SRB), established in 1994, plus other regeneration programmes such as Manchester Regeneration, Coalfield Areas Fund, Urban Development Grant and the European Regional Development Fund. Although many of the programmes in the SRB have been targeted previously at priority urban areas, the new SRB Challenge Fund supports regeneration initiatives anywhere in England.

Indicator f9:   Green spaces in urban areas

No published material.

g   **Water resources**

Indicator g1:   Licensed abstractions and effective rainfall

Sources: NRA; DOE.
References: *Water, Nature's Precious Resource: An Environmentally Sustainable Water Resource Strategy For England and Wales* - NRA, March 1994.
Digest of Environmental Statistics No.17: table 3.22 - HMSO, 1995 [ISBN 0-11-753104-9].

The "1:50 year effective drought rainfall" is defined as the average water resource from rainfall under drought conditions less evaporation which might be expected to occur once in 50 years and is widely used as a benchmark for assessing the availability of water supplies. The NRA licenses abstractions in England and Wales for domestic and agricultural use (excluding spray irrigation) in excess of 20 m³ per day and all abstractions for other purposes from surface, tidal and non-tidal water and groundwater. Licensed abstractions are reported annually by the Regions under Section 201 of the *1991 Water Resources Act.* For the purposes of this indicator licensed abstractions exclude abstractions by power generation companies and those for fish farming and cress growing.

Indicator g2:   Low flow alleviation

Source: NRA.
Reference: *Water, Nature's Precious Resource: An Environmentally Sustainable Water Resource Strategy For England and Wales* - NRA, March 1994.

The NRA define a stretch of river as being affected by over-abstraction when studies indicate abstractions are having an unacceptable impact on the water environment.

Indicator g3:   Abstraction by use

Source: NRA.

Reference: *Digest of Environmental Statistics No.17:* tables 3.22 to 3.25 - HMSO, 1995 [ISBN 0-11-753104-9].

Information on actual abstractions is based on returns from licence holders to the NRA. Only a small and not necessarily representative sample of those holding licences for agricultural purposes (including spray irrigation) and for private water supply purposes make returns. Confidence in the accuracy of the data is therefore low. These uses represent only a small proportion of the total licensed quantity. Returns made by licence holders for all other purposes cover a high proportion of the licensed quantity and confidence in the accuracy of the data is high. Since 1991 the NRA has revised the format of the survey used to collect this information by redefining and clarifying categories and definitions, improving methods used to take account of non-respondents and improving the allocation of licenses to use categories. As a result more confidence can be placed in the data collected since 1991 and these data are not strictly comparable with those collected in earlier years.

Indicator g4:   Abstractions for public water supply

Sources: NRA; WSA; Water Companies Association; OFWAT.

References: *Digest of Environmental Statistics No.17:* tables 3.22, 3.27 and 10.26 - HMSO, 1995 [ISBN 0-11-753104-9].
WaterFacts and Figures - OFWAT, 1995
[Similar publications were produced by WSA from 1988 to 1994]
1993-94 Report on the Cost of Water Delivered and Sewage Collected - OFWAT, December 1994.
[Similar publications were produced by OFWAT in 1992 and 1993]

Estimates of the water put into the public water supply are provided by Water Service Companies and Water Supply Companies. Data for the years after 1990/1 have been compiled by OFWAT. OFWAT compile their data on the basis of strictly defined elements of supply. The application of these criteria has resulted in more accurate figures. Figures for distribution losses refer only to losses from the distribution system for which water companies/water supply companies are responsible. They do not include losses from customers' pipes.

Indicator g5:   Demand and supply of public water

Source: NRA.

Reference: *Water, Nature's Precious Resource: An Environmentally Sustainable Water Resource Strategy For England and Wales* - NRA, March 1994.

The available resource is defined as the reliable yield from the water system under drought conditions which might be expected to occur once in 50 years. Methods used to estimate the available resource differs between the NRA regions because of differences in the structure of the water system. Demand is the water put into the public water supply.

Indicator g6:   Abstractions for spray irrigation

Sources: NRA; MAFF.

References: *Digest of Environmental Statistics No.17:* table 3.22 - HMSO, 1995 [ISBN 0-11-753104-9].
Irrigation of Outdoor Crops - England and Wales Special Enquiry - MAFF, 1992
[Similar bulletins were produced by MAFF in 1982, 1983, 1984, 1987 and 1990].

Irrigation water applied is for spray irrigation only. Figures are averaged over the whole year, although the irrigation season lasts normally only between 1 April - 30 September and will be different for individual crops. The data used by the DOE does not include water taken from the mains supply, trickle irrigation, sub-irrigation through pipes or by raising water tables and the virtually unused surface irrigation. Figures on the area of land irrigated are from a survey of farmers carried out by the Agricultural Census Branch of MAFF. Figures are for outdoor crops only.

h   **Forestry**

Indicator h1:   Forest cover

Source: FC.

Reference: *Digest of Environmental Statistics No.17:* table 8.7 - HMSO, 1995 [ISBN 0-11-753104-9].

About 65 per cent of forests and woodland in GB are privately owned, the remaining 35 per cent owned or managed by the FC. Northern Ireland has only around 5 per cent tree cover of which nearly 80 per cent are state forests.

Indicator h2:   Timber production

Source: FC.

Reference: Home Grown Timber Advisory Committee statistics.

Indicator h3:   Ancient semi-natural woodland

Sources: EN; CCW; SNH.

Reference: Spenser J.W. and Kirby K.J. *An inventory of ancient woodland for England and Wales* - Biological Conservation 62, 77-93, 1992.

Roberts A.J., Russell C., Walker G.J. and Kirby K.J. Regional Variation in the Origin, *Extent and Composition of Scottish Woodland* - Bot. J. Scotl. 46(2), 167-189.

The inventory of ancient semi-natural woodland in GB was compiled by NCC and is maintained by its successor bodies - EN, CCW, and SNH - based on their survey work, together with information supplied by nature conservation organisations, local authorities and woodland owners, as well as through aerial photographs. Analysis of the extent of ancient semi-natural woodland in the past has been attempted using old Ordnance Survey maps, other old maps and other historical evidence. This indicator is based on best information available up to 1992. The inventory is revised periodically as new material becomes available. There are currently no reliable estimates of the area of ancient semi-natural woodland in Northern Ireland.

Indicator h4:   Tree health

Source: FC.

Reference: *Digest of Environmental Statistics No.17:* table 8.8 - HMSO, 1995 [ISBN 0-11-753104-9].

The FC conducts an annual GB survey of between 7,000 and 9,000 individual trees of 5 species - Sitka spruce, Norway spruce, Scots pine, oak, and beech. The results relate to the percentage of trees for each species showing percentage reductions in crown density relative to a "perfect" tree with maximum foliage. This indicator shows trends for each of the 5 tree species surveyed giving the percentage of trees with over 25 per cent reductions in crown density.

Indicator h5:   Forest management

Source: FC.

Reference: *Forestry Commission Facts and Figures 1994/95* - FC, 1995.

Direct measurements of multipurpose forestry are not available at present. Proxy indicators relate to management and grant practices to encourage multipurpose forestry objectives.

j   Fish resources

Indicator j1:   Fish stocks

Source: ICES.

Reference: *Digest of Environmental Statistics No.17:* table 4.15 - HMSO, 1995 [ISBN 0-11-753104-9].

Biomass estimates of major, internationally assessed, fish stocks are produced by ICES, based on mathematical models which use data on international catches and fishing effort, and indices or estimates of abundance from research vessel surveys.

Indicator j2:   Minimum Biological Acceptable Level (MBAL)

Source: ICES.

Reference: *Cooperative Research Report, Advisory Committee on Fishery Management* - ICES, 1994.

Indicator j3:   Fish catches

Source: MAFF.

Reference: *Digest of Environmental Statistics No.17:* table 4.16 - HMSO, 1995 [ISBN 0-11-753104-9].

Catches data are obtained from sampling at UK ports and other countries engaged in the fishery for the species in question, and are based on landings information and estimates of discarded fish.

k   Climate change

Indicator k1:   Global greenhouse gas radiative forcing rate

Source: Hadley Centre.

Reference: *A Climate Research Technology Note (No. 50)* - Hadley Centre, September 1994.

Increases in the concentrations of greenhouse gases lead to a reduction in outgoing infrared radiation, reducing the amount by which the earth cools to space and warming the lower atmosphere and earth's surface. A change in average net radiation at the top of the lower atmosphere is called *radiative forcing*; a positive radiative forcing caused by increased concentrations of greenhouse gases tends to warm the earth's surface and the lower atmosphere.

Annex B

Indicator k2:   Global temperature change

Source: Hadley Centre.
Reference: *The UK Environment: figure 3.13* - HMSO, 1992 [ISBN 0-11-752420-4].

This indicator compares annual mean global temperatures and temperatures over central England with the average temperatures recorded between 1951 and 1980.

Indicator k3:   Emissions of greenhouse gases

Source: NETCEN.
Reference: *Digest of Environmental Statistics No.17:* tables 1.1, 1.2, 1.3 and 1.4 - HMSO, 1995 [ISBN 0-11-753104-9]. [Data for nitrous oxide emissions in *Digest of Environmental Statistics No.18* (to be published) - HMSO, 1996.]
                    Economic Trends Annual Supplement 1996: table 1.2 - HMSO, 1996

The GWP of a given greenhouse gas depends on its efficiency in absorbing infrared radiation from the earth's surface, its lifetime in the atmosphere and its molecular weight. In addition, the relative strength of greenhouse gases will depend on the period over which the effects of the gases are to be considered. For example a short-lived gas that has a strong greenhouse effect will, in the short term, be more effective at changing radiative forcing than a weaker but longer-lived greenhouse gas. Over longer periods, the effect of the weaker greenhouse gas will be greater because of its persistence in the atmosphere.

Indicator k4:   Power station emissions of carbon dioxide

Source: NETCEN; DTI.
Reference: *Digest of Environmental Statistics No.17:* table 1.2 - HMSO, 1995 [ISBN 0-11-753104-9].
                    Digest of United Kingdom Energy Statistics 1995: table A11 - HMSO, 1995 [ISBN 0-11-515368-3].

The left-hand chart depicts time series in emissions and electricity generated from all major UK producers including nuclear; the scales for these 2 series have been designed to start off from the same point in 1970 to convey, thereafter, relative rates of change. The right-hand chart shows the ratio between the 2 series, ie emissions per unit of electricity generated, indexed to a value of 100 in 1970.

l   Ozone layer depletion

Indicator l1:   Calculated chlorine loading

Source: DOE.
Reference: Unpublished.

The effective chlorine loading is the calculated concentration in the lower atmosphere of the chlorine and bromine contained in compounds which could be transported into the upper atmosphere. The relationship between chlorine loading in the lower atmosphere and stratospheric ozone depletion is neither simple nor exact, but in general the higher the chlorine loading the higher the potential for ozone depletion in the stratosphere.

Indicator l2:   Measured ozone depletion

Source: MO.
Reference: Unpublished.

Direct measurements of stratospheric ozone are difficult to make since the stratosphere extends from 15 to 50 km above the earth. Most modern aircraft can just reach the lower stratosphere and balloons can attain heights of around 35 km. As a result, ground-based remote sensing techniques using Dobson spectrophotometers have been developed to measure the total column of ozone above specific locations on the earth's surface.

Indicator l3:   Emissions of ozone-depleting substances

Source: Atmospheric Environment.
Reference: Simmonds, P.G., Derwent R.G., McCulloch A., O'Doherty S., and Gaudry A. *Long-term trends in concentrations of halocarbons and radiatively active trace gases in Atlantic and European air masses at Mace Head, Ireland from 1987-1884* - Atmospheric Environment, 1996 (to be published).

The ODP for a given halocarbon provides a measure of the potential contribution of that compound to stratospheric ozone depletion relative to that of CFC-11. These weights have been applied to the measured concentrations of major halocarbons in European air masses to deduce the trends in regional emissions of these gases since 1987 and the relative potential impact on the ozone layer.

Indicator l4:   CFCs consumption

Source: European Council of Chemical Manufacturers Federation (CEFIC).
Reference: *Digest of Environmental Statistics No.17:* table 1.7 - HMSO, 1995 [ISBN 0-11-753104-9].[Data for 1994 in *Digest of Environmental Statistics No.18* (to be published) - HMSO, 1996].

Data on UK consumption of ODS are not available separately but are included in EC-wide data sets.

m   Acid deposition

Indicator m1:   Exceedences of provisional critical loads for acidity

Source: ITE.
Reference: Unpublished.

In the UK wet deposition is monitored at 32 sites across the country through the collection and analysis of weekly rainfall samples using bulk collectors. At 5 of these sites, rainfall is collected daily and these sites form the UK contribution to the European Monitoring and Evaluation Programme (EMEP). Using these data wet deposition of sulphur and nitrogen can be mapped. Dry deposition of sulphur occurs principally through the absorption of sulphur dioxide. Concentrations of this gas are measured at 41 rural sites across the UK and these data are used to map the distribution of sulphur dioxide. Dry deposition is calculated from these concentrations and estimated deposition velocities, derived from models using results from atmospheric process and field studies. For soils, total acid deposition maps, ie for sulphur and nitrogen combined, are not generally used because of uncertainties in estimating dry deposition values for nitrogen.

Deposition maps for soils are presented at a resolution of 20 km^2 and for freshwater at a resolution of 10 km^2. Deposition exceedences of critical loads are calculated at these levels of areal resolutions and the data aggregated to a UK level to form the basis for this indicator.

Indicator m2:   Power station emissions of sulphur dioxide and nitrogen oxides

Source: NETCEN; DTI.
Reference: *Digest of Environmental Statistics No.17:* tables 2.2 and 2.9 - HMSO, 1995 [ISBN 0-11-753104-9].
                   Digest of United Kingdom Energy Statistics 1995: table A11 - HMSO, 1995 [ISBN 0-11-515368-3].

The left-hand charts depict time series in emissions and electricity generated; the scales for these 2 series have been designed to start off from the same point in 1970 to convey, thereafter, relative rates of change. The right-hand charts show the ratio between the 2 series, ie emissions per unit of electricity generated, indexed to a value of 100 in 1970.

Indicator m3:   Road transport emissions of nitrogen oxides

Source: NETCEN; DOT.
Reference: *Digest of Environmental Statistics No.17:* table 2.9 - HMSO, 1995 [ISBN 0-11-753104-9].
                   Transport Statistics Great Britain 1995: tables 9.1 and 9.3 - HMSO, 1995 [ISBN 0-11-551716-2].

The left-hand charts depict time series in emissions from road passenger and road freight transport in relation to passenger-miles travelled and tonnage-miles of goods moved; the scales for these series have been designed to show the differentials between passenger transport and freight and to start off from the same point in 1970 to convey, thereafter, relative rates of change. The right-hand charts show the ratio between the 2 series, ie emissions per unit of electricity generated, indexed to a value of 100 in 1970. Road passenger transport emissions include those from cars and taxis, buses and coaches, and motorcycles; road freight emissions include those from heavy and light goods vehicles. The data on road transport emissions are for the UK whereas the data on passenger traffic published in *Transport Statistics* are for GB. Equivalent data on road traffic back to 1970 for Northern Ireland are not readily available but this should not invalidate the relative trends shown in the charts.

n   Air

Indicators
n1 to n3:   Ozone, nitrogen dioxide and particulate matter concentrations

Source: NETCEN.
Reference: Unpublished.

A useful aggregate statistic for measuring air quality at a given site is Accumulated exposure Over a Threshold "x" (AOTx). This is calculated for each pollutant by first measuring the extent to which recorded average hourly or daily concentrations, as appropriate, exceed a given threshold, and then summing the results for each year. Such a statistic combines both the magnitude and length of time that concentrations are above the threshold. It is usual for monitoring stations to be not fully operational or for concentration recordings to have not met validation and calibration criteria for part of each year. The AOTs shown in the charts are given only where there has been at least 75 per cent data capture in any given year at the selected sites.

Annex B

Indicator n4:   Volatile organic compound emissions

Source: NETCEN; DOT; CSO.
Reference: *Digest of Environmental Statistics No.17:* table 2.19 - HMSO, 1995 [ISBN 0-11-753104-9].
                  Transport Statistics Great Britain 1995: table 9.1 - HMSO, 1995 [ISBN 0-11-551716-2].
                  United Kingdom National Accounts 1995: table 2.2 - HMSO, 1995 [ISBN 0-11-620710-8].
                  Economic Trends Annual Supplement 1996: tables 1.6 and 2.8 - HMSO, 1996.

The left-hand charts depict VOC emissions from road passenger transport and from industry, compared with road passenger transport mileage and industry's contribution to GDP respectively. The scales for these 2 series have been designed to start off from the same point in 1970 and to convey, thereafter, relative rates of change. The right-hand charts show the ratio between the 2 series, ie road passenger transport emissions per road passenger-miles and emissions from industry per value added, expressed as indices with a base year value of 100 in 1970. The categorisation of VOC emissions from industry may not equate precisely with the source classification used for industrial GDP. The data on road passenger transport emissions are for the UK whereas the data on passenger traffic published in *Transport Statistics* are for GB. Equivalent data on road passenger traffic back to 1970 for Northern Ireland are not readily available but this should not invalidate the relative trends shown in the charts.

Indicator n5:   Carbon monoxide emissions

Source: NETCEN; DOT.
Reference: *Digest of Environmental Statistics No.17:* table 2.12 - HMSO, 1995 [ISBN 0-11-753104-9].
                  Transport Statistics Great Britain 1995: table 9.1 - HMSO, 1995 [ISBN 0-11-551716-2].

The left-hand chart depicts carbon monoxide emissions from road passenger transport compared with road passenger transport mileage. The right-hand chart shows the ratio between the 2 series, ie road passenger transport emissions per road passenger-miles, indexed to a value of 100 in 1970. The data on road passenger transport emissions are for the UK whereas the data on passenger traffic published in *Transport Statistics* are for GB. Equivalent data on road passenger traffic back to 1970 for Northern Ireland are not readily available but this should not invalidate the relative trends shown in the charts.

Indicator n6:   Black smoke emissions

Source: NETCEN; DOT; DOE.
Reference: *Digest of Environmental Statistics No.17:* table 2.6 - HMSO, 1995 [ISBN 0-11-753104-9].
                  Transport Statistics Great Britain 1995: tables 9.3 - HMSO, 1995 [ISBN 0-11-551716-2].
                  [household estimates are unpublished]

The left-hand charts depict black smoke emissions from road freight transport and from domestic sources, compared with road freight mileage and households respectively. The right-hand charts show the ratio between the 2 series, ie road freight emissions per road freight tonne-miles and emissions from domestic sources per household, indexed to a value of 100 in 1970. The data on road freight transport emissions are for the UK, whereas the data on freight traffic published in *Transport Statistics* are for GB. Equivalent data on road freight traffic back to 1970 for Northern Ireland are not readily available but this should not invalidate the relative trends shown in the charts.

Indicator n7:   Lead emissions

Source: DTI.
Reference: *Digest of Environmental Statistics No.17:* tables 2.14 and 2.15 - HMSO, 1995 [ISBN 0-11-753104-9].

Lead emissions from petrol-engined vehicles are based on lead contents of petrol published by the Institute of Petroleum. It has been assumed that 70 per cent of this lead in petrol is emitted from exhaust systems, the remainder being retained in lubricating oil and exhaust systems.

Indicator n8:   Expenditure on air pollution abatement

Source: ECOTEC Research and Consulting Ltd.
Reference: *A Review of UK Environmental Expenditure. A Final Report to the Department of the Environment* - ECOTEC, 1993.

Expenditure on protecting the environment is difficult to quantify and accurate figures on the amount spent do not exist, either in the UK or other countries. This is partly because much of the data has not been collected, but mainly because of the difficulty in defining what is meant by environmental expenditure; such expenditure is often an integral and indistinguishable part of expenditure on goods and services. The estimates of air pollution abatement include both capital and current expenditure incurred by Government, industry and households which can be clearly identified and explicitly attributed to directly improving and maintaining the quality of the environment. The attribution of expenditure has been made on the basis of the actor directly responsible for the expenditure rather than on the actor financing the expenditure.

p   **Freshwater quality**

Indicator p1:   River quality - chemical and biological

Sources: NRA; SO; DOE(NI).
Reference: *Digest of Environmental Statistics No.18* (to be published) - HMSO, 1996.

The general chemical quality of rivers and canal waters in the UK has been monitored in a series of separate national surveys. These surveys have been repeated every 5 years and divide all river and canal lengths into 4 chemical classes. Different systems of classification have been used in these national surveys, so the results are not directly comparable between countries. Since 1970, 3 different systems have been used in England and Wales. The system used in Scotland is broadly comparable to that used in England and Wales from 1970 to 1980, and the system used in Northern Ireland is broadly comparable to that used in England and Wales between 1980 and 1990. A new, more objective survey methodology was introduced in England and Wales in 1990. The figures for earlier years in England and Wales have been adjusted so they are broadly comparable with those for the 1990s.

More recently, the 1990 surveys gave a general biological assessment of quality, also into 4 classes. There are a number of different bases for biological classification, but, in contrast to the chemical gradings, one set of biological gradings are available on the same basis for each of the country's 1990 surveys. However, not all river lengths were biologically tested; eg only about 21 per cent of Scottish rivers sampled for chemistry were also sampled for biology. Using a procedure known as the River Invertebrate Prediction and Classification System (RIVPACS), species groups of small animals (ie invertebrates) which live in or on the bed of the river at each site were compared with those which would be expected to be present in the absence of pollution, allowing for the different environmental characteristics in different parts of the country. Three different summary statistics (known as ecological quality indices) were calculated, and then the biological quality was assigned to one of 4 bands based on a combination of these 3 statistics.

Indicator p2:   Nitrates in rivers and groundwater

Sources: Harmonised (Water) Monitoring Scheme (HMS) for rivers data; NRA for groundwater data
Reference: *Digest of Environmental Statistics No.18* (to be published) - HMSO, 1996.

Rivers monitored under HMS have been broadly grouped into 3 categories according to the type of landscape through which the river mainly flows. Using the Institute of Terrestrial Ecology (ITE) landscape classifications, "typically eastern lowlands" covers rivers flowing mainly through landscapes classified by ITE as "arable", "typically western lowlands" covers those flowing mainly through "pastural" landscapes, and "upland" covers those flowing mainly through "marginal upland" or "upland" landscapes. For each broad landscape group, the average of the annual means at sites at tidal limits has then been calculated, with each site being given equal weight, irrespective of the number of samples taken from that site or the size of the river.

A network of groundwater sites (ie underground aquifers) in England and Wales is in the process of being developed by the NRA as part of a review of groundwater monitoring. Some information is available from work carried out by the NRA in relation to nitrate in boreholes used for abstraction for public water supplies or other processes. From amongst boreholes experiencing elevated nitrate levels close to or above 50 mg/l, 17 sites have been chosen to give a broad geographical coverage of England and Wales, and to utilise continuous, consistent data where available. These sites, however, are not representative of all aquifers, either in their immediate region or in England and Wales as a whole. A combined annual average concentration of nitrate has been calculated for the 17 groundwater sites, with each site being given equal weight, irrespective of the number of samples taken from that site. The broad trends for each site are similar, so, although there were no data for some sites in particular years, the combined average gives a reasonable indication of the overall trend for these 17 selected sites.

Indicator p3:   Phosphorus in rivers

Source: HMS.
Reference: *Digest of Environmental Statistics No.18* (to be published) - HMSO, 1996.

Levels of phosphorus (both total phosphorus and orthophosphate) in rivers in GB have also been monitored since 1975 as part of HMS. The most comprehensive data available are for concentrations of orthophosphates. These data (in terms of phosphorus) have been used for this indicator, as this gives a good indication of the trends in levels for total phosphorus.

Annex B

Indicator p4:   Pesticides in rivers and groundwater

Source: NRA.

Reference: *Digest of Environmental Statistics No.18* (to be published) - HMSO, 1996.

There are currently about 450 active ingredients approved for use as pesticides in the UK (about 340 of these are used as agricultural pesticides). A number of others used in the past are no longer approved because of potential risks to human health or to the environment. The NRA, Scottish River Purification Authorities, and DOE(NI) monitor for about 120 different pesticides. About 100 were detected in rivers in England and Wales during the last 3 years. The vast majority of these pesticides are found in very small quantities in water, and well below any existing or proposed EQSs. For this indicator, 6 herbicides and insecticides have been selected from those most commonly found in water, including examples of those used on non-agricultural land, in agriculture, and in industry. The 6 are:

Atrazine and Diuron: Herbicides primarily used for non-agricultural purposes for general weed and control. The non-agricultural use of atrazine was banned from September 1993. Diuron might now be widely used as a replacement.

Mecoprop and Isoproturon: 2 of the most commonly used agricultural herbicides.

Permethrin and Lindane: Both are insecticides. Permethrin is currently the most commonly found and pyrethroid in water, and is primarily used as a moth proofing agent, but is also used as an insecticide in horticulture and forestry. Lindane is used in agriculture, horticulture, forestry, and in timber treatment.

Only lindane has a statutory EQS for surface waters set under the *EC Dangerous Substances Directive*. Atrazine and permethrin have EQSs proposed by the DOE and the NRA has developed operational EQSs for isoproturon, diuron and mecoprop. There are no EQSs for groundwater. The figures collected are based on all the samples taken by the NRA from rivers in England and Wales. Far fewer results are available for groundwater than for rivers; for 1992 the available information covered only 4 of the 8 NRA regions. Most regions have relied on water company data for groundwater results, and this will continue until the network of national groundwater sites is set up.

Indicator p5:   Pollution incidents

Source: NRA.

Reference: *Digest of Environmental Statistics No.18* (to be published) - HMSO, 1996.

Substantiated incidents are classified into 3 categories according to the severity of their environmental impact:

Category 1:   covers "major" incidents involving any of the following: persistent (or potentially persistent) effects on water quality or aquatic life; extensive fish kills; the need to cease water abstraction; the need for extensive remedial measures; excessive breaches of consent conditions; major effect on amenity value.

Category 2:   covers "significant" incidents involving any of the following: significant fish kills; measurable effect on invertebrate life; water unfit for fish stock; the need to notify abstractors; bed of watercourse contamination; odour or appearance effect on amenity value.

Category 3:   covers "minor" incidents which, on investigation, prove to have little notable effect.

The substantiated numbers of major and significant incidents are not thought to be affected so much by the extent of reporting, so analysis of incidents in these categories are believed to provide a more meaningful indication of actual trends in pollution incidents.

There are some differences in reporting practice in different parts of the country. In particular, some incidents classified as "industry" in 1993 may have previously been classified as "oil". The apparent substantial increase in industrial incidents in this year may be partly explained by this. Figures for significant incidents in the Welsh NRA region for 1991 and 1992 are not available on a comparable basis to those for other regions. Hence, the analysis has been made on an English NRA region basis.

Indicator p6:   Pollution prevention and control

Source: NRA.

References: *Digest of Environmental Statistics No.18* (to be published) - HMSO, 1996.
   Discharge Consents: Monitoring and Compliance in 1993 - NRA, August 1995.

Indicator p7:   Expenditure on water abstraction, treatment and distribution

Sources: WSA; OFWAT.
References: *Waterfacts* - WSA, 1994.
               [Similar publications were produced by WSA from 1988 onwards]
               1993-94 Report on the Cost of Water Delivered and Sewage Collected - OFWAT, December 1994.
               [Similar publications were produced by OFWAT in 1992 and 1993]

National data on the overall costs of drinking water supply are available for England and Wales, with operational costs reported since 1990/91 and capital expenditure since the mid-1970s. These costs include, in addition to those of water treatment, the costs of water resources, abstraction, distribution, and management. The operational costs relating to treatment and resources together have been identified separately from the total costs, and since 1990/91, the capital costs relating to treatment alone have also been identified separately.

The operational and capital cost figures have been adjusted to 1994/95 prices using the GDP deflator. The costs have then been expressed as a cost per cubic metre of drinking water supplied in each year.

Indicator p8:   Expenditure on sewage treatment

Sources: WSA; OFWAT.
References: *Waterfacts* - WSA, 1994.
               [Similar publications were produced by WSA from 1988 onwards]
               1993-94 Report on the Cost of Water Delivered and Sewage Collected - OFWAT, December 1994.
               [Similar publications were produced by OFWAT in 1992 and 1993]

National data on the overall costs of sewage service are available for England and Wales, with operational costs reported since 1990/91 and capital expenditure since the mid-1970s. These costs include, in addition to those of sewage treatment, the costs of sewerage and sewage management. The operational costs relating to treatment have been identified separately.

The operational and capital cost figures have been adjusted to 1994/95 prices using the GDP deflator. The costs have then been expressed as a cost per head of resident population (using mid-year population estimates from OPCS, as published in the Annual Abstract of Statistics).

q   **Marine**

Indicator q1:   Estuarial water quality

Sources: NRA; SO; DOE(NI).
Reference: *Digest of Environmental Statistics No.17:* table 4.4 - HMSO, 1995 [ISBN 0-11-753104-9].

Surveys are reported every 5 years by the NRA (England and Wales), SOEND and DOE(NI). The increase in the percentage of estuaries classed as good in Northern Ireland since 1985 results from the inclusion of the Larne and Strangford Loughs in surveys since 1991. Estuaries are measured by area in Scotland but by distance around estuaries in England and Wales and Northern Ireland.

Indicator q2:   Concentrations of key pollutants

Source: NRA.
Reference: *Digest of Environmental Statistics No.17:* table 4.5 - HMSO, 1995 [ISBN 0-11-753104-9].

Indicator q3:   Contaminants in fish

Source: MAFF Fisheries Laboratory.
Reference: *Digest of Environmental Statistics No.17:* table 4.17 - HMSO, 1995 [ISBN 0-11-753104-9].

Indicator q4:   Bathing water quality

Sources: NRA; SO; DOE(NI).
Reference: *Digest of Environmental Statistics No.17:* table 4.1 - HMSO, 1995 [ISBN 0-11-753104-9].

Samples of bathing waters are taken at regular intervals beginning 2 weeks before and then during the bathing season at bathing waters around the UK covered by the *EC Bathing Water Directive* (464 in 1995). The season runs from mid-May to the end of September in England and Wales and from the beginning of June to mid-September in Scotland and Northern Ireland. A minimum of 20 samples are normally taken at each site. The Directive gives mandatory values for total and faecal coliforms (10,000 and 2,000 per 100 ml respectively). For a bathing water to comply with the coliform standards at least 95 per cent of samples taken for each of these parameters over the bathing season must be less than or equal to the mandatory values. In practice this means that where 20 samples are taken only 1 sample may exceed the mandatory value for the bathing water to comply.

Annex B

Annex B

Indicator q5: Inputs of contaminants

Source: DOE.
Reference: *Digest of Environmental Statistics No.17:* table 4.9 - HMSO, 1995 [ISBN 0-11-753104-9].

The information on inputs is derived from samples at approximately monthly intervals of all main river systems close to but upstream of the tidal limit. Also all major direct discharges of trade or sewage effluent entering estuaries down stream of the sampling points are sampled, as are major coastal discharges. Some samples contain quantities of substances below the detection limits of monitoring instruments. Where this is the case the figures given in the indicator assume that the true concentrations are at the limit of detection and are therefore maximum estimates.

Indicator q6: Oil spills and operational discharges

Sources: ACOP; DTI.
References: *ACOP Surveys of Oil Pollution around the Coasts of the UK, 1983-1993* - ACOP.
Digest of United Kingdom Energy Statistics 1994: table D10 - HMSO, 1995 [ISBN 0-11-515368-3].

Oil spills figures are based on the reporting of incidents and from surveillance. Improved surveillance techniques were introduced in 1986. Figures on spills over 100 gallons are not strictly comparable with the number of incidents reported since not all reports gave information on spill size. Information on tonnages spilt and operational discharges are only available for offshore installations. The amounts of oil discharged from offshore installations depend on the extent of new exploration, the amount of oil produced, on the life cycle of the oil wells used in production, and on improvements and techniques. One of the reasons why oil from drill cuttings has reduced substantially in recent years was the introduction of drilling muds using organic phase other than mineral oil, together with greater use of water-based muds, rather than the use of oil-based muds.

r Wildlife and habitats

Indicator r1: Native species at risk

Source: JNCC.
References: *Digest of Environmental Statistics No.17:* table 9.1 - HMSO, 1995 [ISBN 0-11-753104-9].
British Red Data Book series - JNCC.
Biodiversity Steering Group Report - DOE, December 1995.

The proportions of terrestrial and freshwater species in GB considered to be *endangered*, *vulnerable*, or *rare* (ie included in Red Data Lists) are based on criteria devised by the International Union for the Conservation of Nature (IUCN) - these are *threatened species*. Figures for *nationally scarce* species (where available) cover those species which are recorded as present in only 16-100 10-km squares in GB. The source of both sets of figures is JNCC.

The figures for "fish, etc" relate to the 53 native species of freshwater fish, non-marine reptiles, and amphibians. Information on the number of these species which are nationally scarce are not available. The figures for "invertebrates" cover 15,000 species native to GB (in those groups which are covered in the Red Data Books), while those for "seed plants" relate to 2,300 native species of seed plants, ferns, and related plants, and those for "mosses, etc" relate to 2,700 native species of mosses, liverworts, and lichens. Comparable data on risk for GB populations of mammals and birds are not available since the IUCN threat status of these species is assessed on an international basis and not for GB separately. A large proportion of invertebrates, plants, and other organisms (eg parasitic animals, springtails, fungi, and micro-algae) have not been assessed and so are not included.

Indicator r2: Breeding birds

Sources: BTO; WWT; Seabird Colony Register (JNCC and RSPB).
References: *Digest of Environmental Statistics No.18* (to be published) - HMSO, 1996.
Walsh, P.M., Brindley, E. and Heubeck, M. *Seabird numbers and breeding success in Britain and Ireland, 1994* - JNCC, 1995.
Gibbons, D.W., Reid, J.B. and Chapman, R.A. *The New Atlas of Breeding Birds in Britain and Ireland 1988-1991* - BTO, 1993.

Population size - Data on GB bird population changes are available from a variety of sources. The Common Bird Census estimates the populations of *common* species found on "farmland" and "woodland" sites during summers between 1968 and 1993. This survey has now been superseded by the broader based Breeding Bird Survey. The Wetland Bird Survey monitors wintering wildfowl and waders, and estimates populations for winters between 1978 and 1993. These species have been used as an indicator for "lowland wetlands" habitats. While many waders live in estuaries, for the purposes of this exercise these species have not been included as part of the indicator for "coastal" habitats. The Seabird Colony Register covers seabird colonies on the British and Irish coasts for the years 1969/70 to 1986/87, and has been used as an indicator for "coastal" habitats. This indicator shows the proportion of species in each habitat whose abundance changed by 10 per cent or more over the respective periods of comparison. Species whose abundance changed by less than 10 per cent are assumed to be relatively stable (in population terms) for the purposes of this indicator.

Geographical Distribution - Data on geographical distribution are available for all British breeding birds, and comparisons can be made between the 1988/91 BTO Atlas of Breeding Birds and the previous Atlas for 1968/72. BTO has allocated each species to one of 6 breeding season habitats. 4 of the habitats ("farmland", "woodland", "coastal", and "lowland wetland") have been shown for this indicator, together with a GB total. The choice of habitats was qualitative and kept to a minimum so that the numbers of species in each were sufficiently large. Those species which could not be classified were placed in an "unclassified" category (not shown here). Species recorded in 15 or fewer 10-km squares during each Atlas period, as well as feral and introduced species, have been excluded. For each included species, 10-km squares have been compared between the 2 Atlases, and the presence or absence of the species noted for each square. If the number of squares where the species is present has increased between the 2 Atlases, then that species is said to have "*increased its geographical distribution*". Similarly, if the number of squares has decreased, then it has "*decreased its geographical distribution*". The indicator shows the proportion of species in each habitat whose geographical distribution changed by 10 per cent or more between the 2 Atlases. Species whose geographical distribution changed by less than 10 per cent are assumed to be relatively stable (in distributional terms) for the purposes of this indicator.

The 2 measures are complementary. Adverse population trends may not correspond to adverse geographical distribution trends, and vice versa. However, the habitats shown for each measure are *not* directly comparable as the species groups are not necessarily the same. The population measure includes all common birds found during the summer at "farmland" and "woodland" sites, British and Irish seabirds for the "coastal" habitat, and winter wildfowl for the "lowland wetlands" habitat. The geographical distribution measure *assigns* British breeding birds to "farmland", "woodland", "coastal", and "lowland wetland" habitats. Nevertheless, the groupings for each measure *can* be usefully considered together in *broad* terms.

Indicators r3,
r5, and r8:   Plant diversity in semi-improved grassland, hedgerows, and streamsides
Sources: ITE; IFE.
Reference: Barr, C.J., Bunce, R.G.H., Clarke, R.T., Fuller, R.M., Furse, M.T., Gillespie, M.K., Groom, G.B., Hallam, C.J., Hornung, M., Howard, D.C. and Ness, M.J. *Countryside Survey 1990 Main Report* - DOE, 1993

The 1990 Countryside Survey was conducted by the ITE and the IFE for the DOE. The survey examined diversity in plant species and freshwater animals through field surveys in 508 1-km squares. This followed similar surveys carried out in 1978 and 1984. In 1990, vegetation data were collected from a number of plots in each of the 1-km squares. The main plots each covered 200 m^2, and 5 were randomly chosen in each of the 1-km squares surveyed. Up to 17 10-m by 1-m plots covering linear features such as hedges, roadside verges, and stream banks were also selected within each square. In 1978, similar data were collected from a smaller number of plots in 256 squares. About 1,200 main plots and nearly 900 linear plots were recorded in both the 1978 and 1990 surveys, allowing comparisons to be made for more common types of habitats between the 2 years. However, by their nature these general national surveys cannot be used to assess changes in rarer and localised habitats. Each vegetation plot surveyed was classified into distinct vegetation types characteristic of open fields, woods, moors, hedges, road verges, and stream banks. The main vegetation plots from open fields, woods, and moors were grouped into 6 major types of habitat, 1 of which covered semi-improved grassland.

Indicator r3 shows the gross changes in mean species numbers in main plots recorded as semi-improved grassland in 1978, regardless of whether the habitat type of plot had changed by the 1990 survey. Hence, these changes largely correspond to changes *within* the habitat type and *between* the habitat and other habitat types. The indicator is restricted to lowland landscapes, ie just "arable" and "pastural".

Indicator r5 shows the changes in mean species numbers in linear plots recorded as hedgerows in 1978. The majority (93 per cent) of these plots were also hedgerows in 1990, although a few had become relict hedges. Hence, these changes largely correspond to changes *within* this habitat type. The analysis of change was based on 202 hedge plots sampled in 1978 and reliably relocated and recorded in 1990. Only 14 of these hedge plots recorded in 1978 were no longer recorded as hedges but were relict hedges in the 1990 survey. The indicator is restricted to lowland landscapes, ie just "arable" and "pastural".

Indicator r8 shows changes in linear plots recorded on streamsides in 1978 (ie plots adjacent to ditches, streams, rivers, and canals). This analysis of change for the streamside data was based on 322 plots from 179 squares throughout GB which were recorded in both 1978 and 1990. The changes for indicator r8 are presented for each of the 4 broad ITE landscape types ("arable", "pastural", "marginal upland", and "upland").

In all cases above the mean species numbers cover *all* plant species found in the paired plots. As has been mentioned in the main text, future development might focus on mean numbers based on *only* "characteristic" or representative species of each habitat type or landscape feature.

Indicators r4
and r6:   Area of chalk grassland and habitat fragmentation
Sources: Keymer, R.J. and Leach, S.J. (England Field Unit (EFU), NCC); Blackwood, J.V. and Tubbs, C.R.
References: Keymer, R.J. and Leach, S.J. 'Calcareous grassland - a limited resource in Britain' in Hillier, S.H., Walton, D.W.H. and Wells, D.A. (eds) *Calcareous Grasslands Ecology and Management* - Bluntisham Books, 1990.
Blackwood, J.V. and Tubbs, C.R. 'A quantitative survey of chalk grassland in England' in *Biological Conservation No.3* - 1970.

Annex B

For **indicator r4** the areas for 1966 are taken from the survey by Blackwood and Tubbs, which was the first nationwide survey to attempt to estimate the total area of chalk grassland in England. Figures for 1982-88 are based on various county surveys conducted by the EFU. The 1966 survey recorded any grassland on chalk which appeared 'unsown', and therefore included mesotrophic as well calcareous grasslands. For the EFU surveys in the 1980s the definition of chalk grassland was restricted to all calcareous grassland on chalk, and so the results are not strictly comparable with the 1966 results. Thus, although there was a genuine loss of chalk grassland since the mid-1960s the extent of this overall loss may be over-estimated by the comparison between the 2 surveys.

For **indicator r6** the fragment figures for Dorset in 1966 are again taken from the national survey by Blackwood and Tubbs, see also above. Figures for 1983 are based on the Dorset county survey conducted by the EFU. Again the 1966 and 1983 survey results are not strictly comparable because the 1966 survey used a slightly broader definition of chalk grassland than the more recent EFU survey. For further discussion of both the extent and fragmentation results, see Keymer and Leach.

Indicator r7: Lakes and ponds

Sources: ITE; NCC.

References: Barr C.J., Howard, D.C. and Benefield C.B. *Countryside Survey 1990 Inland Water Bodies* - DOE, October 1994. Swan, M.J.S. and Oldham, R.S. *Amphibian Communities* (CSD report No.1020) - NCC, 1989.

In their 1989 report on amphibian communities, Swan and Oldham included estimates of the number of inland water bodies (ranging in size from 0.75 m^2 to 22 km^2) in GB in 1945 and 1986. The ITE Countryside Surveys in 1984 and 1990 included estimates of the number of water bodies, or parts of water bodies, in GB in 1 km squares. The results of Swan and Oldham and ITE are not directly comparable because of the different survey methodology used (ie historical maps/aerial photography vs field surveys). The Countryside Survey results are also less appropriate for larger water bodies which could be counted more than once. Both sources indicate a decline in water body numbers: Swan and Oldham estimate 38 per cent from 473,000 in 1945 to 291,000 in 1986, while ITE estimate 4 per cent from 346,000 in 1984 to 332,000 in 1990.

1990 was a year of drought conditions in the south and east of GB, and 25,000 water bodies were recorded as 'dried-out' in the ITE survey. The overall 4 per cent decline in numbers since 1984 assumed that these dried-out sites would eventually recover. However, a small re-survey of water bodies in 1993 discovered that some of these sites were in fact permanently 'lost'. ITE concluded that the permanent net reduction in the number of water bodies in GB was between 4 and 9 per cent in the period 1984 to 1990. If the decline was in fact 9 per cent then the estimated total number of water bodies in 1990 becomes about 315,000.

Indicator r9: Mammal populations

Source: JNCC.

References: Harris, S., Morris, P., Wray, S. and Yalden, D. *A Review of British Mammals* - JNCC, 1995. *Digest of Environmental Statistics No. 17:* table 9.5 - HMSO, 1995 [ISBN 0-11-753104-9].

The information in this indicator is based on *A Review of British Mammals* carried out for JNCC (Harris et al, 1995). This review attempted to summarise the available information and knowledge for each species of the 61 terrestrial mammals known or believed to be currently breeding in GB. The report gives changes in mammal populations over the last 30 years, but in most cases these are based on largely subjective criteria, because there are very few species with long-term population data.

The indicator splits British mammals into 4 groups and summarises for each group the number of species known or believed to be increasing in population over the last 30 years, those declining, and those with stable populations. The figures shown for "rodents, etc" relate to the 24 GB species of rodents, insectivores (eg hedgehogs, shrews) and lagomorphs (ie, rabbits and hares) . The figures for "bats" cover 15 species (all but one being native to GB) and those for "carnivores" relate to 11 carnivorous species. Finally, the figures for "deer, etc" relate to 10 species of ungulates, which include 7 deer (only 2 of which are native), the feral goat, feral sheep, and park cattle. The chart excludes the small GB population of the red-necked wallaby.

Indicators r10 and r11: Dragonfly and butterfly distributions

Source: Biological Records Centre (BRC), ITE.

Reference: *Digest of Environmental Statistics No.18* (to be published) - HMSO, 1996.

BRC was set up in 1964 and is now part of ITE. BRC's computerised data sets include about 6 million individual records of some 10,000 taxa, including dragonflies and butterflies. Comparable data have been presented for changes in geographical distribution of **dragonflies in indicator r10** and **butterflies in indicator r11**. The analyses split the data into 5 broad landscape types. These are not directly comparable with those used for indicators R3, R5, and R8 because the "coastal" classification used includes *all* 10-km squares containing coastal waters. BRC analysed data for all dragonfly and butterfly species typically found in each of these broad landscapes. Thus, particular species will be included in more than one landscape. For each dragonfly species in turn, 10-km squares in the relevant habitat type have been compared between 2 periods of data (ie before 1975 and 1975-88), and the presence or absence of the species noted for each square. For butterflies the 2 periods of comparison were slightly earlier (ie, before 1970 and 1970-82). The number of squares for each species was then expressed as a proportion of a measure of the total amount of dragonfly (or butterfly) recording in the period. These "relative proportions" of geographical distribution thus take some account of recorder effort and make the results between different periods more comparable. The indicator shows the number of species found in each landscape type whose "relative proportion" increased or decreased by 10 per cent or more. Species with changes of less than 10 per cent were considered to be relatively stable (in distributional terms) for the purposes of this indicator.

Annex B

In this way a measure was obtained of the balance between species increasing and those decreasing in their geographical distribution. This does not necessarily mean that *populations* are being affected in the same way. It may be that although a species is found to be present in relatively fewer squares from one survey period to the next, its actual population has increased and it is just inhabiting a smaller area. However, the pattern of geographic change mirrors the results of intensive local surveys and detailed site studies, which provide more information on actual populations. Hence, where there are far more species decreasing than increasing their geographical distribution, it is probable that this is indicative of populations in that landscape type also being adversely affected.

The nature of the date source means that some further caution must be exercised in the interpretation of the figures provided for this indicator because:

The data estimates are derived from sample-based surveys and so are subject to sampling errors;

There may be some differences in the way the data have been recorded by different observers in the field, which could affect the geographical coverage of the results.

S   Land cover and landscape

Indicator s1:   Rural land cover

Sources: ITE; NERC.

Reference: Barr, C.J., Bunce, R.G.H., Clarke, R.T., Fuller, R.M., Furse, M.T., Gillespie, M.K., Groom, G.B., Hallam, C.J., Hornung, M., Howard, D.C. and Ness, M.J. *Countryside Survey 1990 Main Report* - DOE, 1993.

The *1990 Countryside Survey of GB* (CS1990) was undertaken by ITE to record the stock of countryside features, to determine changes and to provide a baseline for future comparisons of change. Field surveys were used to map land cover and soil types and record the length of field boundaries such as walls, hedges and fences (see also Indicator s7).

For the CS1990 field survey, survey teams visited a stratified random sample of 508 1-km squares taken from all areas of the British countryside but excluding 1-km squares containing more than 75 per cent urban land. Comparable data from a similar survey by ITE in 1984 were used for assessing change. Changes in land cover were estimated by comparing data from those 1-km squares that were mapped in both 1984 and 1990 (381 1-km squares).

The sample of field survey sites was stratified using a land classification scheme developed by ITE. This scheme comprised 32 distinct land classes, identified by environmental characteristics including geology, topography, soil and climate which were characterised by land cover and ecological data obtained from sample field surveys. Each of the circa 244,000 1-km squares in GB was allocated to a distinct land class. The 32 land classes have been aggregated for Indicator s1 into 2 main landscape types: lowlands and uplands.

Indicator s2:   Designated and protected areas

Sources: EN; CCW; SNH; DOE(NI).

Reference: Unpublished.

Data on the extent of designated and protected areas should be treated with caution since some areas of land may be included in more than one category of designation, eg many Ramsar sites are also designated as Special Protection Areas (SPA) for Birds under the *EC Birds Directive*.

Indicator s3:   Damage to designated and protected areas

Source: JNCC.

References: *Digest of Environmental Statistics No.17:* table 8.18 - HMSO, 1995 [ISBN 0-11-753104-9].

JNCC Annual report 1994-95 - JNCC, 1995 [ISBN 1-86107-4018].

Full loss of the SSSI is classified as damage which will result in denotification of the whole SSSI. Partial loss is classified as damage which will result in denotification of part of the SSSI. Long-term damage is defined as damage causing a lasting reduction in the environmental value of the SSSI, but has the possibility of recovery. Short-term damage is defined as damage from which the SSSI could recover, given favourable management.

Indicator s4:   Agricultural productivity

Source: MAFF.

Reference: Unpublished.

The ratio of gross output of agriculture to total inputs used by the industry, valued at constant prices, is a measure of growth in productivity.

Gross output is the value (net of VAT) of production sold off-farm, plus direct payments, plus the value of physical increases in stocks. Total input comprises farmers' expenditure (net of reclaimed VAT) on current inputs, that is excluding depreciation but including labour.

From 1973 onwards, indices have been derived by revaluing outputs and inputs at 1990 prices. For earlier years, indices of gross output and total input relating to several different base years have been linked to the 1990-based series.

Annex B

Indicator s5: Nitrogen usage

Source: MAFF.
Reference: Unpublished.

The approach adopted is broadly based on guidelines drawn up by the Paris Convention for the Prevention of Marine Pollution (North Sea) (PARCOM). Measured nitrogen inputs are in mineral fertiliser, animal feedstuffs, seed, sewage sludge spread on farmland and nitrogen fixed in the soil by legumes (except clover for which no reliable data were available). No account has been taken of atmospheric deposition of ammonia. Some inputs have been excluded because data are unavailable, eg minor inputs from organic household wastes and from nitrogen fixed in the soil by clover, as well as outputs of some minor crops and crop by-products. Protein outputs are principally in crops and livestock products for human consumption and animal feed. Output crops include cereals, oilseed rape, linseed and sugar beet, field beans and peas, potatoes, vegetables and fruit, and livestock products include meat and meat products, milk, eggs, honey, and wool. The nitrogen content of animal feedstuffs is counted as an input whilst the nitrogen content of crops consumed by animals (eg wheat, barley, field beans and peas) is counted both as an input and an output. Nitrogen in animal manure, grass and forage crops (excluding that fixed in soils by clover and free-living bacteria) is implicitly included in the calculation since all of this nitrogen derives from mineral fertiliser and/or animal feed.

Data on inputs of mineral fertilisers are from the British Survey of Fertiliser Practice. Estimates used in the calculation of feed inputs and product outputs are based mainly on quantity estimates used in the national agricultural accounts from a variety of sources. Nitrogen contents were obtained principally from 3 published sources covering animal feed, food for human consumption, and manures. Data obtained from sample surveys and experimental measurement are also liable to a degree of sampling error.

Indicator s6: Pesticide usage

Source: MAFF.
Reference: Unpublished.

This indicator is based on the results of the regular agricultural pesticide use surveys. Figures are readily available for the years 1974, 1977, 1982, 1988, 1990, 1992 and 1994. Figures presented for each survey year include the total tonnage of active ingredient applied per hectare of cereals for herbicides, fungicides, growth regulators, insecticides and seed treatments, together with a total for all pesticides.

Indicator s7: Length of landscape linear features

Source: ITE.
References: Barr, C., Howard, D., Bunce, R., Gillespie, M. and Hallam, C. *Changes in Hedgerows in Britain between 1984 and 1990* (contract report to DOE) - ITE, 1991.
Barr, C., Gillespie, M. and Howard, D. *Hedgerow Survey 1993* (contract report to DOE) - ITE, 1994.

Indicator s7 shows the estimated extent of hedgerows and walls in GB for 1984 and 1990 and the estimated length of hedgerows in England and Wales in 1993. Data for 1984 have been derived from a field survey of 384 1-km squares taken from all areas of the GB countryside; 1990 data come from the *1990 Countryside Survey of GB* and have been derived from a field survey of 508 1-km squares. The 1993 data for England and Wales are based on a much smaller sample of 108 1-km squares. By their very nature, the survey estimates have margins of error associated with them. To minimise errors, estimates of length have been based on the largest sample available and estimates of change between survey periods, eg 1984-90, have been derived from the largest sample for which comparable data are available at both dates and then weighted to the stock figures from the larger data set, in this case 1990.

Indicator s8: Environmentally managed land

Source: MAFF.
Reference: MAFF Departmental Report.

The figures shown in the graph are for the cumulative area under management agreement in the given year and relate to the areas under management agreement, and not to the designated or eligible areas.

The Environmentally Sensitive Areas Scheme is a voluntary incentive scheme for promoting environmentally sensitive farming. The scheme was first introduced in 1987 with the specific purpose of protecting the landscape, wildlife and historic interest of areas of England identified as being of national environmental significance and whose conservation depends on adopting, maintaining or extending particular farming practices. Under the scheme, annual payments are made to farmers and other land managers under voluntary 10-year management agreements to implement agricultural practices such as the traditional management of hay meadows.

Countryside Stewardship is the main incentive scheme for the countryside outside ESAs. It provides 10-year management agreements to land managers to enhance and conserve important English landscapes, their wildlife habitats and history. Payments are made for changes to farming and land management practices, which provide conservation benefits or improved access to and enjoyment of the countryside. The landscapes habitats and features eligible re Countryside Stewardship include chalk and limestone grassland, lowland heath, waterside land, the coast, uplands, historic landscapes and features, old orchards, old meadows and pastures, countryside around towns, field margins on arable land and field boundaries.

Annex B

t Soil

Indicator t1:   Soil quality

Sources: National Soils Inventory (NSI) - SSLRC; Representative Soils Sampling Scheme (RSSS)
References: McGrath, S. P. and Loveland, P. J. *The Soil Geochemical Atlas of England and Wales* - Blackie, 1992.
Skinner, R.J., Church, B.M.L. and Kershaw, C.D. *'Recent trends in soil pH and nutrient status in England and Wales'* in *Soil Use and Management No.8:* pps 16-20 - 1992.

Organic matter was measured as part of the MAFF-funded NSI undertaken by the Soil Survey and Land Research Centre, ADAS and the Institute of Arable Crops Research Rothamsted. Aggregated soil samples were collected and analysed from sites at the intersects of a 5-km grid across England and Wales. Urban and industrial soils were not sampled. Nearly 5,700 NSI sites were first sampled in the period 1978-1981. A subsequent partial re-sampling exercise, involving 16 per cent of the original NSI sites, was undertaken in 1995 and has enabled comparisons to be made between the 2 periods. The re-sampling focused on those soils under arable and short-term grassland.

The data on pH, phosphorus and potassium in soils are taken from the RSSS, which measures pH and certain nutrients in agricultural soils (excluding unimproved grassland) in England and Wales. Currently, 3,800 sites are selected in each 5-year sampling cycle and are sampled 3 times, at 0, 5 and 10 years. Under the RSSS, soils are either under arable or grass when sampled but they could be different when re-sampled as some fields will be in rotation. At each sampling stage, one-third of new fields are sampled for the first time, one-third for the second time and one-third for the third and last time. Such a sampling scheme helps to minimise bias from farmers adjusting fertiliser and lime management practices.

Organic matter is not measured under the RSSS since changes in content are generally detectable only over 15-20 years. Nutrients and pH by contrast can change more rapidly.

Indicator t2:   Heavy metals in topsoils

Source: National Soils Inventory (NSI) - SSLRC.
Reference: McGrath, S. P. and Loveland, P. J. *The Soil Geochemical Atlas of England and Wales* - Blackie, 1992.

The data for heavy metals have been derived from the NSI which was undertaken in 1978-1981 and covered nearly 5,700 sites. Aggregated samples were collected and analysed from topsoil at the intersects of a 5-km grid across England and Wales. Urban and industrial soils were not sampled.

u Minerals extraction

Indicator u1:   Aggregates output

Source: DOE.
Reference: *Housing and Construction Statistics 1983-93:* table 4.5 - HMSO, 1994.

The time series for primary aggregates output covers crushed rock, sand, and gravel, whereas that for value of construction covers the value of all construction work (in 1990 prices). Crushed rock output figures include exports (but exclude imports), whereas sand and gravel output figures exclude exports (but include imports). The ratio of aggregates to value has been standardised by relating each year's data to the 1972 level (ie 1972 = 100).

Indicator u2:   Aggregates from wastes

Source: DOE
Reference: *Managing Demolition and Construction Wastes* - HMSO, 1994.

Estimates are based on limited data derived from a survey of 50 recycling operations, information provided by Waste Removal Authorities on quantities landfilled in their area and inspection of a sample of landfilling operations. "Secondary aggregates" covers construction wastes used in place of primary aggregates. "Construction sites" covers wastes used at construction or demolition sites as filling for site roads, providing working platforms and improving soft areas. "Landfill engineering" covers construction of haulage and access roads, cell construction and uses as cover. "Other disposal" relates to unlicensed disposal which occurs legally for agriculture wastes and illegally as fly-tipping.

Indicator u3:   Mineral workings on land

Sources: DOE; WO.
References: *Survey of Land for Mineral Workings in England 1994* - HMSO, 1996 (to be published).
Survey of Land for Mineral Workings in Wales 1988 - WO, 1991.
[Similar publications were produced by HMSO and WO for earlier years]

Minerals surveys provide data on the nature and extent of mineral workings, spoil tips and reclamation of mineral workings. There have been surveys of land for mineral workings for England for 1974, 1982, 1988 and 1994. For Wales, there were similar surveys for 1982 and 1988. There are no equivalent surveys covering Scotland or Northern Ireland.

Annex B

Indicator u4:   Land covered by restoration/aftercare conditions

Sources: DOE; WO.
References: *Survey of Land for Mineral Workings in England 1994* - HMSO, 1996 (to be published).
Survey of Land for Mineral Workings in Wales 1988 - WO, 1991.
[Similar publications were produced by HMSO and WO for earlier years]

Indicator u5:   Reclamation of mineral workings

Sources: DOE; WO.
References: *Survey of Land for Mineral Workings in England 1994* - HMSO, 1996 (to be published).
Survey of Land for Mineral Workings in Wales 1988 - WO, 1991.
[Similar publications were produced by HMSO and WO for earlier years]

Restoration of land includes both that which had been worked for surface minerals and the removal of spoil from sites where it had been tipped. The Surveys of Land for Minerals Working provide data on the areas restored, including the resultant land uses.

Indicator u6:   Aggregates dredged from the sea

Source: Crown Estate Commissioners; British Marine Aggregate Producers Association (BMAPA).
Reference: *Why Dredge? Aggregates from the Sea* - BMAPA, 1995.

v   Waste

The statistical database for solid wastes is poor, especially in the historical context. The paucity of reliable statistics on both waste generation and disposal is a global problem. The reasons for the poor statistical base can be attributed to a number of factors. Firstly, responsibility for regulating and managing wastes is diverse, often resting with local administrations where financial constraints and other difficulties impair the establishment of national infrastructures and procedures for data collection. Moreover, as a general rule very little waste is weighed either by producers, carriers or at disposal sites and it is very difficult to establish reliable volume to weight conversion factors for a variety of reasons. The lack of standard classifications and definitions of waste types acts as a further impediment to the development of statistical descriptions of wastes. The complexity of many waste streams in terms of composition, ie many waste streams comprise mixtures of chemicals, exacerbates the problems of waste characterisation and consistent description.

Research programmes within DOE have already initiated projects directed at solving some of these problems. Estimates of the composition of household waste are derived from one such programme and this is one area where little information has previously been available. In the Department's *Waste Strategy for England and Wales* targets have been set for improving the availability and reliability of information needed to refine and monitor progress towards targets set for recovery, recycling and diversion of wastes from landfill.

Indicator v1:   Household waste

Sources: CIPFA; SO; DOE; CSO.
References: *Waste Collection Statistics, 1991/2* - CIPFA, 1993.
[Similar publications were produced in 1983/4-1989/90]
Waste Collection, Disposal and Regulation Statistics 1993 - SO, 1994.
[A similar publication was produced in 1992]
National Household Waste Analysis project Phase 2 - Report on Composition and Weight Data (CWM/082/94) - DOE, 1994.
Economic Trends Annual Supplement 1996: table 1.3 - HMSO, 1996.
Annual Abstract of Statistics 1995: table 2.1 - HMSO, 1995.

This indicator relates only to wastes arising directly from households (dustbin collections) and waste taken by householders to civic amenity sites. Household waste, as defined by Section 75(5) of the *Environmental Protection Act 1990* and the *Controlled Waste Regulations 1992* comprises waste collected from dustbins and through special collections (eg of garden and bulky waste) and waste taken to civic amenity sites. It also includes litter and material cleared from beaches and household-type wastes from residential homes, educational establishments and hospitals (but not clinical waste). Material collected separately from households or taken by households to civic amenity sites or drop-off facilities for recycling is also notionally included.

Information on waste arisings is reported by WCAs in England and Wales as part of a series of surveys on waste management undertaken by CIPFA with support from DOE. In Scotland figures are provided annually to SO as part of a wide ranging survey of waste management in district and island councils. Because local authorities do not necessarily weigh the waste that they handle, there are likely to be errors in estimating quantities of household waste. A review of procedures in England and Wales revealed that over 60 per cent of authorities weighed less than half the waste loads delivered and a further 24 per cent weighed none at all. Figures from Scotland indicate that some 67 per cent of household waste is weighed prior to disposal.

Estimates of the composition of household waste are derived from the Department's National Household Waste Analysis Programme. The premise on which this work is based is that households of similar socio-economic characteristics are likely to have similar behavioural, purchasing and lifestyle characteristics which will be reflected in the composition and quantity of waste they produce. Dustcart loads of waste from collection rounds identified as belonging to particular socio-economic types defined by ACORN, a market research classification tool, are taken for sorting and analysis. So far, 27 samples covering all the ACORN types derived from analysis of 1981 census data have been analysed. Data cover the period 1991/2-1993/4. Other factors, such as local authority waste management practices, are taken into account in sample selection. In Scotland 18 districts have undertaken analyses on a similar basis over the period 1991-93. Data have been combined to provide a single estimate for GB.

Indicator v2: Industrial and commercial waste

Commercial waste is defined in Section 75(7) of the *Environmental Protection Act 1990*. It means waste from premises used wholly or mainly for the purpose of a trade or business or purposes of sport, recreation or entertainment. It excludes household waste, industrial waste from mines and quarries and from premises used for agriculture and sewage sludge or septic tank sludge.

Industrial waste is defined in Section 75(6) of the *Environmental Protection Act 1990*. It is waste from any factory or premises used for, or in connection with:

the provision of transport services to the public by air, land or water,

the supply of gas, water, electricity or sewerage services to the public,

the provision to the public of postal or telecommunication services.

Household, industrial and commercial wastes together with sewage sludge, dredged spoils and construction and demolition wastes are usually referred to as controlled wastes . Controlled wastes are so called because they were first regulated under the control of *Pollution Act 1974*. These wastes are now subject to regulation under the EPA 1990 and the CWR 1992. Other wastes, eg wastes from agriculture or radioactive wastes, are subject to control or regulation under separate legislation and are therefore excluded from the definition of controlled wastes.

Indicator v3: Special waste

Sources: Waste Regulation Authorities (WRAs) in England and Wales; SO; DOE(NI).
Reference: *Digest of Environmental Statistics No.17:* table 7.3 - HMSO, 1995 [ISBN 0-11-753104-9].

The control procedure for special waste is more stringent than for other wastes. All movements of special waste must be accompanied by a Consignment Note containing information on the producer, carrier and recipient of the waste and on the nature of the waste itself. Figures on the arisings, movement and management of these wastes is compiled by WRAs from the consignment notes. Figures reported exclude special wastes treated and disposed of within the curtilage of the site where they arise. Difficulties in compiling national statistics arise because there is no standard classification system for describing the wastes, and because wastes are frequently reported as volumes and other non-standard units. Other errors arise from double counting of wastes sent to transfer stations. Implementation of the *Hazardous Waste Directive*, which will supersede the *1980 Special Waste Regulations* may result in changes to the number and type of wastes to be included as special.

Indicator v4: Household waste recycling and composting

Sources: NETCEN; Audit Commission.
References: NETCEN unpublished.
Audit Commission Local Authority Performance Indicators Volume 2 - HMSO, 1995.

The figure for 1990 is an unpublished best estimate based on work at NETCEN. The figure for 1993 is derived from recycling rates reported by individual local authorities in England and Wales to the Audit Commission. Inaccuracies in the estimate occur because local authorities calculate recycling rates on differing bases.

Indicator v5: Materials recycling

Sources: Iron and Steel Statistics Bureau; Aluminium Federation; World Bureau of Metal Statistics; British Steel; Aluminium Can Recycling Association; The Paper Federation of Great Britain; British Glass Manufacturers Confederation.
Reference: *Digest of Environmental Statistics No.17:* tables 7.12-7.19, 7.21 - HMSO, 1995 [ISBN 0-11-753104-9].

Information on recycling of various materials is provided by trade associations and groups actively promoting the recycling of particular post-consumer items. It is not always possible to make comparisons of recycling performance between different materials. Industry sectors collect different information, use different definitions and assemble the data in different ways to calculate measures of recycling. Technological, process and commercial considerations affect the way in which the data can be collected, as well as limiting the use of secondary materials.

Recycling rates can be calculated in a number of ways. The figures shown reflect the amount of secondary scrap used (scrap collected less exported scrap plus imported scrap) in the UK in a year as a proportion of consumption in that year. This gives an idea of the extent to which secondary material is displacing raw material from the feedstock. A weakness of this definition is that material which is being recycled now and related to current consumption might originally have been delivered to an end market some years ago. Where products have a short lifetime, ie are discarded within 12 months, this of little importance.

Annex B

Indicator v6:   Energy from waste

Sources: DTI; Energy Technology Support Unit (ETSU); AEA Technology.
References: *Digest of United Kingdom Energy Statistics 1995:* table B1 - HMSO, 1995 [ISBN 0-11-515368-3].
                   Energy from Waste News - ETSU, April 1995.

Data on landfill gas exploitation are provided from the Landfill gas Monitoring, Modelling and Communications System (LAMMCOS) maintained by ETSU. Data is reported on a voluntary basis by sites participating in the Non-Fossil Fuel Obligation Scheme (NFFO). Approximately 94 per cent of those participating in the scheme provided information on landfill gas collected and electricity and heat generated. Figures do not include gas used directly in kilns and boilers. Information on sewage sludge digestion is for projects supported under NFFO. Before 1991 data came from the RESTATS project and since 1991 data is provided from the CHAPSTAT database. The figures for straw combustion are estimates based partly on 1990 information and partly on a survey of straw-fired boilers that was carried out in 1993-94. Figures for Municipal Solid Waste Combustion were obtained from data collected using the RESTATS questionnaire. The "other" category includes combustion of general industrial wastes, industrial waste wood, waste tyres, hospital waste and poultry litter, and farm waste digestion. Information on general industrial waste combustion is an estimate based on responses to the RESTATS questionnaire. Information on hospital waste incineration and industrial wood combustion is also derived from RESTATS. Information on tyre combustion is for 3 plants known to be operating in the UK. Figures for poultry litter combustion relate to 2 NFFO projects. Figures for farm waste digestion are based on a review carried out by ADAS in 1991-92 which identified all farm waste digesters in the UK. Information was collected from these projects in 1993 and used to derive estimates for 1994.

Indicator v7:   Waste going to landfill

Source: DOE.
Reference: *Making Waste Work: A strategy for sustainable waste management in England and Wales* - HMSO, 1995.

w Radioactivity

Indicator w1:   Radiation exposure

Source: NRPB.
Reference: Hughes, J.S. and O'Riordan, M.C. *Radiation Exposure of the UK Population - 1993 Review,* NRPB-R263 - HMSO, 1993.
                   [Similar reports reviewing radiation exposure of the UK population were published by NRPB in 1974, 1978, 1984 and 1988]

Radiation doses to the population from discharges and consumer products are based on a number of estimates, eg food consumption rates by individuals and the number and frequency of use of different products. Many of these estimates are subject to large uncertainty and therefore estimates of dose from discharges and products are indicative only and should be treated with caution.

The methodology used for estimating occupational exposure has been refined over the years to reflect improved understanding of the groups of workers exposed to sources of natural and artificial radiation. The data for occupational exposure cover both workers in the nuclear industry and workers in other industries, eg radiographers, miners who are exposed to radon and couriers transporting isotopes for medicine, etc. Radiation doses to individual workers are monitored using detectors such as dosemeters and "film badges"; thus dose estimates are relatively accurate. Average individual dose to the UK population is derived by dividing the total dose received via occupational exposure by the number of people living in the UK.

Food intake is the main pathway for collective exposure from radioactive discharges. The collective dose is estimated by modelling the uptake of different radionuclides in foods and multiplying the concentrations by estimates of consumption rates and data for dose per unit intake. The food concentration data are supported by the results of MAFF environmental monitoring programmes; in the case of fish consumption, collective dose is derived directly from a knowledge of the radionuclide concentrations and fish landings. Average individual dose is derived by dividing the total collective dose from all discharge pathways by the number of people living in the UK.

Consumer products such as gas mantles, smoke alarms, luminous clocks and watches contain small amounts of radionuclides. The collective dose is estimated using typical exposures from such products and the estimated number in use. Average individual dose is then derived as above.

Indicator w2:   Discharges from nuclear installations and nuclear power generation

Sources: DOE; DTI.
References: *Digest of Environmental Statistics No.17:* tables 10.13 and 10.16 - HMSO, 1995 [ISBN 0-11-753104-9].
                   Digest of United Kingdom Energy Statistics 1995 - HMSO, 1995 [ISBN 0-11-515368-3].

Radioactive atmospheric discharges and liquid discharges from nuclear installations are released through specially designed systems. Discharges are continuously monitored using a variety of instrumentation depending on the types of radionuclides being discharged. Representative samples of discharges are taken and assessed in the laboratory to determine actual discharges of individual radionuclides.

Annex B

The data on discharges in this indicator cover all nuclear power and defence activities. Different radionuclides have different toxicities and, therefore to provide proper indications of change over time, all of the discharge data have been weighted using discharges of caesium-137 as the baseline to take account of relative toxicities.

The indices for liquid and atmospheric discharges have been derived from data on discharges published annually in DOE's *Digest of Environmental Statistics*. The index for nuclear power generation have been derived from data on electricity supply from nuclear stations published annually in DTI's *Digest of United Kingdom Energy Statistics*.

Indicator w3: Radioactive waste arisings and disposal

Sources: DOE; Electowatt Engineering Services (for UK Nirex Ltd).
References: *The 1991 United Kingdom Radioactive Waste Inventory* (DOE/RAS/92.010) (UK Nirex Ltd Report No.284) - DOE, November 1992.
                  The 1994 United Kingdom Radioactive Waste Inventory (DOE/RAS/95.001) (UK Nirex Ltd Report No.695) - DOE, 1996 (to be published).
                  [Similar inventories were produced for 1986, 1987, 1988 and 1989]

High level wastes result from the reprocessing of nuclear fuel and are highly radioactive. Intermediate level wastes are less radioactive and include nuclear reactor components and the metal cladding used for nuclear fuel. Unlike high level and intermediate level wastes, low level wastes do not normally require shielding during handling and transport. Examples include rubble, discarded protective clothing and worn out or damaged plant and equipment from nuclear sites.

Data shown in this indicator are mainly collected under inventories commissioned jointly by DOE and UK Nirex Ltd and covering all nuclear operators. The inventory is now well established but is no longer produced annually.

Abbreviations used

ACOP	Advisory Committee on Protection of the Sea
BTO	British Trust for Ornithology
CCW	Countryside Council for Wales
CIPFA	Chartered Institute of Public Finance and Accountancy
CSO	Central Statistical Office[1]
DOE	Department of the Environment
DOE(NI)	Department of the Environment (Northern Ireland)
DOT	Department of Transport
DTI	Department of Trade and Industry
EN	English Nature
FC	Forestry Commission
JNCC	Joint Nature Conservation Committee[2]
ICES	International Council for the Exploration of the Sea
IFE	Institute of Freshwater Ecology
ITE	Institute of Terrestrial Ecology
MAFF	Ministry of Agriculture, Fisheries and Food
MO	Meteorological Office
NERC	Natural Environmental Research Council
NETCEN	National Environmental Technology Centre[3]
NRPB	National Radiological Protection Board
NCC	Nature Conservancy Council[2]
NRA	National Rivers Authority
OFWAT	Office of Water Services
OPCS	Office of Population Censuses and Surveys[1]
RSPB	Royal Society for the Protection of Birds
SNH	Scottish Natural Heritage
SO	Scottish Office
SSLRC	Soil Survey and Land Research Centre
WO	Welsh Office
WSA	Water Services Association
WWT	Wildfowl and Wetlands Trust

1   The "Central Statistical Office" and "Office of Population Censuses and Surveys" is to merge on 1 April 1996 and will henceforth be known as the "Office for National Statistics" (ON).
2   The "Joint Nature Conservation Committee" (JNCC) is the successor coordinating body to the "Nature Conservancy Council" (NCC).
3   Formerly the Warren Spring Laboratory

Annex B

Annex C

Bibliography of related indicator work

Domestically

Pearce D., Turner R.K., Brown D. and Bateman I. *The Development of Environmental Indicators: A Report to the Department of the Environment.* DOE,1991(unpublished).

Anderson V. *Alternative Economic Indicators*, New Economics Foundation, Routledge 1991.

MacGillivray A. (ed) *Environmental Measures: indicators for the UK environment.* Environment Challenge Group (Friends of the Earth, International Institute for Environment and Development, The New Economics Foundation, The Royal Society for Nature Conservation - the Wildlife Trusts' partnership, The Royal Society for the Protection of Birds, World Wide Fund for Nature - UK, Wildlife and Countryside Link), 1994. ISBN 0-90-3138-824.

Green Gauge: indicators for the state of the environment. Environment Challenge Group, 1994.

Rowell T.A., *Ecological Indicators for Nature Conservation Monitoring: JNCC Report No. 196*, Joint Nature Conservation Committee, 1994.

Sustainability Indicators Research Report - Report of Consultants on the Pilot Phase, Local Government Management Board, 1995. ISBN 0-7488-9702X.

Sustainability Indicators Research Report: Indicators for Local Agenda 21 - A Summary, Local Government Management Board, 1995. ISBN 0-7488-9744-5.

Measuring the Unmeasurable, Council for the Protection of Rural England, 1995.

Sustainability Indicators Project: Summary and Recommendations, Fife Regional Council, 1995.

Strathclyde Sustainability Indicators, Strathclyde Regional Council, 1995.

State of the Countryside Indicators, Countryside Commission (to be published).

Abroad

A Report on Canada's Progress Towards a National Set of Environmental Indicators. State of the Environment Report No. 91-1, Environment Canada, Ottawa 1991.

Environmental Indicators: A Preliminary Set. OECD, Paris 1991.

Alfsen K.H., Brekke K.A., Brunvoll F., Luras H., Nyborg K. and Saebo H.V. *Environmental Indicators.* Discussion Paper No. 71. Central Bureau of Statistics, Norway, Oslo 1992.

Sustainable Seattle. *Indicators of Sustainable Community 1992.* Seattle 1992.

Indicators for the Integration of Environmental Concerns into Energy Policies. Environment Monographs No. 79. OECD, Paris 1993.

Indicators for the Integration of Environmental Concerns into Transport Policies. Environment Monographs No. 80. OECD, Paris 1993.

Adriaanse A. *Environmental policy performance indicators: a study on the development of indicators for environmental policy in the Netherlands*, The Hague, 1993. ISBN 90-12-09099-1.

OECD Core Set of Indicators for Environmental Performance Reviews: A synthesis report by the Group on the State of the Environment. Environment Monographs No. 83. OECD, Paris 1993.

Environmental Indicators: OECD Core Set. OECD, Paris 1994. ISBN 92-64-04263-6.

Bakkes J.A., van den Born G.J., Helder J.C., and Swart R.J., National Institute of Public Health and Environmental Protection, Bilthoven, the Netherlands, and Hope C.W., and Parker J.D.E., University of Cambridge, United Kingdom. *An Overview of Environmental Indicators: State of the art and perspectives*, UNEP, Nairobi 1994. ISBN 92-807-1427-9.

Monitoring Environmental Progress: A Report on Work in Progress. The World Bank, 1995. ISBN 0-8213-3365-8.

Hammond A., Adriaanse A., Rodenburg E., Bryant D. and Woodward R. *Environmental Indicators: A Systematic Approach to Measuring and Reporting on Environmental Policy Performance in the Context of Sustainable Development.* World Resources Institute, Washington DC, 1995. ISBN 1-56973-026-1.

Gouzee N., Mazijn B., and Billharz. *Indicators of Sustainable Development for Decision-Making.* Report of the Workshop of Ghent, Belgium 9-11 january 1995 submitted to the UN Commission on Sustainable Development, Federal Planning Office of Belgium, 1995.

Environmental indicators: a systematic approach to measuring and reporting on the environment in the context of sustainable development. Scientific Committee on Problems of the Environment (SCOPE). Discussion paper submitted to the UN Commission on Sustainable Development, 1995.

Annex C

Printed in the United Kingdom for HMSO
Dd 301407   3/96   C12   65536   348879   12/34898